INTRODUCTION TO

# Poetry

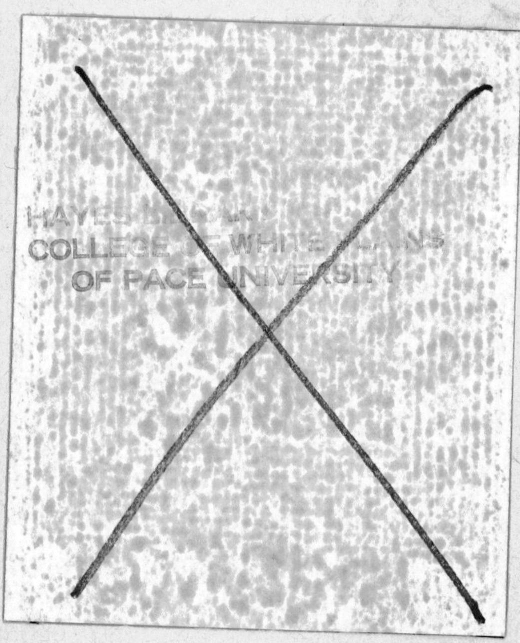

# INTRODUCTION TO

William C. Cavanaugh
DePauw University

WM. C. BROWN COMPANY PUBLISHERS

Dubuque, Iowa

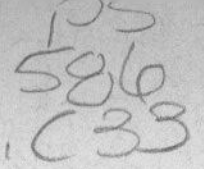



Library of Congress Catalog Card Number: 74–76527

ISBN 0–697–03956–0



Printed in the United States of America

COPYRIGHTS AND ACKNOWLEDGMENTS

SAMUEL ALLEN. "A Moment Please" is reprinted by permission of the author.

ALURISTA. "unexpectedly: my night gloom came," reprinted by permission of the poet.

RICHARD ARMOUR. "Going to Extremes" from *Light Armour* by Richard Armour, copyright 1954 by Richard Armour, reprinted by permission of McGraw-Hill Book Company.

JACK ANDERSON. "A Dream of Metals" from *The Invention of New Jersey*, © 1969 by the University of Pittsburgh Press, reprinted by permission of the University of Pittsburgh Press.

W. H. AUDEN. "A Free One" from *Collected Shorter Poems 1927–1957* by W. H. Auden, copyright 1934 and renewed 1962 by W. H. Auden; "That Night When Joy Began" from *Collected Shorter Poems 1927–1957* by W. H. Auden, copyright 1937 and renewed 1965 by W. H. Auden; "Musée des Beaux Arts" and "The Unknown Citizen" from *Collected Shorter Poems 1927–1957* by W. H. Auden, copyright 1940 and renewed 1968 by W. H. Auden, all reprinted by permission of Random House, Inc., and Faber and Faber, Ltd. of London.

ALFRED GOLDSWORTHY BAILEY. "Algonkian Burial" from *Border River* by Alfred G. Bailey. Reprinted by permission of The Canadian Publishers, McClelland and Stewart Limited, Toronto.

THE BEATLES. "A Day in the Life" (lyrics only), copyright 1967 by Northern Songs, Limited, reprinted by permission of Northern Songs, Limited. All rights reserved.

JOHN BERRYMAN. "Dream Song 15" from *Berryman's Sonnets* by John Berryman, copyright © 1952, 1967 by John Berryman, reprinted by permission of Farrar, Straus and Giroux, Inc.

JOHN BETJEMAN. "Late-Flowering Lust" and "In Westminster Abbey" from *Collected Poems* by John Betjeman, reprinted by permission of John Murray Publishers, Ltd. and Houghton Mifflin Company.

ELIZABETH BISHOP. "The Prodigal" from *The Complete Poems* of Elizabeth Bishop, copyright © 1951, 1969 by Elizabeth Bishop, reprinted by permission of Farrar, Straus and Giroux, Inc.

EARLE BIRNEY. From "Damnation of Vancouver" from *Selected Poems* by Earle Birney, reprinted by permission of The Canadian Publishers, McClelland and Stewart Limited, Toronto.

ROBERT BLY. "After Drinking All Night with a Friend, We Go Out in a Boat at Dawn to See Who Can Write the Best Poem" from *Silence in the Snowy Fields*, Wesleyan University Press, copyright 1962 by Robert Bly, reprinted by permission of the author. "Romans Angry About the Inner World" from *The Light Around the Body* by Robert Bly, copyright © 1967 by Robert Bly, reprinted by permission of Harper & Row, Publishers, Inc.

PHILIP BOOTH. "Ego" from *Letter from a Distant Land* by Philip Booth, copyright © 1956 by Philip Booth, originally appeared in *The New Yorker*, reprinted by permission of The Viking Press, Inc.

GWENDOLYN BROOKS. "We Real Cool" from *The World of Gwendolyn Brooks* by Gwendolyn Brooks, copyright © 1959 by Gwendolyn Brooks, reprinted by permission of Harper & Row, Publishers, Inc.

STERLING A. BROWN. "The Ballad of Joe Meek", reprinted by permission of the author.

JOHN CIARDI. "Gulls Land and Cease to Be" from *Person to Person*, copyright 1964 by Rutgers, The State University, reprinted by permission of the author.

LUCILLE CLIFTON. "The 1st" from *Good Times* by Lucille Clifton, copyright © 1969 by Lucille Clifton, reprinted by permission of Random House, Inc.

GREGORY CORSO. "Marriage" from *The Happy Birthday of Death*, copyright © 1960 by New Directions Publishing Corporation, reprinted by permission of New Directions Publishing Corporation.

HART CRANE. "Chaplinesque" from *The Collected Poems and Selected Letters and Prose of Hart Crane* by Hart Crane, copyright © 1933, 1958, 1966 by Liveright Publishing Corporation, reprinted by permission of Liveright, Publishers, New York.

STEPHEN CRANE. "The Heart" from *Collected Poems of Stephen Crane*, published by Alfred A. Knopf, Inc.

ROBERT CREELEY. "I Know a Man," "Wait for Me," and "The Wife" from *For Love* by Robert Creeley, copyright © 1962 by Robert Creeley, reprinted by permission of Charles Scribner's Sons.

COUNTEE CULLEN. "Incident" from *On These I Stand* by Countee Cullen, copyright 1925 by Harper & Row, Publishers, Inc., renewed 1953 by Ida M. Cullen, reprinted by permission of Harper & Row, Publishers, Inc.

E. E. CUMMINGS. "in Just–" from *Complete Poems 1913–1962* by E. E. Cummings, copyright 1923, 1951 by E. E. Cummings, reprinted by permission of Harcourt Brace Jovanovich, Inc. "next to of course god america i" from *Complete Poems 1913–1962* by E. E. Cummings, copyright 1926 by Horace Liveright, renewed 1954 by E. E. Cummings, reprinted by permission of Harcourt Brace Jovanovich, Inc.

PETER DAVISON. "The Last Word" from *Pretending to Be Asleep* by Peter Davison, copyright © 1970 by Peter Davison, reprinted by permission of Atheneum Publishers.

EMILY DICKINSON. "After great pain, a formal feeling comes" from *The Complete Poems of Emily Dickinson,* edited by Thomas H. Johnson, copyright 1929, © 1957 by Mary L. Hampson, reprinted by permission of Little, Brown and Company. "Belshazzar had a Letter," "There is no Frigate like a Book," "Because I could not stop for Death," and "Apparently with no surprise" from *The Poems of Emily Dickinson,* Thomas H. Johnson, Editor, Cambridge, Mass.: The Belknap Press of Harvard University Press, copyright 1951, 1955 by The President and Fellows of Harvard College, reprinted by permission of the publishers and the Trustees of Amherst College.

RICHARD EBERHART. "New Hampshire, February" and "The Fury of Aerial Bombardment" from *Collected Poems 1930–1960* by Richard Eberhart, copyright © 1960 by Richard Eberhart, reprinted by permission of Oxford University Press.

T. S. ELIOT. "Journey of the Magi," "The Love Song of J. Alfred Prufrock," and "Morning at the Window" from *Collected Poems 1909–1962* by T. S. Eliot, copyright 1936 by Harcourt Brace Jovanovich, Inc. Copyright © 1963, 1964 by T. S. Eliot, reprinted by permission of Harcourt Brace Jovanovich, Inc., and Faber and Faber, Ltd. of London.

LAWRENCE FERLINGHETTI. "Constantly risking absurdity" and "In Goya's greatest scenes" from *A Coney Island of the Mind* by Lawrence Ferlinghetti, copyright © 1958 by Lawrence Ferlinghetti, reprinted by permission of New Directions Publishing Corporation.

EDWARD FIELD. "Unwanted" from *Stand Up, Friend, With Me* by Edward Field, copyright © 1963 by Edward Field, reprinted by permission of Grove Press, Inc.

ROBERT FRANCIS. "Pitcher" and "High Diver" from *The Orb Weaver* by Robert Francis, copyright © 1953 by Robert Francis, reprinted by permission of Wesleyan University Press.

RICHARD FROST. "Climbing the Tower at Pisa" from *Getting Drunk with the Birds,* copyright 1971 by Richard Frost, reprinted by permission of Ohio University Press.

ROBERT FROST. "Out, Out—" and "Stopping by Woods on a Snowy Evening" from *The Poetry of Robert Frost* edited by Edward Connery Lathem, copyright 1916, 1923, © 1969 by Holt, Rinehart and Winston, Inc.; copyright 1944, 1951 by Robert Frost; "Design," "After Apple-Picking," "Tree at My Window," and "Fire and Ice" from *The Poetry of Robert Frost* edited by Edward Connery Lathem, copyright 1923, 1928, 1930, 1939, © 1969 by Holt, Rinehart and Winston, Inc.; copyright 1936, 1951, © 1956, 1958 by Robert Frost; copyright © 1964, 1967 by Lesley Frost Ballantine, reprinted by permission of Holt, Rinehart and Winston, Inc.

ALLEN GINSBERG. "A Supermarket in California" from *Howl and Other Poems* by Allen Ginsberg, copyright © 1956, 1959 by Allen Ginsberg, reprinted by permission of City Lights Books.

ROBERT GRAVES. "Sick Love" from *Collected Poems 1955* by Robert Graves, published by Doubleday & Company, copyright © 1955 by Robert Graves, reprinted by permission of Collins-Knowlton-Wing, Inc.

THOM GUNN. "Black Jackets" from *My Sad Captains* by Thom Gunn, copyright 1961 by Thom Gunn, reprinted by permission of Faber and Faber, Ltd. and the University of Chicago Press.

DONALD HALL. "The Frontier" from *Exiles and Marriages* by Donald Hall, published by The Viking Press, copyright © 1955 by Donald Hall, reprinted by permission of Curtis Brown, Ltd.

ROBERT S. HAHN. "Picture of the Usual Murderer in the Usual Magazine" first published in *The Antioch Review*, Vol. 19, No. 1; copyright © 1969 by The Antioch Review, Inc., reprinted by permission of the editors.

THOMAS HARDY. "Revulsion," "Hap," "In the Restaurant," "The Man He Killed," and "The Darkling Thrush" from *Collected Poems* by Thomas Hardy, copyright 1925 by The Macmillan Company. Reprinted by permission of The Macmillan Company; the Trustees of the Hardy Estate; Macmillan London & Basingstoke; and The Macmillan Company of Canada, Ltd.

ROBERT HAYDEN. "Middle Passage" from *Selected Poems* by Robert Hayden, copyright © 1966 by Robert Hayden, reprinted by permission of October House Inc.

SEAMUS HEANEY. "Digging" from *Death of a Naturalist* by Seamus Heaney, copyright © 1966 by Seamus Heaney, reprinted by permission of Oxford University Press, Inc. and Faber and Faber Ltd.

ANTHONY HECHT. "The Dover Bitch" from *The Hard Hours* by Anthony Hecht, copyright © 1960 by Anthony E. Hecht, reprinted by permission of Atheneum Publishers. Originally appeared in *Transatlantic Review.*

ROBERT HILLYER. "The Bats" from *Collected Poems* by Robert Hillyer, copyright © 1961 by Robert Hillyer, reprinted by permission of Alfred A. Knopf, Inc.

GERARD MANLEY HOPKINS. "The Windhover: To Christ our Lord," "God's Grandeur," "Spring and Fall," and "Felix Randal" from *Poems of Gerard Manley Hopkins*, 4th ed., Ed. by W. H. Gardner and N. H. MacKenzie, published 1967 by Oxford University Press.

A. E. HOUSMAN. "Others, I am not the first" and "On your midnight pallet lying" from "A Shropshire Lad"—Authorized Edition—from *The Collected Poems of A. E. Housman*, copyright 1939, 1940, © 1965 by Holt, Rinehart and Winston, Inc.; copyright © 1967, 1968 by Robert E. Symons, reprinted by permission of Holt, Rinehart and Winston, Inc., The Society of Authors as the literary representative of the Estate of A. E. Housman, and Jonathan Cape, Ltd., publishers of A. E. Housman's *Collected Poems.* "Eight O'Clock" from *The Collected Poems of A. E. Housman*, copyright 1922 by Holt, Rinehart and Winston, Inc., copyright 1950 by Barclays Bank Ltd., reprinted by permission of Holt, Rinehart and Winston, Inc., The Society of Authors as the literary representative of the Estate of A. E. Housman, and Jonathan Cape Ltd., publishers of A. E. Housman's *Collected Poems.*

ROBERT HUDSON. "The Sea within the Ship" reprinted by permission of the author.

TED HUGHES. "Pike" from *Lupercal* (1960) by Ted Hughes, copyright © 1959 by Ted Hughes, reprinted by permission of Harper & Row, Publishers, Inc. and Faber and Faber Ltd. of London. "The Hag" from *The Hawk in the Rain* by Ted Hughes, copyright © 1956 by Ted Hughes, reprinted by permission of Harper & Row, Publishers, Inc. "Truth Kills Everybody" and "Crow's Last Stand" from *Crow* by Ted Hughes, copyright © 1971 by Ted Hughes, reprinted by permission of Harper & Row, Publishers, Inc., and Faber and Faber Ltd. of London.

JOSEPHINE JACOBSEN. "Night Patrol" reprinted by permission; © 1973 The New Yorker Magazine, Inc.

RANDALL JARRELL. "The Death of the Ball Turret Gunner" and "A Camp in the Prussian Forest" from *The Complete Poems* by Randall Jarrell, copyright © 1945, 1946, 1969 by Mrs. Randall Jarrell, reprinted by permission of Farrar, Straus and Giroux, Inc.

TED JOANS. "Why Try?" from *Black Pow-Wow* by Ted Joans, copyright © 1969 by Ted Joans, reprinted by permission of Farrar, Straus and Giroux, Inc.

DONALD JUSTICE. "Metamorphoses of the Vampire" (translated by Donald Justice), reprinted by permission of Donald Justice.

RICHARD KELL. "Fishing Harbour Towards Evening" from *Control Tower* by Richard Kell, reprinted by permission of Chatto & Windus Ltd.

KENNETH KOCH. "You Were Wearing" from *Thank You and Other Poems* by Kenneth Koch, copyright © 1962 by Kenneth Koch, reprinted by permission of Grove Press, Inc.

JOSEPH LANGLAND. "War" from *The Green Town: Poems* by Joseph Langland, copyright 1956 by Joseph Langland, reprinted by permission of Charles Scribner's Sons.

D. H. LAWRENCE. Four lines of "Bat", "Piano," and "To Be Superior" from *The Complete Poems of D. H. Lawrence* ed. by Vivian de Sola Pinto and F. Warren Roberts, copyright © 1964, 1971 by Angelo Ravagli and C. M. Weekley, reprinted by permission of The Viking Press, Inc.

AL LEE. "Going Whoring" first appeared in *Poetry*. Copyright 1971 by The Modern Poetry Association, reprinted by permission of the Editor of *Poetry* and Al Lee.

DENISE LEVERTOV. "A Day Begins" from *The Sorrow Dance*, copyright © 1966 by Denise Levertov Goodman, reprinted by permission of New Directions Publishing Corporation. "To the Snake" from *With Eyes at the Back of Our Heads* by Denise Levertov, copyright © 1958 by Denise Levertov Goodman. "To the Snake" was first published in *Poetry*. Reprinted by permission of New Directions Publishing Corporation.

PHILIP LEVINE. "Animals Are Passing from Our Lives" from *Not This Pig* by Philip Levine, copyright © 1968 by Philip Levine, reprinted by permission of Wesleyan University Press.

LAURENCE LIEBERMAN. "No One to Blame" from *The Unblinding* by Laurence Lieberman, copyright © 1965 by Laurence Lieberman, reprinted by permission of Macmillan Publishing Co., Inc.

AMY LOWELL. "Night Clouds" from *Complete Poetical Works of Amy Lowell*, reprinted by permission of Houghton Mifflin Company.

ROBERT LOWELL. "Ezra Pound" from *Notebook 1967–68* by Robert Lowell, copyright © 1967, 1968, 1969 by Robert Lowell, reprinted by permission of Farrar, Straus and Giroux, Inc.

ARCHIBALD MACLEISH. "You, Andrew Marvell" from *Collected Poems* by Archibald MacLeish, reprinted by permission of Houghton Mifflin Company; "Ars Poetica" from *Collected Poems 1917–1952* by Archibald MacLeish, reprinted by permission of Houghton Mifflin Company; " 'Dover Beach'—A note to that poem" from *Public Speech* by Archibald MacLeish, copyright 1936, © 1964 by Archibald MacLeish, reprinted by permission of Holt, Rinehart and Winston, Inc.

JAY MACPHERSON. "Eurynome" from *The Boatman* by Jay Macpherson, reprinted by permission of the Oxford University Press, Canadian Branch.

DAVID MCFADDEN. "The External Element" reprinted by permission of the author.

JACK MATTHEWS. "The Mill" from *An Almanac for Twilight*, copyright © 1966 by Jack Matthews, reprinted by permission of the University of North Carolina Press.

W. S. MERWIN. "Fog-Horn" from *The Drunk in the Furnace*, copyright © 1958 by W. S. Merwin, reprinted by permission of Harold Ober Associates Incorporated and David Higham Associates, Ltd.

EDNA ST. VINCENT MILLAY. "God's World" from *Collected Poems*, copyright 1917, 1945 by Edna St. Vincent Millay, reprinted by permission of Harper & Row, Publishers, Inc.

RAY MIZER. "Dirge" from *Southern Poetry Review*, Spring, 1968, Vol. 8, No. 2, copyright 1968 by Ray Mizer, reprinted by permission of *Southern Poetry Review*. "Cognate Object" from *College English*, April 1961, copyright © 1961 by the National Council of Teachers of English, reprinted by permission of the publisher and Ray Mizer.

MARIANNE MOORE. "The Mind is an Enchanting Thing" from *Collected Poems* by Marianne Moore, copyright 1944 by Marianne Moore, reprinted by permission of The Macmillan Company. "Spenser's Ireland" from *Collected Poems* by Marianne Moore, copyright 1941 by Marianne Moore, renewed 1969 by Marianne Moore, reprinted by permission of The Macmillan Company.

HOWARD NEMEROV. "The Goose Fish" from *New and Selected Poems*, by Howard Nemerov, copyright 1960 by the University of Chicago, reprinted by permission of Margot Johnson Agency.

JOHN FREDERICK NIMS. "Penny Arcade" from *The Iron Pastoral*, copyright 1947 by John Frederick Nims, reprinted by permission of William Morrow and Company, Inc.

WILFRED OWEN. "Anthem for Doomed Youth" from *Collected Poems* by Wilfred Owen, copyright 1946, 1963 by Chatto & Windus, Ltd., reprinted by permission of New Directions Publishing Corporation and Chatto & Windus, Ltd.; "Dulce et Decorum Est" from *Collected Poems* by Wilfred Owen, copyright 1946, © 1963 by Chatto & Windus Ltd., reprinted by permission of New Directions Publishing Corporation, the Estate of the late Harold Owen and Chatto & Windus Ltd.

AMÉRICO PAREDES. "Guitarreros" from *Southwest Review* (Autumn, 1964), reprinted by permission of the publisher and the author.

SYLVIA PLATH. "Cut" from *Ariel* by Sylvia Plath, copyright © 1963 by Ted Hughes, published by Faber & Faber Ltd., London, reprinted by permission of Harper & Row, Publishers, Inc., and Miss Olwyn Hughes.

RALPH POMEROY. "Corner" from *In the Financial District* by Ralph Pomeroy, copyright © 1961 by Ralph Pomeroy, reprinted by permission of Macmillan Publishing Company, Inc.

EZRA POUND. "In a Station of the Metro" and "Portrait d'une Femme" from *Personae* by Ezra Pound, copyright 1926 by Ezra Pound, reprinted by permission of New Directions Publishing Corporation.

JOHN CROWE RANSOM. "Janet Waking" from *Selected Poems*, Revised Edition, by John Crowe Ransom, copyright 1927 by Alfred A. Knopf, Inc., and renewed 1955 by John Crowe Ransom, reprinted by permission of Alfred A. Knopf, Inc.

HENRY REED. "Naming of Parts" from *A Map of Verona and Other Poems* by Henry Reed, copyright 1947 by Henry Reed, reprinted by permission of Jonathan Cape Ltd.

ISHMAEL REED. "I Am a Cowboy in the Boat of Ra" reprinted by permission of the poet.

EDWIN ARLINGTON ROBINSON. "Richard Cory" if reprinted, by permission of Charles Scribner's Sons from *The Children of the Night* by Edwin Arlington

Robinson (1897). "John Gorham" from *Collected Poems* by Edwin Arlington Robinson, copyright 1916 by Edwin Arlington Robinson, renewed 1944 by Ruth Nivison, reprinted by permission of The Macmillan Company.

THEODORE ROETHKE. "I Knew a Woman" from *The Collected Poems of Theodore Roethke*, copyright © 1954 by Theodore Roethke, reprinted by permission of Doubleday & Company, Inc.; "Dolor" from *The Collected Poems of Theodore Roethke*, copyright 1943 by Modern Poetry Association, Inc., reprinted by permission of Doubleday & Company, Inc.; "Weed Puller" from *The Collected Poems of Theodore Roethke*, copyright 1946 by Editorial Publications, Inc., reprinted by permission of Doubleday & Company, Inc.

CARL SANDBURG. "Splinter" from *Good Morning, America*, by Carl Sandburg, copyright 1928, 1956 by Carl Sandburg, reprinted by permission of Harcourt Brace Jovanovich, Inc.

GEORGE SANTAYANA. "On the Death of a Metaphysician" from *Poems* by George Santayana, copyright 1923 by Charles Scribner's Sons, renewal copyright 1951, reprinted by permission of Charles Scribner's Sons.

SIEGFRIED SASSOON. "Base Details" from *Collected Poems* by Siegfried Sassoon copyright 1918 by E. P. Dutton & Co., 1946 by Siegfried Sassoon, reprinted by permission of The Viking Press, Inc. and Mr. G. T. Sassoon.

DELMORE SCHWARTZ. "The Heavy Bear Who Goes with Me" from *Selected Poems: Summer Knowledge* by Delmore Schwartz, copyright 1938 by New Directions Publishing Corporation, reprinted by permission of New Directions Publishing Corporation.

WINFIELD TOWNLEY SCOTT. "The U.S. Sailor with the Japanese Skull" from *Collected Poems* by Winfield Townley Scott, copyright 1945 by Winfield Townley Scott, reprinted by permission of The Macmillan Company.

ANNE SEXTON. "The Starry Night" from *All My Pretty Ones* by Anne Sexton, reprinted by permission of Houghton Mifflin Company.

KARL SHAPIRO. "Auto Wreck" from *Selected Poems* by Karl Shapiro, copyright 1942 and renewed 1970 by Karl Shapiro, reprinted by permission of Random House, Inc.

W. D. SNODGRASS. "The Operation" from *Heart's Needle* by W. D. Snodgrass, copyright © 1959 by W. D. Snodgrass, reprinted by permission of Alfred A. Knopf, Inc.

GARY SOTO. "Fields" reprinted by permission of the author.

RADCLIFFE SQUIRES. "Old Leaves" from *Waiting in the Bone and Other Poems* by Radcliffe Squires, copyright 1973 by Radcliffe Squires, by permission of Abattoir Editions, The University of Nebraska at Omaha.

WILLIAM STAFFORD. "Traveling through the Dark" from *Traveling Through the Dark* by William Stafford, copyright © 1960 by William Stafford, reprinted by permission of Harper & Row, Publishers, Inc.

GEORGE STARBUCK. "Late Late" from *White Paper* by George Starbuck, copyright © 1962 by George Starbuck, reprinted by permission of Atlantic-Little, Brown and Company; "Cora Punctuated with Strawberries" from *Bone Thoughts* by George Starbuck, copyright 1960 by George Starbuck, reprinted by permission of the Yale University Press.

JAMES STEPHENS. "In Waste Places" from *Collected Poems* by James Stephens, copyright 1915 by The Macmillan Company, renewed 1943 by James Stephens, reprinted by permission of The Macmillan Company, Mrs. Iris

Wise, Macmillan London & Basingstoke, and The Macmillan Company of Canada Limited.

WALLACE STEVENS. "Man Carrying Thing" from *The Collected Poems of Wallace Stevens*, copyright 1947 by Wallace Stevens, reprinted by permission of Alfred A. Knopf, Inc.; "A High-Toned Old Christian Woman," "Sunday Morning," and "Peter Quince at the Clavier" from *The Collected Poems of Wallace Stevens*, copyright 1923 and renewed 1951 by Wallace Stevens, reprinted by permission of Alfred A. Knopf, Inc.

JOHN STONE. "Linda" from *The Smell of Matches* by John Stone, Rutgers University Press, Brunswick, New Jersey, 1972.

MAY SWENSON. "How to Be Old" from *To Mix With Time*, copyright © 1963 by May Swenson, reprinted by permission of Charles Scribner's Sons.

FREDERICK DYER THOMPSON. "A Brief Life" reprinted by permission of Frederick Dyer Thompson.

DYLAN THOMAS. "Do not go gentle into that good night" from *The Poems of Dylan Thomas*, copyright 1952 by Dylan Thomas, reprinted by permission of New Directions Publishing Corporation and the Trustees for the Copyrights of the late Dylan Thomas.

PHYLLIS WEBB. "Marvell's Garden" from *Selected Poems: 1954–1965* (published by Talonbooks, Vancouver, B. C.), copyright 1971 by Phyllis Webb, reprinted by permission of the author.

Definition of "bat." Reprinted by permission from *Webster's Third New International Dictionary*, © 1971 by G. & C. Merriam Co., Publishers of the Merriam-Webster Dictionaries.

RICHARD WILBUR. "Quiet" from *Candide*, copyright 1957 by Richard Wilbur, reprinted by permission of G. Schirmer, Inc.; "Mind" and "A Baroque Wall-Fountain in the Villa Sciarra" from *Things of this World* ("A Baroque Wall-Fountain in the Villa Sciarra" first published in *The New Yorker*), copyright © 1956 by Richard Wilbur, reprinted by permission of Harcourt Brace Jovanovich, Inc.; "Years-End" from *Ceremony and Other Poems* by Richard Wilbur, first published in *The New Yorker*, copyright 1949 by Richard Wilbur, reprinted by permission of Harcourt Brace Jovanovich, Inc.

EMMETT WILLIAMS. "A Festive Marching Song in the Shape of 10 Dixie Cups" from *An Anthology of Concrete Poetry*, copyright 1967 by Something Else Press, Inc., New York, reprinted by permission of the publisher.

WILLIAM CARLOS WILLIAMS. "This Is Just to Say" and "Poem (As the cat . . .)" from *Collected Earlier Poems* by William Carlos Williams, copyright 1938 by William Carlos Williams, reprinted by permission of New Directions Publishing Corporation; "The Red Wheelbarrow" from *Collected Earlier Poems* by William Carlos Williams, copyright 1938 by New Directions Publishing Corporation, reprinted by permission of New Directions Publishing Corporation.

RICHARD WRIGHT, "In The Falling Snow," copyright © by Richard Wright, reprinted by permission of Paul R. Reynolds, Inc., 599 Fifth Avenue, New York, N.Y. 10017.

W. B. YEATS. "Leda and the Swan" from *The Collected Poems of W. B. Yeats*, copyright 1928 by The Macmillan Company, renewed 1956 by Bertha Georgie Yeats, reprinted by permission of The Macmillan Company, M. B. Yeats, Esq., and A. P. Watt & Son, Ltd.; "The Second Coming" and "The Wild Swans at Coole" from *Collected Poems of W. B. Yeats*, copyright 1924,

1919 by The Macmillan Company, renewed 1952, 1947 by Bertha Georgie Yeats, reprinted by permission of The Macmillan Company and M. B. Yeats, Esq.; "Byzantium" from *The Collected Poems of W. B. Yeats,* copyright 1933 by The Macmillan Company, renewed 1961 by Bertha Georgie Yeats, and "Among School Children" from *The Collected Poems of W. B. Yeats*, copyright 1928 by The Macmillan Company, renewed 1956 by Bertha Georgie Yeats, reprinted by permission of The Macmillan Company and M. B. Yeats, Esq.

*For Marjo*

. . . A real tradition is not the relic of a past that is irretrievably gone; it is a living force that animates and informs the present. . . . Far from implying the repetition of what has been, tradition presupposes the reality of what endures. It appears as an heirloom, a heritage that one receives on condition of making it bear fruit before passing it on to one's descendants. . . . Tradition thus assures the continuity of creation.

Igor Stravinsky
POETICS OF MUSIC

# Contents

## Part II

# Preface

In putting this book together, I have tried to accomplish two things: first, to present a method of analysis by which any poem, without consideration of its era or author, can be assessed for its unique merit as meaning and as art; and, second, to inject an awareness of poetry's history into this presentation. Because I believe that almost all students can respond to complex poems from the start, the book does not progress from simple to difficult works, but rather from basic questions of artistic purpose and form, through a treatment of the verbal elements of poetry and on to some of the less forbidding technicalities of sound and stress.

The poems in Part I appear mainly because they make good examples of the poetic elements, but also because they show that poetry is "motionless in time," and that although styles and attitudes change, the elements of poetry, like the elements of any living thing, remain constant. In this selection and arrangement of examples lies the substructure of the text. If the plan works, two kinds of development may go on at the same time, and the student will have had the repeated pleasure of reading poems drawn from a wide historical spectrum. Another part of my plan is the frequent pairing of poems to invite comparisons of content and style, and of old and new approaches to recurring themes. I realize that modern works are often the most interesting ones, and I have tried to include as many of them as possible without ignoring the debt that the present owes to the past. The anthology in Part II presents a sampling of six centuries of poems in English, from Chaucer to the Chicano poets, chosen because they are memorable and because they make excellent works to use with the apparatus in Part I.

Part I has more than 200 poems, half of which are modern. Poems which might prove too long for discussion in a single class session appear in the anthology. Though the chapters come in developmental order, there is no pressing reason why individual chapters, such as those on characterization, meter, and sound effects, should not be taken up at the instructor's discretion. Anyone who wants to concentrate on individual authors will find the index helpful in gathering together works by such major poets as Donne, Keats, or Frost, who appear in both Parts I and II.

From beginning to end, this book holds that the appreciation of art is synonymous with the ability to observe and admire the creative technique of the artist. The first three chapters are "preparatory." They lay the foundation for later analytical processes, reminding the student to build his study of poetry on what he already knows about language and life. In each chapter the introductory comment should establish a reference point for the questions that follow many of the poems. Since this is an introductory text, it aims to convey basic information and to employ a vocabulary that makes it easier to talk about poetry.

W. C. C.

# Part I

# INTRODUCTION TO POETRY

*Chapter 1*

# You and the Tradition

MANY literate people never become perceptive readers of poetry and literature as a fine art. This book presumes that any intelligent person can understand poetry, and that the pleasure of understanding depends on his being able to notice and to discuss the strategies through which poets develop their powerful effects. To this end, the bulk of the text aims at helping the student analyze poems by seeing how the irreducible parts (the *elements*) of poetry contribute to the formation of a unified whole.

But before we become deeply involved in analyzing poetry, we should be sure that we do not expect the wrong things: we should not expect all poems to be pretty or uplifting or clearly informative, and we should not expect an art that has been advancing through thousands of years to be unchallenging.

At times, the main interest in poetry is in the manner of speech, not in its content. Gerard Manley Hopkins maintained that poetry is ". . . speech framed . . . to be heard for its own sake and interest even over and above its interest of meaning." A reader who thinks the only worthwhile writing is clear prose and who expects to "get something out of" his reading may find this idea difficult to accept. Modern poetry will almost certainly disappoint him, and he may find up-to-date writing harder to understand than literature from say, the sixteenth or seventeenth century. He wants to read about what is going on around him; he knows the language, and yet he feels somehow ill-equipped. Should he go back, start at the beginning and work his way up to the present? Probably not, even though there is much to be said for the historical approach. A better course would be to read poetry, old and new, recognizing that the elements of all poems are very much the same, and resisting any urge to abandon difficult works. Historical perspective will come with wide reading, and there is no reason to delay the study of the here-and-now, which has a natural first claim on our interest.

Most literate people of 100 years ago knew what to expect, at least in form, of their poets. The differences between the works of the past and the present at that time were largely external—they reflected differences in the answers to the problems which were out in the open and which could be thought about. People had to contend with the new scientific discoveries of Darwin just as their great-grandfathers had to contend with the radical political theories of Rousseau ad Godwin. But they had in common the belief that their problems might be worked out through reason, and might be conveyed in words.

With the modern age came the discovery that much of both human understanding and confusion results from mental responses that are not rational. There also came a change in the artistic portrayal of man's inner life. The poet may, in trying to depict the mental experience, get beneath the surface meaning of words as we speak and write them, and into the more fundamental mingling of images or symbols. This mingling may resemble dreams more than conscious thought.

Here begins the problem for today's student of poetry. In his general reading, "speed" and "comprehension" are the goals. His aim in writing is clarity and force. But in reading poetry he must change his standards and be willing to adjust to the poem without rushing. He must realize that comprehension, which is rarely total, does not necessarily demand that he can accurately summarize what he reads.

Experienced readers know that no poem is good simply because it is clear, and no poem is bad simply because it is unclear. To enjoy poetry, one must cultivate a quality which poets themselves need and which Keats called the "negative capability," that is, the ability to be "in uncertainties, mysteries, doubts, without any irritable reaching after fact or reason."

With these opening caveats in mind, compare the following two poems, which are both, however different in statement, serious works of art.

## *Richard Cory*

Whenever Richard Cory went down town,
We people on the pavement looked at him:
He was a gentleman from sole to crown,
Clean favored, and imperially slim.

And he was always quietly arrayed,
And he was always human when he talked;
But still he fluttered pulses when he said,
"Good-morning," and he glittered when he walked.

And he was rich—yes, richer than a king—
And admirably schooled in every grace:
In fine, we thought that he was everything
To make us wish that we were in his place.

So on we worked, and waited for the light,
And went without the meat, and cursed the bread;
And Richard Cory, one calm summer night,
Went home and put a bullet through his head.

Edwin Arlington Robinson (1869–1935)

## *A Free One*

Watch any day his nonchalant pauses, see
His dextrous handling of a wrap as he
Steps after into cars, the beggar's envy.

'There is a free one,' many say, but err.
He is not that returning conqueror,
Nor ever the poles' circumnavigator.

But poised between shocking falls on razor-edge
Has taught himself this balancing subterfuge
Of an accosting profile, an erect carriage.

The song, the varied action of the blood,
Would drown the warning from the iron wood,
Would cancel the inertia of the buried:

Travelling by daylight on from house to house
The longest way to an intrinsic peace,
With love's fidelity and with love's weakness.

W. H. Auden (1907–1973)

Both poems deal with the contrast between the outer show and inner life of a man. But each poet, after the initial contrast, makes a different application. Robinson, through pungent definiteness, cuts the poem off with sharp irony. The effect Auden is seeking is less definite. Yet the attraction in these poems does not lie in the clarity of their resolution or ending. In fact, it is the very difference between the poet's way of expressing the thought and any summary we might give that will help us to get at an understanding of the poetry. Both poets are trying to give more than information about their subjects.

A paraphrase of "Richard Cory" might go this way:

Any time Richard Cory made a trip to town
those of us in the streets watched him.
He was from head to toe more than a common man,
good looking and slim in the way aristocrats are slim.

He always wore inconspicuous clothes,
and he never tried to be standoffish in his speech;
yet hearts beat a little faster when he said
"Good morning," and when he walked he stood out brightly.

And he was wealthy, wealthier than a monarch,
and he had mastered all the ways of his class:
in short, we thought that he had whatever it takes
to make us wish we were he.

We just went ahead working, hoping for a brighter day
and we had no meat to eat, and damned the bread;
and Richard Cory, one still night in summer,
went home and shot himself in the head.

Obviously, something is lacking in the paraphrase that was present in the poem. The poem's appeal has something to do with the *way* the poet has put the words together. He has said things to suggest more than a random selection or arrangement of words would allow. Robinson has first of all emphasized the contrast between the speaker and Richard Cory by the choice of words describing or associated with him. After we notice that the very name Richard Cory sounds aristocratic (it may echo the name of Richard I—Richard Coeur de Lion), we see that many words suggest royalty and splendor. Even the preposition in the first line makes a difference, suggesting the levels of society which separate Cory from the throng—he went *down* town. The people are *on* the *pavement* (looking up), rather than in the streets or on the sidewalks.

Reading more closely, the reader may detect a quality in the words apart from meaning that affects him. He may find this more difficult to explain. Take, for example, the lines:

> But still he fluttered pulses when he said,
> "Good-morning," and he glittered when he walked.

Robinson has produced more than a compound sentence here. Without extraordinary words and without unusual speech patterns, he has created a definite rhythm. The similarities in the sounds of "fluttered" and "glittered" echo through the lines while they help define a vivid mental picture of the royal Richard. Throughout the poem, the manner of the speaker, his sense of awe, comes through and is enhanced by the rhythm. In the line, "And he was rich—yes, richer than a king—" the sense of the speaker's search to find the right words comes in part from the stop and go of the phrases. After the poem's surprise ending, the reader's imagination goes on to explore deeper meanings that may be taken from the incident.

A paraphrase of Auden's poem presents more difficulty:

> Notice anytime his seemingly careless stops; watch
> his agile manipulation of a lady's cloak as he
> steps after it into autos—any beggar would be jealous.
>
> "There goes a carefree person" many say, but they are
>     mistaken.
> He is not a victor come home
> nor was he ever the one to sail around the poles.

But carefully holding a position between jarring missteps on
  a sharp blade,
he has trained himself how to do this undercurrent of
  inner edge-walking
which makes itself evident in his striking face and upright walk.

The music, the irregular flow of the blood
would smother the cautioning of the spear,
would set aside the inability to move of that which is
  covered over:

Moving out in the light of day from dwelling to dwelling,
taking the longest way to the inner quiet,
with the faithfulness of love and its frailty.

This poem, like "Richard Cory," begins in a conversational tone. The title, "A Free One," makes no sense until the fourth line when we learn that the label, based on superficial observation, misleads. The person described in the poem seems to have the grace and poise of one who acts, dares, and succeeds almost instinctively. Secretly he is too cautious; if he could respond spontaneously to his emotions, if he could risk letting down his guard, he could achieve a natural steadiness. But this would require chancing the strength and frailty of love.

In trying to paraphrase Auden's poem, one soon realizes that the simple substitution of synonyms is not enough, especially in the last three stanzas, after the poet has provided a fairly vivid picture of the "hero's" manner before the public. Robinson's poem concludes as clearly as it begins. Richard Cory's suicide is evidence of disastrous psychic trouble, but Robinson does not attempt to explain the trouble. Auden goes into the subject's mind; he tries to find words that will somehow contain the meaning he wants. He tries to create a vivid image at last of what goes on in the mind by referring to objects of the external world such as razors, and falls, and balancing. The "blood" mentioned in stanza four does not literally have action or song; but since the heart gives to blood a beat, a rhythm of flow, the reader can understand how the words "song" and "blood" may be associated in the poem. Literally the idea that song "would drown the warning of the iron wood," is nonsense. Perhaps it helps to know that "iron wood" is an ancient way of saying "spear," but the words suggest something physical that can do harm. The song can cancel out the sense of harm, and it can cancel the "inertia of the buried." This is a surprising phrase, since literally nothing can bring the dead to life. But if one keeps in mind that the poet is speaking about what goes on in the inner or emotional life of a man, the idea—that those desires and thoughts which men repress or cover over because of fear can be brought out into the open—is not hard to accept.

In reading the final section of the poem, one must remember that the subject is still a man's inner life. The "travelling" mentioned in line 13 is not literal. It is merely a concrete way of saying how emotions can seem, once they are relieved of confining fears. In the next to the last line the phrase "the longest way" suggests the way one takes when free of anxiety. The "intrinsic" peace is that inward calm that would make a display of self confidence unnecessary. The last line, for all its smoothness, reminds us that love, the source of peace, is not perfect.

The subtlety of the musical effects in Auden's lines goes well with the subtlety of the thought, just as the forthright beat and rhyme of Robinson's poem fits the subject. Whereas Robinson rhymes "town" with "crown," and "talked" with "walked," Auden's rhymes are almost inaudible: "razor-edge," "subterfuge," and "carriage," for example. Both poets try to blend the sense of a line with its rhythm. Auden makes the line about balancing seem to totter with the very word "balancing," which upsets the rhythm—

> Has taught himself this balancing subterfuge.

Both "Richard Cory" and "A Free One" draw upon a wider array of the potential for communicating knowledge and feeling than does prose. Both can be appreciated by any reader who will let the words find free association with one another—by any reader who will let all the words enjoy the widest range of meaning.

Like the poems of Auden and Robinson, the two that follow have certain traits in common. They are both in the *carpe diem* vein (this is a kind of poem which defends living for the moment; the term translated means "seize the day"), but the modern poem adds a disruptive element not apparent in the earlier work. The modern age, so devoted to scientific knowledge, has developed a way of writing which challenges reason because mere reason in language cannot record the play of emotion and the subconscious experience.

### *To the Virgins, to Make Much of Time*

Gather ye rose-buds while ye may,
  Old time is still a-flying:
And this same flower that smiles today,
  Tomorrow will be dying.

The glorious lamp of heaven, the sun,
  The higher he's a-getting,
The sooner will his race be run,
  And nearer he's to setting.

That age is best which is the first,
  When youth and blood are warmer;
But being spent, the worse, and worst
  Times, still succeed the former.

Then be not coy, but use your time;
  And while ye may, go marry:
For having lost but once your prime,
  You may for ever tarry.

Robert Herrick (1591–1674)

### *Sick Love*

O Love, be fed with apples while you may,
And feel the sun and go in royal array,
A smiling innocent on the heavenly causeway,

Though in what listening horror for the cry
That soars in outer blackness dismally,
The dumb blind beast, the paranoiac fury:

Be warm, enjoy the season, lift your head,
Exquisite in the pulse of tainted blood,
That shivering glory not to be despised.

Take your delight in momentariness,
Walk between dark and dark—a shining space
With the grave's narrowness, though not its peace.

Robert Graves (1895– )

## QUESTIONS

1. What evidence do you see which suggests that Graves had Herrick's poem in mind when he wrote "Sick Love"? Herrick offers practical advice; how does Graves's counsel differ? How do the moods set by the two poems differ?

2. Herrick says "Gather ye rose-buds," while Graves advises "be fed on apples." Is there a difference in what these phrases suggest? How does this suggestion and the title of Graves's poem affect your interpretation? What *is* the thing that threatens the innocent love pictured in Graves's first stanza?

3. Paraphrase both poems. Do not simply give a general summary. The *paraphrase* should be a restatement, phrase by phrase, of the original. You may have to amplify when you come to phrases that do not make forthright, literal sense. What does each poem communicate which its paraphrase does not?

4. Do you agree with those "New Critics" who maintain that the true nature of the poem cannot be expressed in any words but its own?

To end this introduction, let us have a look at two poems which may seem unrelated at first glance. Both are modern, both offer some resistance to the understanding, and both make a statement—either directly or indirectly—about dying.

The main sign of modernity in Dylan Thomas's poem is that it finds no need to be perfectly rational. Highly emotional experiences rarely are. But in his use of a very strict form, he makes a firm bond with tradition. This poem is widely considered as one of the finest of all *villanelles* (a highly formal poem of nineteen lines with a set pattern for repeating rhymes and whole lines). The form challenges the poet's ability to use much repetition without seeming repetitious. Yet Thomas is performing no mere exercise in technique; he is recording the intense thought and feeling he experienced as he watched his father die. Before going to the questions, read the poem once to get the feel of the rhythm and sound, then go through it once more, concentrating on thought content. Direct your attention to the middle line in each set of three lines.

*Do not go gentle into that good night*

Do not go gentle into that good night,
Old age should burn and rave at close of day;
Rage, rage against the dying of the light.

Though wise men at their end know dark is right,
Because their words had forked no lightning they
Do not go gentle into that good night.

Good men, the last wave by, crying how bright
Their frail deeds might have danced in a green bay,
Rage, rage against the dying of the light.

Wild men who caught and sang the sun in flight,
And learn, too late, they grieved it on its way,
Do not go gentle into that good night.

Grave men, near death, who see with blinding sight
Blind eyes could blaze like meteors and be gay,
Rage, rage against the dying of the light.

And you, my father, there on the sad height,
Curse, bless, me now with your fierce tears, I pray.
Do not go gentle into that good night.
Rage, rage against the dying of the light.

Dylan Thomas (1914–1953)

QUESTIONS

1. How does the formality, particularly the repetition of lines 1 and 3, contribute to the emotional impact of the poem?

2. What new elements introduced in the second, third, and fourth sets of lines does Thomas use to advance his thought?

3. Paraphrase the poem. What is Thomas's attitude toward death? Does he think that one's willingness to die has anything to do with being wise, good, wild, or grave? Why doesn't he want his father to die willingly?

The following poem by Philip Levine has a definite, limiting form too. He works in set units of four lines, with about seven syllables to the line. Part of the contemporary flavor of this poem comes from its vocabulary and sentence structure, which are deliberately "unpoetic." That is, there is nothing pretty or dressed up about the language. But it is poetic in its rhythm, vividness, and freshness. You will be left with doubts about what, exactly, has been said, but Levine makes a definite impression that there is a zest for life, even though it is full of horror and death.

*Animals Are Passing from Our Lives*

It's wonderful how I jog
on four honed-down ivory toes
my massive buttocks slipping
like oiled parts with each light step.

I'm to market, I can smell
the sour, grooved block, I can smell
the blade that opens the hole
and the pudgy white fingers

that shake out the intestines
like a hankie. In my dreams
the snouts drool on the marble,
suffering children, suffering flies,

suffering the consumers
who won't meet their steady eyes
for fear they could see. The boy
who drives me along believes

that any moment I'll fall
on my side and drum my toes
like a typewriter or squeal
and shit like a new housewife

discovering television,
or that I'll turn like a beast
cleverly to hook his teeth
with my teeth. No. Not this pig.

Philip Levine (1928– )

## QUESTIONS

1. Why does the poet use a pig and all the details of the slaughter house to say something about human existence? How do you know the statement is not literally about a pig?
2. How does the speaker's viewpoint differ from that of a cartoon character or the usual pig in an animal fable?
3. What does the boy (line 15) signify?
4. You may find that the poem becomes difficult to follow around line 10. Begin a paraphrase here. Your search for parallel words may give you some ideas about interpretation. What alternative ways of reading the poem do you see?

Every person interested in poetry will, in time, develop an awareness of how interrelated its past and present are. When he begins to read in a collection of poems drawn from centuries of verse, he will find that it is something like visiting a large museum of art. He realizes that he cannot absorb all of it in a day. He may content himself with browsing at first, and lingering over a few exhibits which strike him as being most pleasing or most perplexing, but he will probably neither enjoy nor understand all that he sees. He will have to come back again and again, just as the reader of poetry must, to nourish the beginnings of his interest. Once he gets beyond the initial response based on personal preference, the growth of his appreciation depends on an understanding of what art is attempting to do, and how it differs from other forms of expression.

*Chapter 2*

# Purpose and Form

TO Boswell's question," What is poetry?" Dr. Johnson replied, "Why, sir, it is much easier to say what it is not. We all *know* what light is, but it is not easy to *tell* what it is." Maybe the best way to tell the difference between the purpose of prose and that of poetry is to say what its purpose is not, then to show the difference.

## *Purpose*

First, poetry is not intended to convey information, even though in the process of doing its work, poetry often does give information. If, for example, you should want a good account of the battle of Balaklava in the Crimean War during which hundreds of English cavalrymen of the 600th Brigade were killed, you may find what you need to know in history. But for a sense of excitement in the event, you will do better to read Tennyson's poem, "The Charge of the Light Brigade." Poetry does not, like history, seek to account for facts; it uses the facts of human experience and tries to create a sharper sensation of experiencing these facts.

The difference between the way an archive preserves experience and the way poetry does is simply that a study of the records informs, and the study of poetry reawakens the life which went into the making of the poem. For example, newspapers pour out a constant barrage of facts about disaster, yet somehow we are insulated against many of these facts because they do not involve us imaginatively. Karl Shapiro's "Auto Wreck" (see p. 376) says more about the subject than the fact that 500 Americans died in auto accidents during the Easter weekend—12 fewer than last year. In 1901 a young boy was killed in an accident reported in *The Littleton* (N.H.) *Courier* as follows:

*Sad Tragedy at Bethlehem*
*Raymond Fitzgerald a Victim*
*of Fatal Accident*

Raymond Tracy Fitzgerald, one of the twin sons of Michael G. and Margaret Fitzgerald of Bethlehem, died at his home Thursday afternoon, March 24, as the result of an accident by which one of his hands was badly hurt in a sawing machine. The young man was assisting in sawing up some wood in his own dooryard with a sawing machine and accidentally hit the loose pulley, causing the saw to descend upon his hand, cutting and lacerating it badly. Raymond was taken into the house and a physician was immediately summoned, but he died very suddenly from the effects of the shock, which produced heart failure. . . .

Robert Frost knew young Fitzgerald, who had played with the Frost children during two summer visits in the Bethlehem area. It was at least nine years before the poet began to make his record of the event, and fifteen years before the poem was published.

*'Out, Out—'*

The buzz saw snarled and rattled in the yard
And made dust and dropped stove-length sticks of wood,
Sweet-scented stuff when the breeze drew across it.
And from there those that lifted eyes could count
Five mountain ranges one behind the other
Under the sunset far into Vermont.

And the saw snarled and rattled, snarled and rattled,
As it ran light, or had to bear a load.
And nothing happened: day was all but done.
Call it a day, I wish they might have said
To please the boy by giving him the half hour
That a boy counts so much when saved from work.
His sister stood beside them in her apron
To tell them "Supper." At the word, the saw,
As if to prove saws knew what supper meant,
Leaped out at the boy's hand, or seemed to leap—
He must have given the hand. However it was,
Neither refused the meeting. But the hand!
The boy's first outcry was a rueful laugh,
As he swung toward them holding up the hand,
Half in appeal, but half as if to keep
The life from spilling. Then the boy saw all—
Since he was old enough to know, big boy
Doing a man's work, though a child at heart—
He saw all spoiled. "Don't let him cut my hand off—
The doctor, when he comes. Don't let him, sister!"
So. But the hand was gone already.
The doctor put him in the dark of ether.
He lay and puffed his lips out with his breath.
And then—the watcher at his pulse took fright.
No one believed. They listened at his heart.
Little—less—nothing!—and that ended it.
No more to build on there. And they, since they
Were not the one dead, turned to their affairs.

Robert Frost (1874–1963)

## QUESTIONS

1. The title calls to mind Macbeth's speech on hearing of the death of Lady Macbeth (see *Macbeth,* Act V, scene v). What meaning does Macbeth see in death? How does this affect the mood of this poem?

2. In general, how do the details in the news article differ from those in the poem?

3. The news article does not engage in any comparisons. What are some of the comparisons Frost makes, and what does this do to the emotional impact of the poem?

4. Poetry is supposed to delight. Can a poem like this cause delight? How?

What you find out about bats in an encyclopedia or book of zoology may even be much fuller of detail than the actual experience of coming upon a bat by surprise. Yet the very best verbal account of the biological facts about bats cannot match the sensation of seeing one. A poem can create in the mind for an instant a vital sense of the creature, though the facts may be, from the point of view of the natural scientist, hazy and general.

Which statement does more to sharpen in your mind's eye a picture of the bat? First, a dictionary definition:

> Any one of numerous flying mammals that constitute the order Chiroptera, the only mammals capable of true flight, having the fore limbs modified to form wings, the metacarpals and finger bones except for the thumb being greatly elongated and supporting like the ribs of an umbrella a cutaneous membrane that also extends a little in front of the arm and also embraces the hind limbs except the feet and sometimes the whole length of the tail; having a thumb and toes with claws by which the animal suspends itself often head downwards when at rest; being nocturnal in habit and among the most perfectly aerial animals, locomotion other than by flying being comparatively difficult for it; occurring most abundantly and attaining the largest size in warm countries; and being mostly insectivorous though some are frugivorous and a few suck the blood of other mammals.
>
> from *Webster's Third International Dictionary*

Then, from D. H. Lawrence's "Bat":

> A twitch, a twitter, an elastic shudder in flight
> And serrated wings against the sky,
> Like a glove, black glove thrown up at the light,
> And falling back.

The poem provides an image of the bat as we know it—in dark and fleeting glimpses, not stretched out on the laboratory table. With words such as "twitch," "twitter," and "shudder," the poem makes its sounds convey both sight, sound, and motion impressions. In addition, it uses associated mental pictures by comparing the bat in flight to a falling black glove. The excellent associated image of the dictionary definition which compares the bat's finger bones to umbrella ribs is vivid, but it vivifies the bat as the zoologist sees it—in the light, and without emotion. Most often the poet is interested in going beyond the creation of a vivid mental image; he may go further, linking his image to that part of experience that lies beneath simple observation. The poem below provides an example of what the poet might do with a vivid mental picture of bats.

*The Bats*

These caverns yield
But vampires upside down.
Better the field or town
Than exploration such as this.
These creatures of antithesis
With webbed unfeathered wings
Will shrink away from our electric wink
Lest they be dazzled to the dark of things.

Through stalactites
Of lancets in reverse
Their muffled flights rehearse
A foray on the world of sleep.
These are our underdreams that keep
Our secrets from ourselves,
The lark become half rodent in that dark
Wherein the downward mountain climber delves.

Seal all, before
In ragged panic driven
These nightwings pour to heaven
And seal us from our natural sun.
Of two forbidden trees, there's one
Untampered with till now,
Where throng, with their inaudibly high song,
The bats headdown from roots that are its bough.

Robert Hillyer (1895– )

QUESTIONS

1. What closely observed details about bats and their natural environment do you find? In what sense are bats "creatures of antithesis" (line 5)?

2. What emotional responses does the speaker try to arouse? What is the speaker's attitude toward the exploring of caverns? Which words in the first division of the poem reflect this attitude?

3. The contrast between caverns and the open landscape parallels a contrast in human consciousness. Explain. What kind of mental activity does the flight of bats stand for? What does "our natural sun" (line 20) suggest? Does this imply that the dark world of bats is unnatural?

4. The speaker seems to disapprove of probing the subconscious. Is the poet trying to convince the reader to accept this attitude, or is he trying to construct a mental picture and a mood?

5. The two trees alluded to in line 21 are a reference to the tree of knowledge and the tree of life or to the tree of knowledge of good and evil. The picture suggested is of two trees growing from a single surface, one above the ground and the other into the ground. Does this biblical reference make an appropriate ending?

## *Form*

Poetry and prose differ not only in purpose, but also in form. The first thing anyone notices about printed matter is the way it looks; in one kind of writing the words fill up the page, and in the other kind, poetry, the words are arranged. This arrangement signals that the writing is "different," that it will do something unusual. But giving form to poetry is more than a matter of making it look different—the difference must have significance.

Poetry, like all art, is formal. The arrangement of its parts can never be mere chance, and its design follows some purpose in the artist's mind. One reason for poetry's formality is that form adds a dimension to ordinary speech which helps it capture even the most evasive experience in words. This strength in poetry owes much to the power that comes only through the discipline of form. Another reason for having form is that design, even when used for its own sake, is a source of pleasure.

The following poem, though it is not at all rigid, illustrates a modern poet's way of finding freedom within formality. Keep in mind that any kind of repetition is an aspect of form.

*After Drinking All Night with a Friend,*
*We Go Out in a Boat at Dawn*
*to See Who Can Write the Best Poem*

These pines, these fall oaks, these rocks,
This water dark and touched by wind—
I am like you, you dark boat,
Drifting over water fed by cool springs.

Beneath the waters, since I was a boy,
I have dreamt of strange and dark treasures,
Not of gold, or strange stones, but the true
Gift, beneath the pale lakes of Minnesota.

This morning also, drifting in the dawn wind,
I sense my hands, and my shoes, and this ink—
Drifting, as all of this body drifts,
Above the clouds of the flesh and the stone.

A few friendships, a few dawns, a few glimpses of grass,
A few oars weathered by the snow and the heat,
So we drift toward shore, over cold waters,
No longer caring if we drift or go straight.

Robert Bly (1926– )

QUESTIONS

1. What would be the effect if there were no spacing between the sets of lines? What, if anything, would be lost if the poem had four sets of three lines and one four-line set? Would eight sets of two lines work as well?

2. Contrast is an element of formality used in this poem. What is the poet's point in making the title, a prose sentence, so different from the four sentences in the poem?

3. Notice that the poet uses seven words to a line at first, then begins to drift away from this pattern. Does this deviation have any significance?

4. Bly uses much repetition of words. Point out these repetitions and infer what the purpose is.

## *Internal and External Structure*

Unlike prose, which has only internal structure, every composition in verse has both internal and external form. The *internal form* lies in the organization of thought; the *external form* is the structure evident to the senses such as the shape of the poem on the page and the patterns of sound evident to the ear. When, in reading prose, one sees how the sub-parts of an essay or argument are arranged, he is noticing structure. In writing a poem with a thesis, the poet might, for example, move from particular details to a general conclusion, or he might move from general to particular just as a writer of prose would do. A playwright arranges the pieces of action and dialogue into scenes and acts, and a writer of fiction into chapters and episodes. Most prose, however, does not have external structuring such as the arrangement of print on a page or the pattern of sound repetitions. Poetry has this together with its subtle linkage among words and its arrangement of symbols and figurative comparisons which contribute to internal structure. Ideally, the internal and external patterns should support one another.

Without going into great technical detail, let us take the *sonnet* as an example. It is a poem of fourteen lines, usually with ten syllables to a line and with some kind of grouping of lines according to sound. This describes only the sonnet's external structure, which is relatively fixed. Once the poet commits himself to write in this form, he works out the plan of his statement, which constitutes the internal form. Consider the following.

### *Sonnet 60*

Like as the waves make towards the pebbled shore,
So do our minutes hasten to their end;
Each changing place with that which goes before,
In sequent toil all forwards do contend.
Nativity, once in the main of light,
Crawls to maturity, wherewith being crowned,
Crooked eclipses 'gainst his glory fight,
And time that gave doth now his gift confound.
Time doth transfix the flourish set on youth
And delves the parallels in beauty's brow,
Feeds on the rarities of nature's truth,
And nothing stands but for his scythe to mow.
  And yet to times in hope my verse shall stand,
  Praising thy worth, despite his cruel hand.

William Shakespeare (1564–1616)

## QUESTIONS

1. Notice that Shakespeare uses three sets of four lines, with each set introducing a new idea about time. Do you agree that the groupings grow less and less remote? Explain.

2. In developing his idea, Shakespeare refers to the passage of time as it is evident in the sea, in the sky, and on the land. Explain how this shift of attention from one phase of nature to the next parallels a shift in the poem's external structure.

3. The vocabulary in this sonnet emphasizes a strong sense of action. How does Shakespeare's choice of nouns, adjectives, adverbs, and prepositions contribute to the impression of activity? Notice particularly the verbs used as nouns and adjectives. Since the poet employs so many words which either are verbs or can be used as verbs, could it be argued that word choice is an aspect of the internal design of the poem?

The sonnet below, written in 1973, uses an old form for a timeless theme, but with a definitely modern slant. The rhymes follow the same pattern as Shakespeare's, but the lines are grouped into one set of eight and another of six lines, as in the *Petrarchan sonnet* (named after the Italian poet, Petrarch). Petrarch himself used the idea of love as being like a shipwreck, and the poem given here is a conscious echo of both the old form and subject.

### *The Sea within the Ship*

It is the sea within the ship I fear;
This fluttering of blood into the breach
Beats shipwreck through the lines and such a dear
Disaster rattles in the heart that each
Slow rope and vein is shaken from its knots;
The elements of love bring ruin to
The nerves and currents in the muscled slots
Until the rigging in the limbs falls through.

Imagined passions scatter such debris
Across my sleep that I have come to ache
For devastation; for it is the sea
Within the ship that whispers me awake
And fingers through my thoughts until I rise
To write the ocean out before it dries.

Robert Hudson (1954–     )

QUESTIONS

1. Does the external structure (for example, the sets of eight and six lines) support the internal structure (the thought development)? Explain.

2. Can you see any repetitive patterns in vocabulary that contribute to the poem's structure?

3. Is the poem about real or imagined experience? Explain the meaning of the last line.

If you feel inclined to write a strictly formal poem, the Japanese *haiku* might be a good form to try. Haiku has been a favorite for centuries in Japan, where it was written by such famous poets as Bashô and Buson and by millions of common people. The rules are fairly simple: 1. Write three lines with five syllables in the first and third lines and seven syllables in the middle line. 2. Include detail drawn, directly or indirectly, from nature, particularly the seasons of the year. 3. Concentrate on what the words suggest rather than on what they explain; avoid generalization.

Here is one of our best haiku.

*In the Falling Snow*

In the falling snow
A laughing boy holds out his palms
Until they are white.

Richard Wright (1908–1960)

## *Patterns of Organization*

Prose and poetry actually have much in common in the way they order thought. If one has an understanding of how this order operates in prose, he has a good start in learning about the formal arrangement of ideas in poetry.

Certain patterns of organization have developed to serve the purposes of speech and writing which has some definite objective. This means of using language, called *discourse,* always has a recognizable beginning, middle, and end, and is to be distinguished from random talk or conversation which may be logical and clear without being planned. Poetry is always planned, and like prose discourse it usually has a story to tell, an idea or emotion to convey, an argument to present, or some mental picture to portray. Yet poetry, whether it is narrating, explaining, arguing, or describing, always seeks in addition to awaken in the reader a more vivid sense of life. As the Greek philosopher Longinus put it, "in poetry the end is enthrallment, in prose, clarity." Regardless of what the rhetorical end of a poem may be, its ultimate purpose is to create pleasure. If, as in the poem given below, the poet uses argument, builds a word picture, conveys ideas, and implies a story, his rhetorical structuring is the means, not the end.

Once again we have a *carpe diem* ("seize the day") poem. Most readers take it as an argument in favor of overcoming all obstacles to lovemaking, but some see the speaker in the poem as a suitor who deviously avoids any mention of the advantages of the "chaste courtship." How do you read it?

### *To His Coy Mistress*

Had we but world enough, and time,
This coyness, lady, were no crime.
We would sit down, and think which way
To walk, and pass our long love's day.
Thou by the Indian Ganges' side
Should'st rubies find; I by the tide
of Humber would complain. I would
Love you ten years before the Flood;
And you should, if you please, refuse
Till the conversion of the Jews.
My vegetable love should grow
Vaster than empires, and more slow.
An hundred years should go to praise
Thine eyes, and on thy forehead gaze;
Two hundred to adore each breast;
But thirty thousand to the rest:
An age at least to every part,
And the last age should show your heart.
For, lady, you deserve this state,
Nor would I love at lower rate.
   But at my back I always hear
Time's wingèd chariot hurrying near;
And yonder all before us lie
Deserts of vast eternity.

Thy beauty shall no more be found,
Nor in thy marble vault shall sound
My echoing song; then worms shall try
That long-preserved virginity;
And your quaint honor turn to dust,
And into ashes all my lust.
The grave's a fine and private place,
But none, I think, do there embrace.
   Now, therefore, while the youthful hue
Sits on thy skin like morning dew,
And while thy willing soul transpires
At every pore with instant fires,
Now let us sport us while we may;
And now, like amorous birds of prey,
Rather at once our time devour,
Than languish in his slow-chapped power.
Let us roll all our strength and all
Our sweetness up into one ball;
And tear our pleasures with rough strife
Through the iron gates of life.
Thus, though we cannot make our sun
Stand still, yet we will make him run.

Andrew Marvell (1621–1678)

## QUESTIONS

1. What are the terms of the proposition argued by the speaker? Notice that each verse paragraph represents a separate stage: "If——, but——, so——."

2. When the speaker tries to create a mental picture in descriptive terms, what does he hope to accomplish? In comparing the picture of the first paragraph with that of the second, which is more realistic? Do you see any motive in this?

3. What does the speaker think stands in the way of his conquest? What side of the lady's personality does he attempt to win over? Does he respect her?

4. Consider the argument of the second verse paragraph, particularly the lines

> . . . then worms shall try
> That long-preserved virginity;
> And your quaint honor turn to dust,
> And into ashes all my lust.

Do you see any deviousness in the logic? Does the speaker equate "honor" with physical virginity?

5. Some of the sexuality in this poem is explicitly stated, as in lines 13–20, but some is there by implication. Explain the implications in lines 27–28, 41–44. Why is the poet not always aiming at clarity?

6. How does the poet build up a sense of urgency from paragraph to paragraph? Does the tempo change? Does the change of the mental pictures built contribute to the emotional crescendo?

7. You have noticed when traveling in a car or train that the distant view changes more slowly than the close-up view. Do you see any way in which this idea of the relativity of speed, time, and distance has a place in this poem?

8. In Marvell's time it was impossible to travel fast enough to make the "sun stand still." How can this actually be accomplished? Does this notion of making time stand still make a suitable ending? Does it blend with other details in the poem?

9. Considering that Marvell was a "Puritan" poet, what would you say his attitude toward the speaker in the poem is?

10. How would you respond to someone who maintained that Marvell, in depicting the seducer as a sly but convincing speaker, is implying a warning to anyone who might be taken in by an attractive but devious temptation?

If the foregoing questions have served their purpose, they have directed your attention to those rhetorical traits poetry has in common with prose. They may also have drawn out into relief those traits of emotional and intellectual stimulation common to poetry. Because poetry communicates through a chain of unfolding implications, it is concise. To achieve clarity, a prose writer holds suggestibility in check. Whereas concise prose admits no superfluous word, the conciseness of poetry derives from that which may be guided but not necessarily spelled out.

Poetry is always closer to being an experience than to being an explanation. Often, as one reflects back over a meeting, an encounter, a crucial event, he sees the experience in a different way, for even past experience tends to keep unfolding. But clear explanations achieve a stable place in the mind, as when one learns that water has three forms: solid, liquid, and gas. When poetry has that pellucid quality, which can be found in some of the lyrics of Ben Jonson or Walter Savage Landor, for example, the interest as poetry more likely will lie in the words as sounds and the evocative quality of music and manner than it will in the meaning.

## *Lyrical and Narrative*

Most of the poems in this book might be classed as *lyrical* rather than narrative; that is, their aim is more often to express some feeling or idea than it is to tell a story. The difference between lyric and narrative verse involves both purpose and structure. In *narration,* chronology has special importance, for the reader's interest is focused on what will happen to a character who is involved in a problem. Simple narratives arrange the pieces of action in order of time, and plotted narratives may rearrange the events to emphasize the high points or to create suspense.

Since a story may be told to musical accompaniment, narrative and lyric poetry are not mutually exclusive. In our century, novelists and short story writers do most of the storytelling. But in earlier periods, Chaucer's day for example, long narrative poems such as *Troilus and Cressida* and the many varieties of shorter ones, such as may be found in *The Canterbury Tales,* were the most favored means of storytelling.

## *The Ballad*

One brief form of verse narrative which has survived from the earliest days of poetry in English is the *ballad.* It usually focuses on some vivid crisis and devotes little attention to an elaborate exposition or denouement; that is, there are few preliminaries, no background filling-in or character sketches, and no final unraveling; there is no need.

No one knows whether the ballad came into being as the work of individual poets, a part of the written tradition, or whether it originated as a kind of communal art, handed on as recitations and being modified by the various performers who spoke it. Many of the best old ballads are anonymous. From the beginning, they were poems meant for singing, and so they are today. Calypso ballads of the West Indies, American mountain music, and Australian "bush" ballads are all working to keep the old forms alive.

Sometimes the ballad will be a forthright telling of the story, but it may leave much to the reader's ability to piece things together. Unlike most prose narratives, the ballad relies on musical effects and the suggestiveness of narrating limited detail. The poem below illustrates that a story can be compact without becoming a slight or inconsiderable thing.

*Sir Patrick Spens*

The king sits in Dumferling toune,
  Drinking the blude-reid wine:
"O whar will I get guid sailor,
  To sail this schip of mine?"

Up and spak an eldern knicht,° *old knight*
  Sat at the kings richt kne:
"Sir Patrick Spens is the best sailor
  That sails upon the se."

The king has written a braid° letter, *large*
  And signd it wi his hand,
And sent it to Sir Patrick Spens,
  Was walking on the sand.

The first line that Sir Patrick red,
  A loud lauch° lauched he; *laugh*
The next line that Sir Patrick red,
  The teir blinded his ee.° *eye*

"O wha is this has don this deid,
  This ill deid don to me,
To send me out this time o' the yeir,
  To sail upon the se!

"Mak hast, mak haste, my mirry men all,
  Our guid schip sails the morne":
"O say na sae,° my master deir, *say not so*
  For I feir a deadlie storme.

"Late late yestreen° I saw the new moone, *last evening*
  Wi the auld moone in hir arme,
And I feir, I feir, my deir master,
  That we will cum to harme."

O our Scots nobles wer richt laith° *very unwilling*
  To wet their cork-heild schoone;° *cork-heeled shoes*
Bot lang owre a' the play wer playd,
  Thair hats they swam aboone.° *above*

O lang, lang may their ladies sit,
Wi thair fans into their hand,
Or eir they se Sir Patrick Spens
Cum sailing to the land.

O lang, lang may the ladies stand,
Wi thair gold kems° in their hair, *combs*
Waiting for thair ain deir lords,
For they'll se thame na mair.

Haf owre, haf owre to Aberdour,
It's fiftie fadom deip,
And thair lies guid Sir Patrick Spens,
Wi the Scots lords at his feit.

Anonymous

This story, through its poetic form, is vivid without being elaborate. The poem contains a series of scenes that indirectly tell the reader what he needs to know about the hero.

The King speaks of his need for a good sailor.
An old knight recommends Sir Patrick.
The message is sent.
Sir Patrick laughs, then cries on reading the letter.
His men express fear.
Sir Patrick gives orders to sail.
The hats of the lords swim about in the sea.
The ladies wait for the sailors' return.
The sailors lie drowned at Sir Patrick's feet.

Without drawing for the reader any conclusions about the character of Sir Patrick Spens, the poet has, with something like the indirectness and objectivity of a playwright, led the reader to make his own interpretation.

Doubtlessly a prose version of this story would fill in many missing details, but these would not improve the effectiveness of the poem. More than likely, the detail would render the tale unmemorably trite. Neither the specific nature of the purpose behind Sir Patrick's journey nor the specific circumstances accompanying his death at sea are clarified. Very little of the speech in the poem is uttered by Sir Patrick, yet every detail, either by dramatic foreshadowing or by contrast, is devoted to forming the reader's attitude about the hero and the situation in which he finds himself.

The poet depends upon few but memorable details. Most of what is said of the King is general, but his "blude-reid wine" is specified to fatefully suggest violence to come. The "eldern knicht . . . at the king's richt kne" makes a surprising contrast with the drowned Scots lords at Sir Patrick's feet in the last stanza. Sir Patrick's boldness is pointed up as much by his "teir" as by his quick obedience to an order which he knows spells his doom. The vivid image of the "new moone/Wi the auld moone in hir arme" foreshadows the storm. Ironically, the Scots nobles whom Sir Patrick must escort and who would prefer to keep their cork-heeled shoes dry are soon drowned, and the only evidence of either storm or wreck is their hats floating about. How vividly the hats and shoes characterize both the sight of and the fate of the lords. Likewise do the fans and golden combs of the waiting ladies contrast them with Sir Patrick and his men. This deliberately sparse use of detail keeps in check an emotional scene that could easily be overdone.

The basic design of this plot has been adapted to many stories, in which some soldier, flier, or cowboy who lives by a strict code of honor accepts a dangerous, even suicidal, mission. What "Sir Patrick Spens" has that most such stories in prose lack, is great compression—word economy and a strictly delimited pattern of sound. The care with which not only the plot but also the sounds are arranged make the story a poem. With the effects of sound arrangement the form of rhetoric takes on the form of poetry.

The next poem, however modern its subject, is a direct descendant in form and content of the earliest stories in English.

### *The Ballad of Joe Meek*

1

You cain't never tell
   How far a frog will jump,
When you jes' see him planted
   On his big broad rump.

Nor what a monkey's thinking
By the working of his jaws—
You jes' cain't figger;
And I knows, because

Had me a buddy,
Soft as pie
Joe Meek they called him
And they didn't lie.

The good book say
"Turn the other cheek,"
But that warn't no turning
To my boy Joe Meek.

He turned up all parts,
And baigged you to spank,
Pulled down his breeches,
And supplied the plank.

The worm that didn't turn
Was a rattlesnake to Joe:
Wasn't scary—jes' meek, suh,
Was made up so.

2

It was late in August
What dey calls dog days,
Made even beetle hounds
Git bulldog ways.

Would make a pet bunny
Chase a bad blood-hound,
Make a new-born baby
Slap his grandpa down.

The air it was muggy
And heavy with heat,
The people all sizzled
Like frying meat.

The icehouse was heaven
The pavements was hell
Even Joe didn't feel
So agreeable.

Strolling down Claiborne
  In the wrong end of town
Joe saw two policemen
  Knock a po' gal down.

    He didn't know her at all,
      Never saw her befo'
    But that didn't make no difference,
      To my ole boy Joe.

Walks up to the cops,
  And, very polite,
Ast them ef they thought
  They had done *just right.*

    One cracked him with his billy
      Above the left eye,
    One thugged him with his pistol
      And let him lie.

3

When he woke up, and knew
  What the cops had done,
Went to a hockshop
  Got hisself a gun.

    Felt mo' out of sorts
      Than ever befo',
    So he went on a rampage
      My ole boy Joe.

Shot his way to the station house,
  Rushed right in,
Wasn't nothing but space
  Where the cops had been.

    They called the reserves,
      And the national guard,
    Joe was in a cell
      Overlooking the yard.

The machine guns sputtered,
  Didn't faze Joe at all—
But evvytime *he* fired
  A cop would fall.

The tear-gas made him laugh
When they left it fly,
Laughing gas made him hang
His head an' cry.

He threw the hand grenades back
With a outshoot drop,
An' evvytime he threw
They was one less cop.

The Chief of Police said
"What kinda *man* is this?"
And held up his shirt
For a armistice.

"Stop gunning black boy,
And we'll let you go."
"I thank you very kindly,"
Said my ole boy Joe.

"We promise you safety
If you'll leave us be—"
Joe said: "That's agreeable
Sir, by me. . . ."

4

The sun had gone down
The air it was cool,
Joe stepped out on the pavement
A fighting fool.

Had walked from the jail
About half a square,
When a cop behind a post
Let him have it fair.

Put a bullet in his left side
And one in his thigh,
But Joe didn't lose
His shootin' eye.

Drew a cool bead
On the cop's broad head;
"I returns you yo' favor"
And the cop fell dead.

The next to last words
  He was heard to speak
Was just what you would look for
  From my boy Joe Meek.

Spoke real polite
  To de folks standing by:
"Would you please do me one kindness,
  Fo' I die?"

"Won't be here much longer
  To bother you so,
Would you bring me a drink of water,
  Fo' I go?"

The very last words
  He was heard to say,
Showed a different Joe talking
  In a different way.

"Ef my bullets weren't gone,
  An' my strength all spent—
I'd send the chief something
  With a compliment."

"And we'd race to hell,
  And I'd best him there,
Like I would of done here
  Ef he'd played me fair."

5

So you cain't never tell
  How fas' a dog can run
When you see him a-sleeping,
  In the sun.

Sterling A. Brown (1901–     )

QUESTIONS

1. The story might have been told in many ways. Why do you think Sterling Brown chose to put it in ballad form? In your response, consider the similarities between this and "Sir Patrick Spens."

2. Part of the appeal of the folk ballad is that it creates the impression of being the ordinary speech of ordinary people. How does Brown (a professor of English at Howard University for forty years) accomplish this?

## *A Festive Marching Song in the Shape of 10 Dixie Cups*

```
m                   m
mi                 im
mis               sim
miss             ssim
missi           issim
missis         sissim
mississ       ssissim
mississi     ississim
mississip   pississim
mississipp ppississim
mississippippississim
 i                 i
 is               si
 iss             ssi
 issi           issi
 issis         sissi
 ississ       ssissi
 ississi     ississi
 ississip   pississi
 ississipp ppississi
 ississippippississi
  s               s
  ss             ss
  ssi           iss
  ssis         siss
  ssiss       ssiss
  ssissi     ississ
  ssissip   pississ
  ssissipp ppississ
  ssissippippississ
   s             s
   si           is
   sis         sis
   siss       ssis
   sissi     issis
   sissip   pissis
   sissipp ppissis
   sissippippissis
    i           i
    is         si
    iss       ssi
    issi     issi
    issip   pissi
    issipp ppissi
    issippippissi
     s         s
     ss       ss
     ssi     iss
     ssip   piss
     ssipp ppiss
     ssippippiss
      s       s
      si     is
      sip   pis
      sipp ppis
      sippippis
       i     i
       ip   pi
       ipp ppi
       ippippi
        p   p
        pp pp
        ppipp
         p p
         pip
          i
```

Emmett Williams (1925– )

*Pop Forms*

In the midst of much serious talk about "what poetry is," many writers have gone their own experimental ways and come up with some intriguing and entertaining compositions. Two of the better known developments are concrete poetry and found poetry.

*Concrete poetry* works something like an ideogram or pictograph in which words, parts of words, or letters are arranged on the page in such a way as to cause some communication. For example, Richard Kostelanetz has drawn a four lane cloverleaf design with "T's" and "A's" which represent cars moving along the lanes. The poem is entitled "Tribute to Henry Ford 3." The "T's" and "A's" of course represent the Model A and Model T Fords. The fun in this is like the fun in guessing a riddle. Strictly speaking, you do not read this sort of work, you look at the design to see what meaning is there. The completely nonverbal poem *is* new, but riddles and the kind of wit which involves the arrangement of words on the page to represent a silhouette are not.

The term *"found poem"* explains itself. The poet, instead of inventing a work, puts it together from pieces of speech he has found. The process might resemble the artist's collage or the sculptor's welding together pieces of scrap metal to form an artifact. Words for the found poem may come from traffic signs, whiskey ads, candy wrappers—anyplace. The test of success, however, is whether the found composition moves or excites the reader in a fresh way. The found poem may repeat, omit, and rearrange the original material, but may not add to it.

Here is an excerpt taken at random from *Aubrey's Brief Lives.* It is about an English Jesuit who was supposedly executed during the religious troubles of the seventeenth century. Actually, he escaped to Holland, but Aubrey did not know this when he wrote his straight-faced account.

*A Brief Life*
from *Aubrey*

When Father Harcourt suffered at Tyburne
And his bowells, etc.
Throwne into the fire,

A butcher boy standing by
Resolved to have the kidney
Which was broyling in the fire.

He burnt his fingers much, but got it;
Then Roydon, the Southwark brewer bought it
(a kind of Presbyterian).
A wonder!
'Tis now absolutely
Petrified.
But was not so when he first had it.

In his pocket, by degrees, it hardened
Better than by fire
Like an Agate polished.
I have seen it.
He values it much.

Frederick Dyer Thompson (1932– )

Concrete and found poems, like other aspects of pop art, thrive because so many people can enjoy them. They give every reader a chance to get involved himself. There is no reason why everyone should not be able to make his own poem. Are pop forms really poems? The answer depends on how you prefer to define poetry. A more pertinent question would be: "Am I interested"? There is no use in condemning a thing for not accomplishing effects it never intended to achieve, and the pop forms are not running in competition with *Hamlet* or *Paradise Lost*.

*Chapter 3*

# How to Read a Poem

POETRY, like drama, is an auditory art; it must be heard, at least in the mind's ear, to be enjoyed. Perhaps a good way to begin reading poetry is to read it as if it were a playscript.

Since words require a voice and an author, the fullest understanding of them requires that you let your reading be guided by your knowledge of who the speaker is. You may read intelligently without knowing the identity of an author, but you need some clear notion of whether the speaker in the poem is young or old, hero or villain, man or woman, contemporary or historical. Poetry, like prose, has a point of view, and perceptive reading requires that you understand whether you are listening to an omniscient author or to a more limited voice of an observer or of a participant in some action.

The poet is much less likely than a prose writer to be explicit about his speaker's identity and quite often an awareness in the reader of who the speaker is grows in the process of reading, just as if the reader were overhearing some fragment of conversation uttered by a stranger in a moment of crisis. Just as in life, poetry requires that you use your imagination to fit the bits of experience into a coherent understanding.

Read the following poems through several times, then answer the questions that follow.

*So We'll Go No More A-Roving*

So we'll go no more a-roving
  So late into the night,
Though the heart be still as loving,
  And the moon be still as bright.

For the sword outwears its sheath,
And the soul wears out the breast,
And the heart must pause to breathe,
And love itself have rest.

Though the night was made for loving,
And the day returns too soon,
Yet we'll go no more a-roving
By the light of the moon.

George Gordon, Lord Byron (1788–1824)

QUESTIONS

1. How would you describe the situation of the speaker in the poem?
2. Is the speaker bidding farewell to a living person or to one who has died?
3. Why does the speaker say that he will "go no more a-roving"? Is his explanation convincing?
4. In what way does the soul outwear the breast? How does the sword's outwearing the sheath have anything to do with the matter?
5. Is the mood of the speaker sad and wistful because he must leave or because he wants to leave? Does your answer to this have anything to do with the way the poem should be read?

Remember that all words have some purpose and some occasion, and let your reading express your comprehension of the complete context of the words as far as you can understand it. Most poetry is dramatic in this sense. To read a speech such as the "To be or not to be" soliloquy from *Hamlet,* one has some notion of what kind of a person Hamlet is and at the same time feels his understanding of Hamlet growing. But the author, Shakespeare, may never be clearly understood. One word of caution in connection with this mention of poetry's dramatic nature: take the advice of any actor to the reader of poetry—do not overdo the lines. Let the feeling inherent in the words do most of the work of expressing emotion.

*Since there's no help, come let us kiss and part*

Since there's no help, come let us kiss and part—
Nay, I have done: you get no more of me;
And I am glad, yea, glad with all my heart,
That thus so cleanly I myself can free.

Shake hands for ever, cancel all our vows,
And when we meet at any time again,
Be it not seen in either of our brows
That we one jot of former love retain.
Now at the last gasp of love's latest breath,
When, his pulse failing, Passion speechless lies,
When Faith is kneeling by his bed of death,
And Innocence is closing up his eyes,—
  Now, if thou wouldst, when all have given him over,
  From death to life thou might'st him yet recover!

Michael Drayton (1563–1631)

QUESTIONS

1. In the first eight lines of this poem the speaker is bidding farewell. How does his mood differ from that of the speaker in Byron's poem?

2. What state of mind in the speaker would cause him to shift his tone so quickly between lines one and two?

3. Is the speaker convincing about the gladness in his heart (line 3)?

4. If the speaker is addressing the beloved aloud in the first eight lines, what is the situation in the last six lines? Does the speaker continue to address the beloved? What kind of contrast are the last six lines intended to represent?

5. Is the situation described in the later part of the poem physical, or does it go on in the speaker's imagination?

6. Does your reading of the poem depend on your understanding of the situation? Do you find that your reading is modified by repetition?

## *The Musical Effects*

Frequently a person who reads prose well finds that somehow his attempts at reading poetry are disastrous. When this happens, it is usually the result of an exaggeration of the superficial difference between prose and poetry—the arrangement in lines and the grouping of lines in regular patterns. The poet's way of arranging words on the page is definitely related to the way he wants the words to sound when read aloud, but the poet depends on his readers' recognizing that the words belong to a language that has patterns of stress and rhythms. The poet uses the sounds of the language without distorting them. He is rarely interested in perfectly smooth rhythm, but the reader might distort accents or sounds of words to make them fit a regular pattern never intended. The result of this distortion is the singsong of a nursery rhyme. The poet intends every word to be pronounced as a normal part of the language. If, on occasion, he wants you to alter pronunciation, he will give some sign. The word "blessed" may be one or two syllables, for example, pronounced blest or bless èd; the poet will usually show an accent sign. But such variations are rare. In the poem following, to read the irregular rhymes as if they were regular would spoil the delightful effect of the deliberate disorder. The poem's lilting rhythms would be disrupted by exaggerated pauses at the ends of lines which have no punctuation.

*Delight in Disorder*

A sweet disorder in the dress
Kindles in clothes a wantoness:
A lawn about the shoulders thrown
Into a fine distraction;
An erring lace which here and there
Enthralls the crimson stomacher;
A cuff neglectfull, and thereby
Ribands to flow confusedly;
A winning wave, deserving note,
In the tempestuous petticoat;
A careless shoe-string, in whose tie
I see a wild civility,—
Do more bewitch me, than when art
Is too precise in every part.

Robert Herrick (1591–1674)

In trying not to exaggerate the regularity of rhythm in poetry, the reader should not reduce the lines to a monotone. Absence of rise and fall in the voice is just as unreal and disconcerting as singsong. Poetry is not prose and should not be read as if it were. In any good poem, such as the one above, the distinctly different arrangement of words on the page is not arbitrary. Its formality has a number of purposes designed to fit the subject at hand. Two of the most obvious purposes are the ordering of words for their musical qualities, and the ordering of words for unity and emphasis in meaning.

The inexperienced reader may pervert the arrangement by emphasizing one aspect of order to the exclusion of the other; he may lose the meaning by overdoing the formality of rhythm. Rarely, however, will he lose the musical effects if he reads a poem as a statement that uses words, phrases, and sentences with much the same fundamental connections of grammar and syntax used in writing that is not poetry.

Except for minor variations, the poet uses the same word groupings as a prose writer, but besides using standard marks of punctuation to indicate these groupings, a poet uses each *line* (called a verse), whether punctuated or not, as a further device for grouping. Moreover, groups of verses may be spaced (set apart from other groups) to indicate a shift or advance in the development of thought. Just as a paragraph indentation is, in effect, a mark of punctuation in prose, the spacing of groups of lines is in poetry.

The reader should let what he knows about reading prose and listening to speech be his first guide in reading poetry. He should read in words, phrases, clauses, and sentences; then let the reading be modified by the arrangement of the lines as poetry.

Going back to "Delight in Disorder" as an example, we see that Herrick has punctuated his poem (both in standard punctuation marks and in line division) to show exactly how it should be read. The whole is a sentence with seven principal subdivisions arranged as rhymed couplets. After every other line comes a punctuated strong pause, but a slight drop in the voice may come at the end of unpunctuated lines. The first couplet makes an independent statement summarizing the general idea; the next five couplets are all parts of a compound subject to go with the predicate in the final couplet.

For a poem about disorder, this is remarkably neat—except perhaps for the imperfection in the rhymes which are consciously disarrayed by the poet to supply us with the delight in the disorder of his art, something like the delight he gets in the slight irregularity of a lady's dress. The well-placed imperfection sets off the whole as a beauty mark strategically placed enhances the best features. "Dress" does not rhyme perfectly with "wantoness" because, though the sounds are similar and are spelled alike, the stress of the voice in pronouncing "dress" is unlike that in pronouncing "wantoness." A reader needs no technical knowledge about rhyme to know how to read these lines. Pronounce all words in poetry as you would pronounce them in prose.

Try reading the next poem aloud. Notice how the sounds, as well as the meanings of the words, set the tone and tell you what attitude to strike in your reading.

*Late Late*

Where tomahawks flash in the powwow
and tommyguns deepen the hubbub
and panzers patrol, is the horror
I live without sleep for the love of,

whose A-bombs respond to the tom-tom,
whose halberds react to the ack-ack,
while I, as if slugged with a dumdum,
sit back and sit back and sit back

until the last gunman is drawn on,
last murderous rustler druv loco,
last prisoncamp commandant spat at,
and somehow, and poco a poco,

the bottles are gone from the sixpack,
sensation is gone from the buttocks,
Old Glory dissolves into static,
the box is a box is a box.

George Starbuck (1931– )

So far, the discussion has centered on oral interpretation of poetry. The conclusions are that (1) poetry should be read aloud, (2) the reading should be influenced by what you can surmise about the character of the speaker, (3) the regularity of verse should not be rendered as singsong, and (4) the reader's interpretation should be guided by what he knows of the natural word groupings and speech patterns of the language.

### *Word Meaning*

Another consideration about how to read poetry has to do with meaning, for poetry is not composed only of sound. Any intelligible reading requires an understanding of vocabulary in a poem. Since the poet's craft resides in his ability to use all the resources of the language, he tends to go off and beyond familiar word trails. He avoids clichés and, in his choice of words, tries to enliven thought with fresh language. Even when the right word happens not to be familiar, he still chooses the right one. This is not to say his language is strange or bookish. Nevertheless, the reader must prepare himself to meet the artist's demands by having always nearby a good dictionary. Quite often he will also need a mythology reference book and a copy of the Bible.

Part of the vocabulary problem may arise from the poet's unusual command of words, but part grows too from the fact that poetry is long lived. Vocabulary is constantly changing, but the permanent value of the poetry of any given time does not depend on the permanence of word usage or meanings. The familiar words of Shakespeare's or Byron's day may not be the familiar words of today. In Herrick's "Delight in Disorder," for example, such uncommon words as "stomacher," "lawn," and "ribands" are uncommon because the names of articles of clothing change with styles, not because Herrick was using rare words. In any event, a dictionary will solve most difficulties. Shakespeare would be no less baffled by the names of the things a twentieth-century person uses than we are by the names of things he might have used.

Other aspects of vocabulary may be explained by historical changes in peoples' sense of what is suitable in the language of poetry. Some periods, such as the eighteenth century, have relied more heavily than others on "poetic" words and elegant phrasing. Some, the seventeenth century, for example, seem to demand a great familiarity with the Bible and Greek and Roman classics. So as not to be excluded from appreciating the art of these times, and in order to build up a fund of useful information, the student should have ready access to reference books. In reading older poems, you will find the *Oxford English Dictionary* your best source of information about words that have changed in meaning.

Once the reader goes beyond the first unfamiliar word, his loss of understanding is progressive, and even though he may recognize all the other words in a poem, he has no way of knowing the possible relationships between the rest of the poem and the unfamiliar part.

This familiar quatrain by Edward FitzGerald, for example, ends with a word which, if misunderstood, changes the lines:

A Book of Verses underneath the Bough,
A Jug of Wine, a Loaf of Bread—and Thou
  Beside me singing in the Wilderness—
Oh, Wilderness were Paradise enow!

from *The Rubáiyát of Omar Khayyám*

"Enow," an archaic word meaning "enough," may suggest the word "now," but the reader who makes the incorrect guess that it *means* "now," misses the line. He may, of course, enjoy the quatrain as much as someone who understands it correctly.

Poetry depends on a kind of verbal precision entirely unlike that of the laboratory scientist for whom any symbol, to be useful at all, must have no more than one meaning. The silver and gold of the chemist gather limitless associated meaning in the world of the poet. A poem's success may depend on the multiple meanings to which the reader must be attuned. For a person who habitually misses jokes, there is little likelihood that a dictionary will bring any mirth to his life. So it is with reading poetry. A dictionary will only help a reader who knows he does not know a word.

Consider what would be lost in the following poem to a reader who tries to get along without a dictionary.

*A High-Toned Old Christian Woman*

Poetry is the supreme fiction, madame.
Take the moral law and make a nave of it
And from the nave build haunted heaven. Thus,
The conscience is converted into palms,
Like windy citherns hankering for hymns.
We agree in principle. That's clear. But take
The opposing law and make a peristyle,
And from the peristyle project a masque
Beyond the planets. Thus, our bawdiness,
Unpurged by epitaph, indulged at last,

Is equally converted into palms,
Squiggling like saxophones. And palm for palm,
Madame, we are where we began. Allow,
Therefore, that in the planetary scene
Your disaffected flagellants, well-stuffed,
Smacking their muzzy bellies in parade,
Proud of such novelties of the sublime,
Such tink and tank and tunk-a-tunk-tunk,
May, merely may, madame, whip from themselves
A jovial hullabaloo among the spheres.
This will make widows wince. But fictive things
Wink as they will. Wink most when widows wince.

Wallace Stevens (1879–1955)

## QUESTIONS

1. Check the meaning of "nave," "peristyle," "flagellant," "epitaph," and "citherns."

2. In this poem, the speaker seems to be teasing the old woman by pointing out similarities he finds between her religion and its apparent opposites. His comparison has the sound of reason, is playful, and yet difficult to follow. What is suggested by the words "high-toned"?

3. Which words lower the tone or disturb the formality of the poem's beginning? What happens if you substitute "longing" for "hankering" (line 5); "wickedness" for "bawdiness" (line 9); "waving" for "squiggling" (line 12); "well-fed" for "well-stuffed" (line 15); "tapping" for "smacking" (line 16); and "abdomens" for "muzzy bellies" (line 16)?

4. Does line 18 have any dictionary meaning?

5. How does an epitaph purge bawdiness (lines 9, 10)?

6. Words such as "nave," "moral law," "hymns," and "flaggelant" are associated with Christianity. Look these words up to see how they might possibly contrast with "peristyle," "bawdiness," and "masques." Is there anything particularly pagan about the "jovial hullabaloo" mentioned in line 20?

7. With what attitude is a "wink" associated? What are the "fictive things," and why do they "wink most when widows wince"?

8. A palmer was a pilgrim who carried a palm as a sign that he had been to the holy land. When in medieval times palmers met, they greeted one another by pressing palm of hand to palm of hand. Does this background have any bearing on the poem? See lines 4, 11, and 12.

The dictionary, however indispensable in the reading of poetry, is no key to meaning, but, when used properly, will make the area within which meaning lies more accessible. It should be clear at the start that some poems are more definite in their meaning than this one of Stevens's. He took the risk of being misunderstood when he selected such generally unfamiliar words. But he knew that the audience he was likely to reach (people who enjoy complexity) would welcome this challenge to thought. As Stevens himself has said of poetry, "Things that have their origin in the imagination or in the emotions (poems) very often have meanings that differ in nature from the meanings of things that have their origin in reason. They have imaginative or emotional meanings to people who are susceptible to imagination or emotional meanings." For us, the main thing is not to blame the poet for being willfully obscure and not to blame ourselves for failing to understand distinctly an experience the poet himself may never have distinctly understood.

*Rehearsing the Poem*

The reading of most poems, especialy those with uncommon words, cannot be rushed. For the most part, poems require not one, but many readings. This may be less so for long narrative poems, but at those high points of any work, where the verse is least like prose, the reading process should slow down to become more deliberate. The most compact poems need the kind of treatment given a musical score by a musician. He may be competent to sight read, but for the player only practice and imaginative repetition will bring out all the score may hold. In poetry, as in music, only practice will bring fluency. A reader of poetry is no more satisfied with a rough idea of an ode than a musician is satisfied with the gist of a symphony.

Two poems which may be studied side by side to some advantage as we take up the question of how important it is to have a definite mental picture of the speaker in a poem are "To A Mouse" and "The Solitary Reaper." Even though a reader might pick up these poems at random and read them with pleasure without having any idea of who wrote them or when they were written, some notion of these facts might be helpful in establishing an idea of what the speaker is like. The poems were written within eighteen years of one another—Burns's in 1785 and Wordsworth's in 1803. Burns was at the time of his composition still an unknown Scottish farmer squeezing an existence out of the unprosperous land. His father had recently died and his brothers had emigrated to America. He had spent some time off the farm as a flax dresser in Irvene. Burns himself described the life he led up to the age of sixteen as being marked by "the cheerless gloom of a hermit and the unceasing toil of a galley slave." Wordsworth, at the time he wrote "The Solitary Reaper," held a university degree, was an acknowledged poet of great merit, and was comfortably settled, living on a modest legacy. He had traveled widely, and it was during an excursion into the Highlands that he was moved to write the poem in question.

Both of the poems have Scottish pastoral settings, and both are the works of poets who have been classed as "romantics." It is generally assumed that both were intended to represent the voice of the poet. Obviously the two poems represent two contrasting views of the pastoral life—the plowman's view versus the tourist's. They may be of equal value as human experience, and both poems are among the best loved in British literature. Whether or not the reader is aware of the identity of the authors, he should derive from the poem a definite impression of the attitude of the speaker. His impression of this attitude should influence his reading. First, let us analyze the poems, concentrating on the way the speaker's sense of his own situation influences the impact of his words.

### *To A Mouse*

Wee, sleekit°, cow'rin', tim'rous beastie, — *sleek*
O what a panic's in thy breastie!
Thou need na start awa sae hasty,
  Wi' bickering brattle°! — *hurrying scamper*
I wad be laith° to rin and chase thee — *loath*
  Wi' murdering pattle!° — *spade*

I'm truly sorry man's dominion
Has broken nature's social union,
And justifies that ill opinion,
  Which makes thee startle
At me, thy poor earth-born companion,
  And fellow-mortal!

I doubt na, whyles°, but thou may thieve — *sometimes*
What then? boor beastie, thou maun° live — *must*
A daimen icker in a thrave° — *an occasional ear from a sheaf of corn*
'S a sma request:
I'll get a blessin' wi' the laive,° — *the rest*
And never miss't!

Thy wee bit housie, too, in ruin!
Its silly wa's the win's are strewin'!
And naething now to big a new ane
O'foggage° green, — *coarse grass*
And bleak December's winds ensuin',
Baith snell° and keen! — *sharp*

Thou saw the fields laid bare and waste,
And weary winter comin' fast,
And cozie here, beneath the blast,
Thou thought to dwell,
Till, crash! the cruel coulter° passed — *cutter attached to a plow*
Out through thy cell.

That wee bit heap o' leaves and stibble
Has cost thee mony a weary nibble!
Now thou's turned out for a' thy trouble,
But house or hald°, — *abode*
To thole° the winter's sleety dribble, — *endure*
And cranreuch° cauld! — *hoar-frost*

But, Mousie, thou art no thy lane° — *not alone*
In proving foresight may be vain:
The best-laid schemes o' mice and men
Gang aft a-gley°, — *often go astray*
And lea'e us nought but grief and pain
For promised joy.

Still thou art blest, compared wi' me!
The present only toucheth thee:
But och! I backward cast my e'e
On prospects drear!
And forward, though I canna see,
I guess and fear.

Robert Burns (1759–1796)

## QUESTIONS

1. Why does the poet use dialect words so extensively? Try paraphrasing the first stanza in modern English. What effect, if any, is lost?

2. Note that the standard English of the second stanza would be for the Scottish farmer a departure from his normal way of expression. Why does the plowman "change his voice" to express the idea contained in this stanza?

3. To what extent would a farmer be likely to sympathize with the troubles of an animal? Do you think the speaker is reacting to the mouse or to what the mouse reminds him of?

4. Some readers claim that this poem expresses regret about the lack of feeling humans have to dumb animals and about the lost sense of the oneness of nature. Do you agree?

5. To what degree do you think the speaker attributes the qualities of man to the animal? When in line 39 he mentions "the best laid plans of mice," do you read this to mean that he thinks that mice make plans?

6. Do you find after reading this poem aloud several times that your reading is modified by your idea of the speaker's mood? Try reading the poem gaily, then read it solemnly. Which of your interpretations best suits the overall impact of the poem?

"The Solitary Reaper" records an English traveler's personal response to hearing a young woman sing in the strange Scottish tongue as she worked alone in the fields. Let your first reading of the poem help you form some idea about the speaker's attitude, then reread the poem.

### *The Solitary Reaper*

Behold her, single in the field,
Yon solitary highland lass!
Reaping and singing by herself;
Stop here, or gently pass!
Alone she cuts and binds the grain,
And sings a melancholy strain;
O listen! for the vale profound
Is overflowing with the sound.

No nightingale did ever chaunt
More welcome notes to weary bands
Of travellers in some shady haunt,
Among Arabian sands:
A voice so thrilling ne'er was heard
In spring-time from the cuckoo-bird,
Breaking the silence of the seas
Among the farthest Hebrides.

Will no one tell me what she sings?—
Perhaps the plaintive numbers flow
For old, unhappy, far-off things,
And battles long ago:
Or is it some more humble lay,
Familiar matter of to-day?
Some natural sorrow, loss, or pain,
That has been, and may be again?

Whate'er the theme, the maiden sang
As if her song could have no ending;
I saw her singing at her work,
And o'er the sickle bending;—
I listened, motionless and still;
And, as I mounted up the hill,
The music in my heart I bore,
Long after it was heard no more.

William Wordsworth (1770–1850)

## QUESTIONS

1. How does the musical effect of the rhyme in this poem contribute to the overall impression?
2. In what way does the poem seem true to the facts of emotional experience?
3. The speaker says that the song is both melancholy and welcome. How does your understanding of this mood in which sad songs are enjoyable affect your reading?

Some poems present seemingly insurmountable obstacles to readers who expect a poem to read like a nursery rhyme. Yet, as with written music, all pieces may not come easily. Few who read Gerard Manley Hopkins's "The Windhover" for the first time are able to appreciate fully the artistry in the sound effects. Nevertheless, after deliberately working out the phrasing, the reader is apt to get much pleasure from the "feel" of the poem. Read the poem through several times, and when you have some idea of what the poet is trying to accomplish, react to the questions that follow.

*The Windhover:*
*To Christ our Lord*

I caught this morning morning's minion, king-
dom of daylight's dauphin, dapple-dawn-drawn Falcon, in
his riding
Of the rolling level underneath him steady air, and striding
High there, how he rung upon the rein of a wimpling wing
In his ecstasy! then off, off forth on swing,
As a skate's heel sweeps smooth on a bow-bend: the hurl
and gliding
Rebuffed the big wind. My heart in hiding
Stirred for a bird,—the achieve of, the mastery of the thing!

Brute beauty and valour and act,
oh, air, pride,
plume,
here
Buckle! *and* the fire that breaks from thee then,
a billion
Times told lovelier, more dangerous, O my chevalier!

No wonder of it: shéer plód makes plough down sillion
Shine, and blue-bleak embers, ah my dear,
Fall, gall themselves, and gash gold-vermilion.

Gerard Manley Hopkins (1844–1889)

QUESTIONS

1. If the first sentence, covering six and a half lines, were prose, we would probably say that it lacked unity and coherence. Why do you think the poet takes such license with sentence structure?

2. Why is the poet so apparently intent on keeping the lines in the first division of the poem from ending with a dropping off of the voice? How does the motion of the voice in reading this poem coincide with the motion of the hawk, the horseman and the skater?

3. Why does the poet use so many explosive sounds such as the "d" sound in line 2, the "b" sound in lines 6 to 10, and the "g" sound in line 14?

4. In what ways is the falcon dawn-drawn? In what sense does the speaker mean his heart was in hiding (lines 7–8)? What does "buckle" in line 10 mean?

How does the fact that a plow moving through the furrow (sillion) makes the earth smooth and shiny figure in the explanation of the last three lines?

5. Is it possible to have a pleasurable response to the poem even without being able to resolve the meaning of all the details?

## *The Eagle*

He clasps the crag with crooked hands;
Close to the sun in lonely lands,
Ringed with the azure world, he stands.

The wrinkled sea beneath him crawls;
He watches from his mountain walls,
And like a thunderbolt he falls.

Alfred, Lord Tennyson (1809–1892)

### QUESTIONS

1. What does this poem have in common with "The Windhover"?
2. Why has the poet made the first line so difficult to say? Does the contrast of this awkwardness with the relative smoothness of the second line have a useful purpose?

With a little experience in reading poetry one discovers that every poem demands some new adjustment of the reader. The reader must adapt his voice to the voice of the poet. It would not do to read all poetry as if it were a serious, philosophical reflection. A drinking song obviously needs a different treatment than a speech; a hymn requires a response drastically unlike the response to a satire. Ordinarily, a single reading will not bring out all the tonal variations intended by the poet. Read the following poem aloud and notice how the attitudes of the poet infect your own oral rendition.

## *The Operation*

From stainless steel basins of water
They brought warm cloths and they washed me,
From spun aluminum bowls, cold Zephiran sponges,
    fuming;
Gripped in the dead yellow glove, a bright straight razor
Inched on my stomach, down my groin,

Paring the brown hair off. They left me
White as a child, not frightened. I was not
Ashamed. They clothed me, then,
In the thin, loose, light, white garments,
The delicate sandals of poor Pierrot,
A schoolgirl first offering her sacrament.

I was drifting, inexorably, on toward sleep.
In skullcaps, masked, in blue-green gowns, attendants
Towed my cart, afloat in its white cloths,
The body with its tributary poisons borne
Down corridors of the diseased, thronging:
The scrofulous faces, contagious grim boys,
The huddled families, weeping, a staring woman
Arched to her gnarled stick,—a child was somewhere
Screaming, screaming—then, blind silence, the elevator rising
To the arena, humming, vast with lights; blank hero,
Shackled and spellbound, to enact my deed.

Into flowers, into women, I have awakened.
Too weak to think of strength, I have thought all day,
Or dozed among standing friends. I lie in night, now,
A small mound under linen like the drifted snow.
Only by nurses visited, in radiance, saying, Rest.
Opposite, ranked office windows glare; headlamps, below,
Trace out our highways; their cargoes under dark tarpaulins,
Trucks climb, thundering, and sirens may
Wail for the fugitive. It is very still. In my brandy bowl
Of sweet peas at the window, the crystal world
Is inverted, slow and gay.

W. D. Snodgrass (1926–     )

## *Quality and Tone*

The question of how to read a poem cannot be divorced from the problem of how to judge a poem. Every qualified reader of poetry is a critic in that his ability to evaluate what he reads helps him to enjoy it. Generous readers, who look for what pleasure the poet has attempted to provide, do not delight in sneering at unsuccessful attempts, but they do have standards of judgment which are not entirely arbitrary.

Since poetry does aspire to find words for experience that is difficult to express, it is no surprise that all attempts do not succeed. Readers with a clear understanding of poetic technique may be able to point out flawed lines, or rhymes, or diction (which may or may not spoil a poem), but the fundamental cause of failure is more likely to be inappropriateness, which any reader might discern, even without much knowledge of technique.

Every poem calls on the reader to respond with his mind and his feelings, but if the voice of the poet seems untrustworthy—if it sounds too holy, too full of self-pity, too shallow, or too sure of itself—the poem fails, at least for the reader who senses insincerity or excess. What we are talking about here is *tone:* that quality in any work of literature which reflects the author's feelings toward his subject, himself, and his reader.

Just as, in conversation, one knows how to "take" a remark as much by how it is said as by what it means, so in poetry the "how" of a statement is the crux. In poetry, tone emerges from all the shadings of manner and meaning which gather through the interplay of rhythms, word choice, sound effects, and all the other poetic elements. Misreading the tone of a poem is like mistaking a remark in conversation because you missed some shade of facial expression or vocal inflection which qualified the meaning.

The analysis of tone requires some understanding of the workings of poetry. Since the analysis of tone explains fully the interdependence of all the parts of a work, it would seem appropriate to save "tone" for discussion later, yet the awareness of a poem's tone may be one of the reader's first responses. This awareness influences both the understanding and the judgment of the reader, and should not, therefore, be put off. Precision in analysis will come in time, with a mastery of the poetic elements. In describing the tone of a poem the words you will use will resemble the words that are customary for describing any speaker's attitude, for example, "irate," "sad," "exuberant," "seductive," "morose," and so forth.

Read the following poems with these questions in mind: What is the tone? How do I know? Is it the right tone to elicit the response which the poet probably intends?

*Others, I am not the first*

Others, I am not the first,
Have willed more mischief than they durst:
If in the breathless night I too
Shiver now, 'tis nothing new.

More than I, if truth were told,
Have stood and sweated hot and cold,
And through their veins in ice and fire
Fear contended with desire.

Agued once like me were they,
But I like them shall win my way
Lastly to the bed of mould
Where there's neither heat nor cold.

But from my grave across my brow
Plays no wind of healing now,
And fire and ice within me fight
Beneath the suffocating night.

A. E. Housman (1859–1936)

QUESTIONS

1. What is the speaker trying to console himself about? Speculate on how old the speaker might be, how he feels, and what time and where he is when he speaks.

2. Why does he not come right out and say what is frustrating him? Is there anything about his choice of words which leads you to deduce the cause of his feverishness? Why does he say "mischief" (line 2) rather than "sin"? Why "desire" (line 8) rather than "ambition"? Why "bed of mould" (line 11) rather than "coffin"? What mental picture do you get from lines 7 and 8?

3. When do you discover who the "others" really are? What would be the effect if, from the start, the speaker said "those who have died"?

4. What details in the first four lines are repeated in the last four? Has the speaker resolved his difficulty by the end of the poem? What dominant impression are you left with?

Housman does not tell us what to think about his speaker's predicament, as an expository prose writer would; he reproduces a sense of the thing and lets us judge for ourselves. And therein lies the difference.

### *Revulsion*

Though I waste watches framing words to fetter
Some unknown spirit to mine in clasp and kiss,
Out of the night there looms a sense 'twere better
To fail obtaining whom one fails to miss.

For winning love we win the risk of losing,
And losing love is as one's life were riven;
It cuts like contumely and keen ill-using
To cede what was superfluously given.

Let me then never feel the fateful thrilling
That devastates the love-worn wooer's frame,
The hot ado of fevered hopes, the chilling
That agonizes disappointed aim!
So may I live no junctive law fulfilling,
And my heart's table bear no woman's name.

Thomas Hardy (1840–1928)

QUESTIONS

1. What does this poem have in common with "Others, I am not the first"? Describe the speaker's tone. Does this resemble the tone of the speaker in "Others, I am not the first"?

2. Which speaker is more self-aware? How do you know? Do you think Hardy is in sympathy with his speaker?

3. Which poem, on the basis of the appropriateness of the tone, do you prefer? Explain.

*Chapter 4*

# Diction

LANGUAGE has a system of operation, called grammar, by which the components of language, the words, interconnect. The system remains relatively static, but the words constantly and noticeably grow and change. If we were to compare language with a plant, we might say that the principle of its organization remains constant, while its fibers continuously grow and change. All men have an inborn potential to understand the basic system of language; without it, they could never be taught to speak. The fiber of language, its vocabulary, is the part that grows and changes uniquely with each person.

When the poet uses language, he does so as an artist, drawing upon his hoard of words with a fitness we do not expect from most men. There is, of course, much more to poetry than word selection. The musicality and the unspoken relationships of words which operate outside the system of sentences are, without a doubt, part of poetry's essence. But we must begin with the basic matter of *diction*—the choice of words.

## *Diction in Everyday Speech*

In choosing words, your selection will depend upon whether you are inclined to be, or wish to seem, (a) formal or informal, (b) favorable or unfavorable, or (c) concrete or abstract. The most important choices deal with nouns, verbs, adjectives and adverbs, for these are the most numerous kinds of words, and English is especially rich in its abundance of synonyms. Suppose, for example, you need an adjective to describe a man of settled opinions. You will choose your word according to the mental picture you have of him and the picture you hope to evoke. If the man in question has decided that in the next presidental election he will vote for whoever the Republican candidate may be, there is no scarcity of terms; consider the following:

A

| | | |
|---|---|---|
| resolute | faithful | dependable |
| steadfast | determined | true-blue |
| staunch | loyal | squared-away |
| principled | consistent | |

B

| | |
|---|---|
| obstinate | stiff-necked |
| headstrong | mulish |
| willful | bullheaded |
| stubborn | pigheaded |
| brainwashed | |

A thoughtless Democrat might call him "mulish"; an independent might say "headstrong"; and a fellow Republican, "staunch." "Resolute" would be formal, favorable, and abstract; "pigheaded" would be informal, unfavorable, and concrete.

### *Diction in Poetry*

Words are the poet's paint—they are his musical notes. Sometimes he wants the reader to look past the words and directly into the life he is portraying, and sometimes he seems to call attention—to say, "Notice the words, see how the mind struggles to find meaning." When the reader responds to poetry, he does not begin by accepting all that is readily available to him and rejecting that which lies behind a curtain of words. His question is more likely to be: "Is the texture and selection of words fitted for the purpose of the poem?"

Yet, whether the poet makes us think deeply or pleases us with just the right notice of some simple thing, his selection of words has a direct bearing on our reactions. Some study of his word choice is almost certain to produce a fuller awareness of the poet's art.

Perhaps the best way to illustrate this is to present you with some alternatives that might face a poet and let you try to choose as he would.

*Sonnet 65*

Since brass, nor stone, nor earth, nor boundless sea,
But sad mortality o'er-sways their power,
How with this rage shall beauty hold a plea,
Whose———is no stronger than a flower? **action, or body?*
O, how shall summer's honey breath hold out
Against the wrackful siege of———days, **battering, or withering?*
When rocks———are not so stout, **impregnable, or*
Nor gates of steel so strong, but Time decays? *immoveable?*
O fearful meditation! where, alack,
Shall Time's best jewel from Time's chest lie hid?
Or what strong hand can hold his swift foot back?
Or who his———of beauty can forbid? **spoil, or loot?*
O, none, unless this miracle have might,
That in black ink my love may still shine bright.

William Shakespeare (1564–1616)

Whether or not you chose as Shakespeare did in every instance here, your choices were probably based on

1. how the word sounded,
2. how precisely it conveyed meaning, and
3. how well it suggested those feelings which blend with the meaning.

In short, your choice is based on the three properties of most words: sound, denotative meaning, and connotative meaning.

The words that Shakespeare used were "action" (line 4), "battering" (line 6), "impregnable" (line 7), and "spoil" (line 12). Each of these words has some association with battle, but so, too, you might say, do "body," "withering," "immoveable," and "loot." In the logic of the poem, however, "beauty" is an ideal with many forms, but no body, and thus "body" would be an unsuitable word. "Action" is an aptly harsh-sounding word associated with fortification and siege. It, along with "holds a plea" (line 3), also goes with the diction of the legal world. "Withering" may go with "flower," but it is almost too smooth sounding for the siege context. The explosive sound of "battering" seems a better choice. "Immoveable" and "impregnable" may both apply to rocks, but the picture intended is one of crashing through, not setting aside. Though "spoil" and "loot" both fit in with the context of "siege," "spoil" has the other meaning of "mar" or "rot," which gives it the better claim. All of the words fit the rhythm pattern of the poem.

### from *The Holy Sonnets*

#### 14

Batter my heart, three-personed God; for you
As yet but knock, breathe, shine, and seek to mend;
That I may rise and stand, o'erthrow me, and bend
Your force to break, blow, burn, and make me new.
I, like an usurped town t'another due,
Labor t'admit you, but oh, to no end.
Reason, your viceroy in me, me should defend,
But is captived, and proves weak or untrue.
Yet dearly I love you, and would be loved fain,
But am betrothed unto your enemy;
Divorce me, untie or break that knot again;
Take me to you, imprison me, for I,
Except you enthrall me, never shall be free,
Nor ever chaste, except you ravish me.

John Donne (1572–1631)

QUESTIONS

1. How did the sound of the words influence Donne's diction in the first four lines?
2. Two aspects of God—His power and His love—provide the axis for word choice in this poem. Which words cluster around the aspect of power? Which around the aspect of love?
3. Why does Donne go to the vocabulary of sex and violence to write a prayer-poem?

## *Denotation and Connotation*

*Denotation* is the exact and explicit meaning of a word. *Connotation* is the implicit, suggestive meaning associated with a word. No piece of writing can be effective unless the writer knows how his words will be taken both in what they state and in what they suggest. A skillful writer can build the core of his thought and surround this with the mood he wishes to create through well-considered word choice.

Since English is so rich in synonyms, writers find it possible to preserve the core meaning while they choose a word with the fittest set of associations. Denotatively, "boy" equals "youngster," "youth," kid," "young fellow," "swain," and "lad." All denote a young male, yet the terms are not interchangeable because they have more than denotative meanings.

In the process of language change, both the denotation and the connotation may undergo alterations, but denotation is a more conservative element. A mill, for example, was once a place where things were made by grinding. The product of this grinding was a related word, "meal." Eventually the word "mill" came to mean a place where things—steel and cotton as well as meal—are made. The facts of industry, it seems, have altered the denotation.

With connotation, the growth of meaning has more to do with the attitude people have toward the facts. The word "criticism" began by meaning the act of making judgments based on discerning observation, but the general dislike of *being* judged has given the word the unfavorable sense of "fault finding." "Pig," "hog," and "swine" all have their shading of unfavorable connotation. The diminutive "piggy," associated as it is with nursery rhymes, has a favorable connotation. The connotation of "pork," like most words, depends on context.

As you move out from the core meaning of any word, you come to regions of meaning less and less bound to the central meaning. Associations of meaning become looser and looser so that the suggestions developed by different words come to overlap or mingle. Careful writers choose their words because of these overlappings, putting ambiguities and light word play to work.

*Days*

Daughters of Time, the hypocritic Days,
Muffled and dumb like barefoot dervishes,

And marching single in an endless file,
Bring diadems and fagots in their hands.
To each they offer gifts after his will,
Bread, kingdoms, stars, and sky that holds them all.
I, in my pleachèd garden, watched the pomp,
Forgot my morning wishes, hastily
Took a few herbs and apples, and the Day
Turned and departed silent. I, too late,
Under her solemn fillet saw the scorn.

Ralph Waldo Emerson (1803–1882)

QUESTIONS

1. In your own words, summarize the comment this poem makes about human judgment.
2. What is the poet's attitude toward days? What words suggest this attitude?
3. In the following list of words from the poem, which are favorable in their connotation? Which unfavorable?

| dervishes | muffled | endless | diadems |
|---|---|---|---|
| pomp | fagots | pleachèd | |

Can you think of synonyms which would alter the connotation?

4. What would be the effect if:
   a. Instead of "daughters" in line 1, the word read "children"?
   b. Instead of "hypocritic" in line 1, the word were "indifferent"?
5. Does "hypocritic" seem right to you denotatively?

## *Abstract Versus Concrete*

When students are learning how to write effectively, their most common fault is a tendency to use abstract words. Too heavy a reliance on abstractions tends to cloud the thought of both reader and writer; exclusive reliance on concrete terms will produce little more than a list. The word "abstract" implies a process by which the mind builds a conception from selected traits shared by a group of subjects. Abstract terms, then, are built upon observation of the concrete. They make thought more efficient, but they need the constant support of concrete terms. Since concrete diction usually involves some actual thing which can be physically experienced, it is constantly needed to verify abstractions.

The mind can relate more definitely and quickly to the concrete than to the abstract. The mention of an abstract word may set the mind groping, while the mention of the concrete satisfies.

| | | |
|---|---|---|
| inscrutable | | polished chrome |
| abominable | versus | kinky hair |
| judgment | | firm biceps |
| honor | | hot coffee |

Most of the poems treated thus far in this chapter have had the strong support of concrete terms. Very abstract statements, however, may be effective in poetry. John Donne, in the following poem, requires his reader to follow a sequence of tightly related abstract statements.

### *Love's Deity*

I long to talk with some old lover's ghost,
  Who died before the god of love was born:
I cannot think that he, who then lov'd most,
  Sunk so low, as to love one which did scorn.
But since this god produc'd a destiny,
And that vice-nature, custom, lets it be,
  I must love her, that loves not me.

Sure, they which made him god, meant not so much,
  Nor he, in his young godhead practis'd it;
But when an even flame two hearts did touch,
  His office was indulgently to fit
Actives to passives. Correspondency
Only his subject was. It cannot be
  Love, till I love her, that loves me.

But every modern god will now extend
  His vast prerogative, as far as Jove.
To rage, to lust, to write to, to commend,
  All is the purlieu of the god of love.
O were we waken'd by this tyranny
T' ungod this child again, it could not be
  I should love her, who loves not me.

Rebel and atheist too, why murmur I,
As though I felt the worst that love could do?
Love might make me leave loving, or might try
A deeper plague, to make her love me too,
Which, since she loves before, I'm loath to see;
Falsehood is worse than hate; and that must be
If she whom I love, should love me.

John Donne (1572–1631)

## QUESTIONS

1. Love's deity in this poem is Cupid, usually pictured as a naked, winged infant with a bow, arrows, and blindfold. He is the son of Jupiter and Venus, and like others of the gods, he was capable of assuming many forms. What are the effects of having such a personage as the god of love?

2. Why is the god not concerned with making perfect matches? What words in the poem describe the role played by love's deity?

3. What is the effect of these words: "vice-nature" (line 6), "custom" (line 6), "practis'd" (line 9), "office" (line 11), "actives" (line 12), "passives" (line 12), "subject" (line 13), "prerogative" (line 16), "purlieu" (line 18), "tyranny" (line 19)? Is there anything incongruous about words like this in a poem about love?

4. What added dimension to the speaker's problem becomes evident in the final stanza?

## *Dolor*

I have known the inexorable sadness of pencils,
Neat in their boxes, dolor of pad and paper-weight,
All the misery of manilla folders and mucilage,
Desolation in immaculate public places,
Lonely reception room, lavatory, switchboard,
The unalterable pathos of basin and pitcher,
Ritual of multigraph, paper-clip, comma,
Endless duplication of lives and objects.
And I have seen dust from the walls of institutions,
Finer than flour, alive, more dangerous than silica,
Sift, almost invisible, through long afternoons of tedium,
Dropping a fine film on nails and delicate eyebrows,
Glazing the pale hair, the duplicate gray standard faces.

Theodore Roethke (1908–1963)

## QUESTIONS

1. Which words are usually associated with office work? Are these words definitely positive, negative, or neutral in connotation?

2. Point out the abstract nouns in the poem. Do these words influence the reader's attitude toward the concrete words?

3. How do the words pertaining to *persons* in the last three lines of the poem affect the words pertaining to *things* in the rest of the poem?

4. The poet often links abstract nouns with concrete ones as in line 1, "sadness of pencils." What other examples of this do you see? What is the general effect?

## *It Is a Beauteous Evening*

It is a beauteous evening, calm and free,
The holy time is quiet as a Nun
Breathless with adoration; the broad sun
Is sinking down in its tranquillity;
The gentleness of heaven broods o'er the Sea:
Listen! the mighty Being is awake,
And doth with his eternal motion make
A sound like thunder—everlastingly.
Dear Child! dear Girl! that walkest with me here,
If thou appear untouched by solemn thought,
Thy nature is not therefore less divine:
Thou liest in Abraham's bosom all the year;
And worship'st at the Temple's inner shrine,
God being with thee when we know it not.

William Wordsworth (1770–1850)

## QUESTIONS

1. This poem is addressed by Wordsworth to his daughter, Anne, whom he met first when she was nine years old. Wordsworth and the child's mother had been kept apart by the events of the French Revolution, and by the time they could be reunited, marriage seemed ill-advised to both. At the time of his meeting with the child, Wordsworth may have been feeling the contrast between conventional morality and the real goodness of the child herself. To what extent is the dominant impression of this poem dependent on abstract words?

2. What words in the poem suggest the poet's inner conflict?

3. Which words suggest tranquillity? Which turbulence?

4. Which words suggest religious significance? What would be the effect if "beauteous" in line 1 were changed to "wonderful" or to "beautiful"? If "nun" in line 2 were changed to "monk"?

### *Tension*

In poetry, as in experience, feelings are seldom uncomplicated —the pleasant and the unpleasant are rarely sorted out, and yet through the confused and unintegrated facts of experience, the mind builds its dominant impressions. In order to understand how poetry resembles life in its ability to resolve opposites, the student should analyze the way words which build conflicting moods resolve themselves into a dominant mental impression.

A term used in poetic criticism to mean the rich unity which arises through resolved opposites is *tension.* The tension of a poem may lie between what is concrete and abstract, what is meant and what is stated, what is specified in the vocabulary (denotation) and what is implicit (connotation). In the following poems, try to see in how many ways such opposites are resolved.

## *A Moment Please*

*When I gaze at the sun*
I walked to the subway booth
for change for a dime.
*and know that this great earth*
Two adolescent girls stood there
alive with eagerness to know
*is but a fragment from it thrown*
all in their new found world
there was for them to know
*in heat and flame a billion years ago,*
they looked at me and brightly asked
"Are you Arabian?"
*that then this world was lifeless*
I smiled and cautiously
—for one grows cautious—
shook my head.
*as, a billion hence,*
"Egyptian?"
*it shall again be,*
Again I smiled and shook my head
and walked away.
*what moment is it that I am betrayed,*
I've gone but seven paces now
*oppressed, cast down,*

and from behind comes swift the sneer
*or warm with love or triumph?*
"Or Nigger?"

A moment, please
*What is it that to fury I am roused?*
for still it takes a moment
*What meaning for me*
now
*in this homeless clan*
I'll turn
*the dupe of space*
and smile
*the toy of time?*
and nod my head.

Samuel Allen (Paul Vesey) (1917– )

QUESTIONS

1. Why does the poet use italics for some lines and roman letters for others? Try reading the italicized lines separately. Do they make more sense? Do the same with the roman lettered lines.

2. Thinking back to your first reading of the poem, which part stayed most vividly in your memory? The philosophical or the practical?

3. Does the poem illustrate the idea that the real and the ideal don't mix? Discuss.

In the next poem the emotional tension finds support in counterpoint of language. The blending of two tongues has a strange fluency that is both musically appealing and troublesome in thought and feeling. Even if you do not understand Spanish, the sense of the poem comes through because Alurista uses mostly cognate words and because the Spanish words echo and vivify the speaker's cultural dilemma.

*unexpectedly: my night gloom came*

Unexpectedly
my night gloom came
injusta capa fúnebre *unfair funereal cloak*
I realized
devoured me
y mis tripas gnawed at *and my guts (tripes)*
la luna y su eclipse *the moon and its eclipse*

the cultural assassination
of my people
  de mis abuelos    *of my grandparents*
y corrí hacia el sol    *and I run to the sun*
  el de mis padres    *that of my fathers*
the one that printed
  on my sarape
fantastic colors
  through the prism
  —la pirámide del sol    *the pyramid of the sun*
at the sacrificial Teocatl    *pre-Columbian temple*
my fathers wore their plumage
  to listen
and soplaron vida con sus solares rayos    *breathe life with its solar rays*
en mi raza    *into my people*

Alurista (1947–    )

### *Naming of Parts*

To-day we have naming of parts. Yesterday,
We had daily cleaning. And to-morrow morning,
We shall have what to do after firing. But to-day,
To-day we have naming of parts. Japonica
Glistens like coral in all of the neighboring gardens,
  And to-day we have naming of parts.

This is the lower sling swivel. And this
Is the upper sling swivel, whose use you will see,
When you are given your slings. And this is the piling swivel,
Which in your case you have not got. The branches
Hold in the gardens their silent, eloquent gestures,
  Which in our case we have not got.

This is the safety-catch, which is always released
With an easy flick of the thumb. And please do not let me
See anyone using his finger. You can do it quite easy
If you have any strength in your thumb. The blossoms
Are fragile and motionless, never letting anyone see
  Any of them using their finger.

And this you can see is the bolt. The purpose of this
Is to open the breach, as you see. We can slide it
Rapidly backwards and forwards: we call this
Easing the spring. And rapidly backwards and forwards
The early bees are assaulting and fumbling the flowers:
  They call it easing the Spring.

They call it easing the Spring: it is perfectly easy
If you have any strength in your thumb: like the bolt,
And the breech, and the cocking-piece, and the point of
 balance,
Which in our case we have not got; and the almond-blossom
Silent in all of the gardens and the bees going backwards and
 forwards,
 For to-day we have naming of parts.

Henry Reed (1914– )

## QUESTIONS

1. At some point in each stanza the mechanical diction is interrupted by words related to growth and life. Where is the interruption?

2. Does a shift of rhythm accompany a shift of language? What is the effect of this?

3. Both the rifle whose parts are being named and the objects in the gardens have sexual connotations. What tension does this produce in the poem?

4. How many words or phrases in the poem have double meanings? How is this related to the tension?

## from *Modern Love*

### 29

Am I failing? For no longer can I cast
A glory round about this head of gold.
Glory she wears, but springing from the mould;
Not like the consecration of the Past!
Is my soul beggared? Something more than earth
I cry for still: I cannot be at peace
In having Love upon a mortal lease.
I cannot take the woman at her worth!
Where is the ancient wealth wherewith I clothed
Our human nakedness, and could endow
With spiritual splendour a white brow
That else had grinned at me the fact I loathed?
A kiss is but a kiss now! and no wave
Of a great flood that whirls me to the sea.
But, as you will! we'll sit contentedly,
And eat our pot of honey on the grave.

George Meredith (1828–1909)

QUESTIONS

1. This poem is from *Modern Love,* a series of sonnet-like lyrics that trace the emotions of a man whose marriage is disintegrating. What is the source of the conflict in the speaker's mind?

2. Which words in the poem describe what is missing from the relationship? Which words have pessimistic overtones?

3. The question beginning in line 9 and ending with line 12 is obscure. Is there any reason why the question should not be phrased more directly? "Nakedness" and "clothed" may suggest the idea of shame. What is the cause of the speaker's shame?

4. How does the speaker resolve his problem? Do the conflicting connotations of "pot of honey" and "grave" in the final line suggest that the speaker is making the best of things? If the contradictions do not neutralize one another, what do they do?

## *"Poetic" Diction*

Poetry is so different from prose in many respects that separate vocabularies developed. Along with this went the thought that some subjects are inherently poetic or unpoetic. With these premises, a theory of decorum, which held that excellence in art depends on a true sense of propriety or fitness, helped to shape the poetry of the Augustan Age (eighteenth century). Thomas Gray (1716–1771), in a passage that describes children swimming and playing by the riverside, found that the dignity of his subject ruled out using such ordinary terms as "children," "swim," "catch birds," "roll hoops," or "throw balls." Instead, he says:

Say, Father Thames, for thou has seen
   Full many a sprightly race
Disporting on thy margent green
   The paths of pleasure trace,
Who foremost now delight to cleave
With pliant arm thy glassy wave?
   The captive linnet which enthrall?
What idle progeny succeed
To chase the rolling circle's speed,
   Or urge the flying ball?

from "Ode on a Distant Prospect of Eton College"

QUESTIONS

1. What would the everyday word be for: "sprightly race" (line 2), "disporting" (line 3), "margent" (line 3), "cleave with pliant arm thy glassy wave" (lines 5 and 6), "idle progeny" (line 8)?
2. What did Gray hope to accomplish with such vocabulary?

No doubt Gray meant his poem to be elegantly clear, not obscure, but young Americans may find him more difficult to follow than a deliberately eccentric contemporary poet. E. E. Cummings, in the poem below, is intelligible to many young readers today because he speaks in their idiom.

*in Just-*

In Just-
spring          when the world is mud-
luscious the little
lame balloonman

whistles          far          and wee

and eddieandbill come
running from marbles and
piracies and it's
spring

when the world is puddle-wonderful

the queer
old balloonman whistles
far          and          wee
and bettyandisbel come dancing

from hop-scotch and jump-rope and

it's
spring
and
          the

                    goat-footed

balloonMan          whistles
far
and
wee

e. e. cummings (1894–1962)

QUESTIONS

1. What sort of person might be the speaker of this poem?

2. How is his sense of excitement related to the poem's word order? Why is there no punctuation? Do you think the poem represents a statement or a stream of thought? What do you lose if you make three complete sentences ending with lines 9, 17 and 24?

3. Sort out the words associated with the children from those associated with the balloonman. What points of contrast do you see?

4. The "goat-footed" balloonman who whistles suggests the Greek god Pan, who was chief of the minor deities. The lower half of his body resembled a goat, and the music he played on his pipes could charm gods or *panic* the enemies of Greece. He is usually associated with the rites of spring. If you did not recognize the reference to Pan in your first reading of the poem, what effect does it have on your later readings?

## *Classic and Romantic*

The foregoing contrast between Gray and Cummings discloses how much difference 200 years can make in what is accepted as good language in poetry. Yet, at any given time, one may find exceptional poets who are poles apart in their approach to diction. For convenience' sake we use the terms "classic" and "romantic" in referring to one important distinction.

*Classical diction* (that is, diction which in imitation of Greek and Roman poetry exercises great emotional restraint by using formal vocabulary) may be contrasted with *romantic diction* which, theoretically at least, tends to be more personal and emotional, though sometimes simple and sometimes ornate. Customarily, the term classical is linked with the eighteenth century (one of the neoclassical periods), and romantic with the early nineteenth century, but any age has its spectrum of diction ranging from the individual and personal to the conventional and formal. Much more than word choice influences the classical or romantic character of a poem, but you will notice in some poets a tendency to use highly charged emotional words sparingly while others make a more direct appeal to your feelings.

The two poems that follow are typical of neoclassical and romantic diction. Notice how, by taking different routes, they both make a strong impression.

## *Ode Written in the Beginning of the Year 1746*

How sleep the brave, who sink to rest,
By all their country's wishes blest!
When Spring, with dewy fingers cold,
Returns to deck their hallowed mold,
She there shall dress a sweeter sod,
Than Fancy's feet have ever trod.

By fairy hands their knell is rung,
By forms unseen their dirge is sung;
There Honour comes, a pilgrim grey,
To bless the turf that wraps their clay,
And Freedom shall awhile repair,
To dwell a weeping hermit there!

William Collins (1721–1759)

## *To Sleep*

O soft embalmer of the still midnight,
  Shutting, with careful fingers and benign,
Our gloom-pleas'd eyes, embower'd from the light,
  Enshaded in forgetfulness divine:
O soothest Sleep! if so it please thee, close
  In midst of this thine hymn my willing eyes,
Or wait the "Amen," ere thy poppy throws
  Around my bed its lulling charities.
Then save me, or the passèd day will shine
Upon my pillow, breeding many woes,—
  Save me from curious Conscience, that still lords
Its strength for darkness, burrowing like a mole;
  Turn the key deftly in the oiled wards,
And seal the hushèd Casket of my Soul.

John Keats (1795–1821)

### QUESTIONS

1. Which of the poems seem most to involve the speaker personally? Which words lead you to your conclusion?
2. Contrast the nouns and verbs in these poems. Which seems more concrete?

3. Death and sleep are implicitly compared in both poems. How does Collins's comparison differ from Keats's?

4. Would you say that one of these poems is soothing, and the other disturbing? What accounts for this? Is one effect preferable to another? Why?

## *Contemporary Diction*

If it is possible to generalize about diction in the present age, the drift is away from formality, poeticisms, and all preconceptions of what kind of language ought to appear in poems. This does not mean that poetry has no more room for elegance, but simply that poetry and elegance are far from synonymous. More and more, poets incline to take their words from the vocabulary of speech and thought, and less from that which is mostly written. If this is indeed the trend, it is nothing new in the history of poetry which has again and again swung between formal and colloquial (spoken) diction. Looking back, we find Skelton, Donne, and Wordsworth rebelling against the too studied elegance of their day. Yet, if we forget about historical perspective, even these rebels may seem self-conscious about poetic proprieties.

As a part of this general drift in diction, many modern poets find their words in unfamiliar places while others have tried to attune themselves to spoken language. Complexity in modern poetry develops more often from the relationship among words than from strangeness of vocabulary. Some selections from both of these types are given below.

### *Romans Angry about the Inner World*

What shall the world do with its children?
There are lives the executives
Know nothing of,
A leaping of the body,
The body rolling—and I have felt it—
And we float
Joyfully on the dark places;
But the executioners
Move toward Drusia. They tie her legs
On the iron horse. "Here is a woman
Who has seen our mother

In the other world!" Next they warm
The hooks. The two Romans had put their trust
In the outer world. Irons glowed
Like teeth. They wanted her
To assure them. She refused. Finally they took burning
Pine sticks, and pushed them
Into her sides. Her breath rose
And she died. The executioners
Rolled her off onto the ground.
A light snow began to fall
And covered the mangled body,
And the executives, astonished, withdrew.
The other world is like a thorn
In the ear of a tiny beast!
The fingers of the executives are too thick
To pull it out!
It is like a jagged stone
Flying toward them out of the darkness.

Robert Bly (1926– )

## QUESTIONS

1. If you find this poem unclear, would you say the difficulty arises from unusual vocabulary, or from the way the poet advances his idea?

2. What is the connection between the middle section (lines 8–23) and the beginning and end sections? What is the scene of Romans torturing a woman supposed to represent? Why does Bly use "executives" and "executioners" almost interchangeably? Why Romans rather than, say, Spartans or Americans?

3. What would be the effect if Bly had chosen some Christian saint martyred by the Romans rather than the apparently unhistorical Drusia?

## *Traveling through the Dark*

Traveling through the dark I found a deer
dead on the edge of the Wilson River road.
It is usually best to roll them into the canyon:
that road is narrow; to swerve might make more dead.

By glow of the tail-light I stumbled back of the car
and stood by the heap, a doe, a recent killing;
she had stiffened already, almost cold.
I dragged her off; she was large in the belly.

My fingers touching her side brought me the reason—
her side was warm; her fawn lay there waiting,
alive, still, never to be born.
Beside that mountain road I hesitated.

The car aimed ahead its lowered parking lights;
under the hood purred the steady engine.
I stood in the glare of the warm exhaust turning red;
around our group I could hear the wilderness listen.

I thought hard for us all—my only swerving—,
then pushed her over the edge into the river.

William Stafford (1914–    )

QUESTIONS

1. This poem obviously does not present any obstacle in vocabulary, yet it has its own sense of mystery. What is the "swerving" mentioned in line 17? How is this related to "swerve" in line 4?

2. Why does the poet say "still," instead of "quiet" in line 11?

3. What is the effect of the verb "purred" in line 14?

4. What is striking about the expression "warm exhaust turning red" in line 15?

Though the word choice in the two foregoing poems differs, the resistance to clear understanding offered by Bly's poem derives more from the way in which the thoughts are related than from the obscurity of individual words. A writer may be cryptic or *surrealistic* (that is, emphasizing the experience of dream images not consciously controlled) without departing from the diction of everyday speech. The two poems that follow illustrate two contemporary styles, one plain and one ornate, but both complex.

*A Dream of Metals*

It was then I dreamed
of small metal objects
tacks to secure
casters to run on

I sorted locks, hooks
bolts and brads
staples loaded in a staple gun

I fill a bureau drawer
with clamps, valves
little wheels, springs
of no known source
or use
which nag to be used

on which I cut myself
and my blood tastes
of copper, silver, and tin

It was then I dreamed
of small metal objects

hinges like cocoons
on the sides of doors
screws thirsty for wood
the hibernation of spikes
on the roadbed

The small metals
trembling as though magnetized
rise one by one
out of the houses they hold together
out of the girders
out of the floorboards
out of the wings of tables

rise up in a cloud / merging
returned to their ore in mid-air
while the cities below them
fall like folded paper

clips, iron filings
the fillings of teeth
sawteeth, tenpenny nails
nuts, pins, and cogs
the strips around the lids of coffee cans

ascending transfigured
like small angels toward the sun

Jack Anderson (1935– )

## QUESTIONS

1. Are there any unfamiliar words in this poem? Most of the words name metal objects; are there any words referring to living things? Experiment with interchanging the names of objects. Is anything lost by this?

2. Taken at face value, this is a fanciful poem about what would happen if all the little bits which lie around or hold things together were magnetized by something up in the sky. Could some other meaning be suggested?

3. Does the phrase "returned to their ore" (line 32) have any parallel with the expression "dust to dust"? What do "cocoons" (line 18) and "hibernation" (line 22) have in common?

4. How do the connotations of "loaded . . . gun" (line 7), "nag" (line 13), "cut" (line 14), "blood" (line 15), "thirsty" (line 21), "trembling" (line 25) affect the reader's emotional response? How do the words listed above relate to the following: "rise" (line 26), "hold together" (line 27), "wings" (line 30), "rise up" (line 31), "ascending transfigured" (line 40), and "angels" and "sun" (line 41)?

5. Can you see any rationale behind the fact that some of the objects have a known purpose and some have unknown purposes? Does this suggest anything about human purpose?

### *A Baroque Wall-Fountain in the Villa Sciarra*

Under the bronze crown
Too big for the head of the stone cherub whose feet
A serpent has begun to eat,
Sweet water brims a cockle and braids down

Past spattered mosses, breaks
On the tipped edge of a second shell, and fills
The massive third below. It spills
In threads then from the scalloped rim, and makes

A scrim or summery tent
For a faun-ménage and their familiar goose.
Happy in all that ragged, loose
Collapse of water, its effortless descent

And flatteries of spray,
The stocky god upholds the shell with ease,
Watching, about his shaggy knees,
The goatish innocence of his babes at play;

His fauness all the while
Leans forward, slightly, into a clambering mesh

Of water-lights, her sparkling flesh
In a saecular ecstasy, her blinded smile

Bent on the sand floor
Of the trefoil pool, where ripple-shadows come
And go in swift reticulum,
More addling to the eye than wine, and more

Interminable to thought
Than pleasure's calculus. Yet since this all
Is pleasure, flash, and waterfall,
Must it not be too simple? Are we not

More intricately expressed
In the plain fountains that Maderna set
Before St. Peter's—the main jet
Struggling aloft until it seems at rest

In the act of rising, until
The very wish of water is reversed,
That heaviness borne up to burst
In a clear, high, cavorting head, to fill

With blaze, and then in gauze
Delays, in a gnatlike shimmering, in a fine
Illumined version of itself, decline,
And patter on the stones its own applause?

If that is what men are
Or should be, if those water-saints display
The pattern of our areté,
What of these showered fauns in their bizarre,

Spangled, and plunging house?
They are at rest in fulness of desire
For what is given, they do not tire
Of the smart of the sun, the pleasant water-douse

And riddled pool below,
Reproving our disgust and our ennui
With humble insatiety.
Francis, perhaps, who lay in sister snow

Before the wealthy gate
Freezing and praising, might have seen in this
No trifle, but a shade of bliss—
That land of tolerable flowers, that state

As near and far as grass
Where eyes become the sunlight, and the hand
Is worthy of water: the dreamt land
Toward which all hungers leap, all pleasures pass.

Richard Wilbur (1921– )

VOCABULARY NOTES

Title "Baroque": the very ornate and irregular style (1550–1750), full of curves, associated with decadent art.
line 4 "brims a cockle": flows over a basin in the form of a shell.
line 9 "scrim": loosely woven cotton or linen cloth.
line 10 "faun-ménage": dwelling place for fauns, mythical creatures with a man's body and the horns and hind legs of a goat.
line 19 "her sparkling flesh": the water here treated as the ecstatic woman over whom the faun is leaning.
line 22 "trefoil": shaped like three leaves.
line 23 "reticulum": a net-like design made by criss-crossing ripples.
line 24 "addling": confusing, intoxicating.
line 30 "Maderna": architect (1556–1629).
line 43 "areté": Greek word for virtue (Wilbur's note).
line 50 "ennui": bored weariness.
line 51 "insatiety": state of never being satisfied.

QUESTIONS

1. Two fountains in Rome, one at the Villa Sciarra and one at St. Peter's cathedral, are described here. Do you see any shift of word choice as the poet turns his attention from one fountain to another? What is the difference? Characterize the difference between Anderson's and Wilbur's vocabulary.
2. What two views of life do these fountains reflect? How do the fauns differ from St. Francis? Why does the poet use St. Francis rather than some other saint? What is the significance of "snow," line 52, among the water details?
3. Does the poet suggest that the true aspiration of the human spirit disregards earthly beauty and pleasure?
4. How are the opposites in the poem resolved in the last three stanzas? Could the conclusion be stated more clearly?
5. The terms classical and romantic may not strictly apply here, but if you had to say Anderson and Wilbur were one or the other, what would you say? Why?

## *The Right Word*

Too much has been made of the idea that successful poems have such intricacies of balance and interdependence in their word choice, that even the slightest alteration would ruin them. But in fact, there usually are alternatives. Some poets constantly revise their works or seem hard pressed to make a decision about the truly "right" word. Perhaps it is good that enthusiastic readers would not have a syllable of their favorite words altered. It may even be that with art, as with life, we can be charmed by the very imperfections of that which we most admire.

Nevertheless, comparing variant versions of a poem makes an instructive exercise because we can deduce from the comparison why the poet chose a few individual words as he did. Read the following two versions of Housman's poem and try to assess which is the poet's final draft.[1] The lines which differ in word choice are marked with an asterisk (*).

A

* On your midnight pallet lying,
Listen, and undo the door:
Lads that waste the night in sighing
In the dark should sigh no more;
* Night should ease a lover's sorrow;
* Therefore, since I go to-morrow,
Pity me before.

In the land to which I travel,
* The far dwelling, let me say—
Once, if here the couch is gravel,
* In a kinder bed I lay,
* And the breast the darnel smothers
* Rested once upon another's
When it was not clay.

B

On your bed at midnight lying,
Listen and undo the door
Lads that waste the night in sighing
In the dark should sigh no more;
Night should sain a lover's sorrow;—
So, because I part tomorrow,
Pity me before.

In the land to which I travel,
When I come there, let me say:
Once, if here the couch is gravel
In a softer bed I lay
Once the breast the cerecloth covers
Breathed against a happy lover's
When it was not clay.

A. E. Housman (1859–1936)

QUESTIONS

1. Compare the connotations of "bed" and "pallet" in line 1.
2. "Sain" (line 5) is an archaic word meaning to bless, as with a sign of the cross. What are its relative merits compared with "ease"?
3. What shade of meaning, if any, lies between the two versions of line 6?

1. Version "B" incorporates detail from several of Housman's working drafts which may be seen in Tom Burns Haber, *The Making of A Shropshire Lad* (Seattle: University of Washington Press, 1966), pp. 79–81.

4. Which version of line 9 seems more meaningful? Do you see any obvious padding in either variation?

5. Compare the relative merits of "darnel" and "cerecloth"; of "smothers" and "covers" (line 12). Before he made his final choice of "darnel," Housman also considered "knotgrass" and "tombstone." Why did he disregard these?

6. One version of line 13 is more concrete. Which is it, and is it therefore preferable? Why? Why not?

## *Diction: Improper and Indecent*

The question of impropriety is not altogether resolved, even for many who are devoted to poetry and who understand it. Most people are conditioned to respond with revulsion to words which, for example, take away the dignity of sexuality. Not long ago the very subject of sex was either avoided altogether or cloaked in terms formal or indirect enough to avoid giving offense. Every generation, it seems, has its built-in tolerance for frank language, and the present day, which seems to have dared all preconceptions and inhibitions, has its limits. Many readers who have no wish to restrict vocabulary in poetry find that after awhile obscenities lose even their shock value. Serious artists, however, are less concerned with taboos than with using language—all language—effectively.

The poem below uses shocking detail deliberately and to a high moral purpose. Notice the pun in the title and the manner in which the poet transforms the adolescent and irresponsible voice in the first part of the poem into a pained statement about the obscenity of war.

### *Going Whoring*

Thank the wonders of penicillin
when you are 20 and can get it up
five or six times a night.
If you are rich or are somewhere cheap
and can sleep all day tomorrow,
strut out with two or three buddies:
there are shabby one-way streets
where girls stand with their chests high
and look straight ahead until you nod.

Babies, boyfriends, bad teeth—
they have also those lazy afternoons

to be themselves, watching television
or shopping like Army wives.
They are like night-shift nurses,
only happier, their clothes are smarter.

You can leave your socks on,
or not, or just unzip,
she will be pleased that you are young
and you come fast.
You do it in a mug of Vaseline.
When you have soaped clean,
have some beer and sausages with your buddies
before peeling an eye for the next one.

She comes from a run-down factory town,
or lost her husband in the war—
she'll tell you anything.
For all you know, she's stuffed
a pared potato up there
with a sliver of razor in it pointed out.

As you lurch above her
raised on your arms as for a push-up,
you are 20 years old, you hear
men shuffling behind the mirrors.
If only you could speak the language!

Sometimes you are so alone, it feels
like falling naked from a helicopter.
You have dreamed of watching blood
spit from a hole in your belly,
nobody could put it back.
Strong as a horse in a meadow
and happy you didn't step
where Johnnie did,
you just go numb when a lead tooth
shoves you into the weeds.
It's so small, you're so big!
The holes were all through him
when your buddy died that way.
You could fuck a girl for free
if you made up your mind,
if you had help.

She wriggles like a mealworm
when you try to set the hook.
You remember fishing for bluegills
and the wailing of crows.
The people are wailing
and the bells are tinkling in the temple.
The noise is awful. The bone is scattering
in a shower of grease, the arms
are flapping like a flight of ducks
beating the air and kicking
until they rest quiet on the water.
They jerk in the dirt
and you stop it.
God, you are happy
nobody shoots back!

The houses are burning, the children
have stiffened, the women's
blood has dried on your clothes.
Your buddies are shooting cows.
Somebody takes your picture
chasing a duck down the road
with a bayonet in your fist.

Al Lee (1938–     )

For contrast, read the following poem by Richard Lovelace. He was a Cavalier poet, one of those loyal to King Charles I in the English Civil War. The ideal courtier of his day, he was twice imprisoned, wounded, and finally impoverished in his service to the king. One legend goes that this poem was written when he left Lucy Sacheverell, his fiance, to fight in Holland with the French army. Before he returned she heard that he was killed and so married someone else.

This poem, one of the best and most romantic of its sort, illustrates the aristocrat's attitude about diction, form, and war in the middle of the seventeenth century.

### *To Lucasta, Going to the Wars*

Tell me not, Sweet, I am unkind,
  That from the nunnery
Of thy chaste breast and quiet mind
  To war and arms I fly.

True, a new mistress now I chase,
  The first foe in the field;
And with a stronger faith embrace
  A sword, a horse, a shield.

Yet this inconstancy is such
  As you too shall adore;
I could not love thee, Dear, so much,
  Loved I not Honor more.

Richard Lovelace (1618–1658)

*Chapter 5*

# Imagery

It was excellently said of Plutarch, Poetry is a speaking Picture, and Picture a mute Poesie . . . Yet of the two, the Pen is more noble, then the Pencill. For that can speake to the Understanding; the other, but to the sense.

Ben Jonson

IN poetry an *image* is produced when a word names or suggests some sensory experience. It may be that imagery is the one solid link between life and art—and the soul of poetry—because it is the animating principle. Imagery is at once the most obvious and the most mysterious element of poetry—obvious, because it appeals directly to the senses, and mysterious because no more is known exactly about how it works in art than is known about how the human mind registers perceptions. An idea of how this works can be illustrated in the political cartoons. With a few lines to represent a shock of hair or a part of a profile, the cartoonist can suggest the whole man plus an idea about the man. The presence of all the details of a face portrayed is less important than the presence of the right details. A few lines, a color, a motion—these are all the mind may need to register a complete response. Images in poetry, like the lines in a cartoon, set off a complex set of mental responses that fill in the necessary ingredients to construct a complete and vital experience.

Notice how the following poem, with a few well-chosen images, manages to recreate a vivid and complex emotional experience.

## *Piano*

Softly, in the dusk, a woman is singing to me;
Taking me back down the vista of years, till I see
A child sitting under the piano, in the boom of the tingling strings
And pressing the small, poised feet of a mother who smiles as she sings.

In spite of myself, the insidious mastery of song
Betrays me back, till the heart of me weeps to belong
To the old Sunday evenings at home, with winter outside
And hymns in the cosy parlor, the tinkling piano our guide.

So now it is vain for the singer to burst into clamour
With the great black piano appassionato. The glamour
Of childish days is upon me, my manhood is cast
Down in the flood of remembrance, I weep like a child for the past.

D. H. Lawrence (1885–1930)

### QUESTIONS

1. What sense impressions of sound, touch, and sight do you find in the first four lines?
2. When you read these lines aloud, does the sound of the words reinforce the meaning? Do the lines go slowly or do they seem to rush? Can an impression of speed in itself be a sense impression?
3. Sound, for the speaker in this poem, is a link between past and present. What signs of contrast do you find between the second and third stanzas?
4. Summarize the meaning of this poem and assess the importance of the sensory details in creating the feeling evoked by this poem.
5. Would you say the sensory effects are well done or overdone?

The theme of memory in Lawrence's "Piano" reminds us that all of the experience of the past is inscribed in the mind as images. Just as there is no meaning or memory without imagery, there is no art without it, any more than there can be beauty without substance. Otherwise we would have an empty paradigm —a blueprint without a building.

### *A Lockean View of Imagery*

The English philosopher John Locke (1632–1704) theorized in his *Essay Concerning Human Understanding* that the human mind, having no inborn ideas, begins as a *tabula rasa,* or smoothed wax tablet ready to be written on. Throughout life the mind forms its ideas from sense impressions made on the tablet. In order to appreciate fully the part played by imagery in poetry, it might help to recall Locke's ideas of the role of sense impressions in thought and the relationship between imagery and experience.

From earliest infancy the individual has inscribed in his nervous system a record of all his encounters with environment in the form of sense impressions. From the beginning he has the potential to think, but not until the tracings of experience provide subjects does he have material to work with. The encounters come at random and they multiply so that each encounter helps the individual meet the next one by a system of trial and error. Thus a child might find that the white crystals on the table are sweet, but go on to discover by experience that other white crystals are salt. Up to a point, the encounters of one person resemble those of another, especially if their surroundings are similar and if their sensory equipment is alike. An Eskimo's encounters would differ from an Arab's, and a deaf person would have different tracings from one who hears. But regardless of the differences, the resemblances between the growth of one human's stock of mental tracings and another's enables all of us to communicate. And the level at which all humanity certainly shares much is the level of recorded sensory responses.

### *Imagery: The Common Bond*

Art communicates by bringing human beings together in heart and in mind. Perhaps, as Leo Tolstoy held, the one unmistakable mark of true art is its infectiousness—its ability to bring people together in feeling. This quality is not for the select few, because any person, educated or not, can join in the basic responses to any art, to feel the effect of a song, a story, or a dance. Poetry derives much of its infectiousness from imagery because images supply us with the stock of words whose meanings are most unequivocally shared. The images are the names of the actions, things, and qualities most accessible to all men, and hence the use of these in any act of communication connects reader and writer in a tighter bond than abstract words can make. Emotional responses are so inseparable from imagery that to mention the image is to create the emotion—the screech of chalk on a blackboard, the sense of warm wetness that turns out to be blood. Such images recreate physical and emotional experience.

Scientists have identified about twenty different types of sense impressions; the most easily recognized are those of sight, sound, taste, smell, touch, temperature, distance, and movement. The constant intake and integration of sensory data make the possibilities of complex thought virtually incalculable. In seventy years, according to one theory, the brain receives fifteen trillion units of information for storage. All this begins with simple, unintegrated sense impressions—fundamental images, without which thought and communication would be impossible.

*Imagery Classified and Illustrated*

Sometimes a systematic study of diction helps us understand the distinctive features of a given poet's style. Things to notice are the proportion of concrete and abstract words, the kinds of imagery, and the poet's tendency to involve or not to involve images in comparisons. As an aid to analysis, a classification of types of imagery, illustrated by excerpts from Byron's poetry, is given below.

| | |
|---|---|
| 1. Sight (color, shape, size, position, and motion) | With the blood running like a little brook<br>From two smart saber gashes, deep and red— |
| 2. Sound | It has a strange quick jar upon the ear,<br>That cocking of a pistol |
| 3. Touch | . . . and then she strayed<br>O'er the sharp shingles with her bleeding feet |
| 4. Motion | 'Til as the snake late coiled, who pours his length<br>And hurls at once his venom and his strength |
| 5. Smell | Not a breath crept through the rosy air |

| | |
|---|---|
| 6. Taste | And life's enchanted cup but sparkles near the brim<br>His had been quaffed too quickly, and he found<br>The dregs were wormwood; but he quaffed again. |
| 7. Kinesthetic (tension and relaxation) | And her head drooped as when the lily lies<br>O'ercharged with rain . . . |
| 8. Internal sensation | But worst of all is nausea, or a pain<br>About the lower region of the bowels |
| 9. Thermal | . . . a deep clear stream<br>Within an Alpine hollow . . . |

With a basic system of classification, you can begin an analysis of many poems. You may discover that the poet uses a pattern of recurring imagery, and that the imagery enables him to construct a mood. Each poem has a kind of temperament that is the result of the poet's having mixed in due proportion the element of imagery. Frequently the key to fullest understanding may be reached through examining the images. It should not be assumed, however, that all poems will have a profusion of images or that statements without imagery are necessarily unpoetic.

Though sensory experience is commonly shared by all men, it would be wrong to conclude that all men react similarly to it. The two poems that follow should show that similar images can, according to the will of the poet, construct opposite thoughts.

### *Dover Beach*

The sea is calm tonight,
The tide is full, the moon lies fair
Upon the straits;—on the French coast the light
Gleams and is gone; the cliffs of England stand,
Glimmering and vast, out in the tranquil bay.
Come to the window, sweet is the night-air!
Only, from the long line of spray
Where the sea meets the moon-blanched land,
Listen! you hear the grating roar
Of pebbles which the waves draw back, and fling,
At their return, up the high strand,
Begin, and cease, and then again begin,
With tremulous cadence slow, and bring
The eternal note of sadness in.

Sophocles long ago
Heard it on the Aegean, and it brought
Into his mind the turbid ebb and flow
Of human misery; we
Find also in the sound a thought,
Hearing it by this distant northern sea.

The Sea of Faith
Was once, too, at the full, and round earth's shore
Lay like the folds of a bright girdle furled.
But now I only hear
Its melancholy, long, withdrawing roar,
Retreating, to the breath
Of the night-wind, down the vast edges drear
And naked shingles° of the world. *stony beaches*

Ah, love, let us be true
To one another! for the world, which seems
To lie before us like a land of dreams,
So various, so beautiful, so new,
Hath really neither joy, nor love, nor light,
Nor certitude, nor peace, nor help for pain;
And we are here as on a darkling plain
Swept with alarms of struggle and flight,
Where ignorant armies clash by night.

Matthew Arnold (1822–1888)

## QUESTIONS

1. What details of sight, sound, smell, taste, touch, and motion do you find in the first section of this poem? What words does the poet use to reveal his attitude to the sensory experience, for example, "calm" (line 1)?
2. What abstract words in the third section of the poem show Arnold leading the reader to a thought about the scene?
3. In the final section Arnold uses more abstract terms followed by a memorable set of images, drawn not from the immediate scene but from his imagination. What is the effect of this?
4. When you read the poem aloud, do the sounds and the motion of the lines contribute to the effect? Could you say that the sound of any poem is part of the sensory experience which affects the reader?
5. This poem reflects the attitudes of many intellectuals in the Victorian era (1832–1901) who were troubled by religious doubts brought on by scientific discoveries and the study of the Bible as history. Arnold is seeking to find the objective equivalent of his emotions in his imagery. Comment on how the

reference to Sophocles and the detail of the last division of the poem affect the emotional impact.

### *"Dover Beach"—A note to that poem*

The wave withdrawing
Withers with seaward rustle of flimsy water
Sucking the sand down, dragging at empty shells.
The roil after it settling, too smooth, smothered . . .

After forty a man's a fool to wait in the
Sea's face for the full force and the roaring of
Surf to come over him: droves of careening water.
After forty the tug's out and the salt and the
Sea follow it: less sound and violence.
Nevertheless the ebb has its own beauty—
Shells sand and all and the whispering rustle.
There's earth in it then and the bubbles of foam gone.

Moreover—and this too has its lovely uses—
It's the outward wave that spills the inward forward
Tripping the proud piled mute virginal
Mountain of water in wallowing welter of light and
Sound enough—thunder for miles back. It's a fine and a
Wild smother to vanish in: pulling down—
Tripping with outward ebb the urgent inward.

Speaking alone for myself it's the steep hill and the
Toppling lift of the young men I am toward now,
Waiting for that as the wave for the next wave.
Let them go over us all I say with the thunder of
What's to be next in the world. It's we will be under it!

Archibald MacLeish (1892– )

QUESTIONS

1. What are some of the details shared by this poem and Arnold's?

2. The two poets are seeing waves from a different vantage point. What is the difference?

3. The speaker in Arnold's poem is addressing another person who is present; MacLeish's speaker is making a less private announcement. How does this affect the poem?

4. Describe in detail the sensory phenomena about waves in this poem.

5. How do the qualifying words and the sound and movement of the lines as you say them aloud influence the attitude built by this poem?

6. What kind of a "note" is MacLeish's poem? What does it say about the way men in the twentieth century have met the Victorian crisis of faith as revealed in "Dover Beach"?

We might conclude from this that although images are very definite, they themselves are rarely the message. What the poet does with the images produces the communication, even when he makes no explicit subjective comment.

*The Economy of Imagery*

A poem has the difficult job of expressing the rarest of experiences without seeming talkative. If it accomplishes its desired effect it takes over the reader's awareness of the words and penetrates experience directly—something like music which, when it is most effectively moving us with sounds, leaves us least aware that anything so physical as sound is responsible for our pleasure. This is, I think, what Archibald MacLeish means when he says, in lines which state and illustrate his thought,

> A poem should be palpable and mute
> As a globed fruit,
>
> . . . . . . . . . . . . . . .
>
> wordless
> As the flight of birds.

The poem should make experience, not talk about it. And the tool most useful in creating this experience is imagery—words, true enough, but words so deeply rooted in the physical perception that they cannot be thought or spoken without awakening experience. In the lines above two images bear the weight of poetic expression. The poet claims "A poem should be palpable and mute . . . wordless"; yet until the images are introduced, all we have is an idea, a statement about poetry which is puzzling and which has, even when stated without the imagery, a certain musical appeal.

It is not until the senses of sight, taste, and touch are evoked that the concept becomes experience. Instinctively, the poet knows that people respond instantly and in one accord to certain things. Full, round fruit, to be held, seen and tasted, automatically stirs a favorable, wordless, response. Likewise, the flight of birds, suggesting solemnity and silent grace, is a part of every person's visual memory. The very mention of it recreates the experience. The image gets at the thought without seeming to "give an explanation."

Now consider MacLeish's poem as a whole.

*Ars Poetica*

A poem should be palpable and mute
As a globed fruit,

Dumb
As old medallions to the thumb,

Silent as the sleeve-worn stone
Of casement ledges where the moss has grown—

A poem should be wordless
As the flight of birds.

*

A poem should be motionless in time
As the moon climbs,

Leaving, as the moon releases
Twig by twig the night-entangled trees,

Leaving, as the moon behind the winter leaves,
Memory by memory the mind—

A poem should be motionless in time
As the moon climbs.

*

A poem should be equal to:
Not true.

For all the history of grief
An empty doorway and a maple leaf.

For love
The leaning grasses and two lights above the sea—

A poem should not mean
But be.

Archibald MacLeish (1892– )

QUESTIONS

1. What variety of imagery do you find in the first sixteen lines? Do you think the poet is trying to include all the major types of sensory perception? Why?

2. At what points do you find the lines difficult to understand? Do you think the poet has been deliberately obscure? Why?

3. One subtle sense we have is the feeling of time passing. What details in the poem seem to awaken this sense?

4. Do any of the images create a negative, unpleasing reaction? What would the presence of such images do to the tone?

5. Do you find any contradiction between the central idea in this poem and the fact that the poem *states* a theory *about* poetry?

## *Other Types of Imagery*

The term "imagery" is frequently used in such combinations as "war imagery," "sexual imagery," or "religious imagery" in speaking of images classed according to subject rather than according to sense perception. Since images have denotation and connotation, they often play a unifying role in poetry as well as a vivifying role. Tension in the following poem lies in the interplay between the war imagery and the imagery of religion. Strictly speaking, all the words involved may not involve sense impressions, but in the aggregate they may call up a very real sensation of sound.

### *Anthem for Doomed Youth*

What passing-bells for these who die as cattle?
Only the monstrous anger of the guns.
Only the stuttering rifles' rapid rattle
Can patter out their hasty orisons.

No mockeries for them; no prayers nor bells,
Nor any voice of mourning save the choirs,—
The shrill, demented choirs of wailing shells;
And bugles calling for them from sad shires.

What candles may be held to speed them all?
Not in the hands of boys, but in their eyes
Shall shine the holy glimmers of good-byes.
The pallor of girls' brows shall be their pall;
Their flowers the tenderness of patient minds,
And each slow dusk a drawing-down of blinds.

Wilfred Owen (1893–1918)

QUESTIONS

1. Which words suggest the sounds of prayer? Are these actual sound images, or words which suggest images?
2. Point out the funeral imagery.
3. How does the imagery of light and darkness operate in the poem?

Sylvia Plath's poem, "Cut," which follows, is at first glance a record of her reactions to an ordinary kitchen accident. The vivid imagery helps us to follow the rapid and complex flow of emotion from the first, strange exhilaration to the final revulsion. But folded into this, you will find a subtle pattern of violence and war imagery.

*Cut*
*For Susan O'Neill Roe*

What a thrill—
My thumb instead of an onion.
The top quite gone
Except for a sort of a hinge

Of skin,
A flap like a hat,
Dead white.
Then that red plush.

Little pilgrim,
The Indian's axed your scalp.

Your turkey wattle
Carpet rolls

Straight from the heart.
I step on it,
Clutching my bottle
Of pink fizz.

A celebration, this is.
Out of a gap
A million soldiers run,
Redcoats, every one.

Whose side are they on?
O my
Homunculus, I am ill.
I have taken a pill to kill

The thin
Papery feeling.
Saboteur,
Kamikaze man—

The stain on your
Gauze Ku Klux Klan
Babushka
Darkens and tarnishes and when

The balled
Pulp of your heart
Confronts its small
Mill of silence

How you jump—
Trepanned veteran,
Dirty girl,
Thumb stump.

Sylvia Plath (1932–1963)

## QUESTIONS

1. Which words contribute to the tone of levity? Which words counteract this? What effect is gained by having the speaker address her thumb as if it were a series of people?

2. Sort out the images of violence. Do they suggest to you any general idea about the role of violence in our lives?

3. Be certain to look up definitions of unfamiliar words such as "wattle" (line 11), "homunculus" (line 23), and "trepanned" (line 38). What do they contribute in sound, connotation, and imagery?

## *The Objective Correlative*

In contemporary criticism, the term *"objective correlative"* is often used to describe the *things* that go into the making of a particular emotion. T. S. Eliot introduced the term, claiming that the objective correlative was the sole means of producing emotion in art. If the artist sets forth objects and events in the proper configuration, he will not have to "talk about" the emotions of yearnings, revulsion, and joy; he will have recreated them. The most effective poetry does not merely stimulate emotion, however; it must communicate emotions as the poet intends them to be felt. Of course, the poet's control over objects and their related emotions may never be perfect because of the shades of response in individual readers. We do not all make mental pictures in the same way.

Notice in the following poem how often the things mentioned are not part of the actual scene, but rather parts of an emotional scene in the mind's eye. The man in the poem wonders if his wife is crying in her sleep, but discovers that she is awake when, at his touch, she stifles her sobs.

### from *Modern Love*

1

By this he knew she wept with waking eyes:
That, at his hand's light quiver by her head,
The strange low sobs that shook their common bed
Were called into her with a sharp surprise,
And strangled mute, like little gaping snakes,
Dreadfully venomous to him. She lay
Stone-still, and the long darkness flowed away
With muffled pulses. Then, as midnight makes
Her giant heart of Memory and Tears
Drink the pale drug of silence, and so beat

Sleep's heavy measure, they from head to feet
Were moveless, looking through their dead black years,
By vain regret scrawled over the blank wall.
Like sculptured effigies they might be seen
Upon their marriage-tomb, the sword between;
Each wishing for the sword that severs all.

George Meredith (1828–1909)

QUESTIONS

1. What is the dominant emotional impression left by this poem? Keeping your answer to this question in mind, how do the following words from the poem contribute to that impression?

a. strangled
b. gaping snakes
c. venomous
d. muffled
e. black
f. scrawled
g. blank wall
h. marriage-tomb
i. sword between

2. Which of the words in the list above are actually and literally pertinent in the bedroom scene? Is the poet describing a room or a state of mind? Can you generalize from this to say that imagery in a poem is a product of the imagination as well as of physical observation?

3. List the words in the poem having to do with trembling or physical motion. What considerations of the poet do you think went into his selection of these words? How might the idea of the objective correlative help you to analyze the kinesthetic imagery?

The next poem offers several points of comparison with the selection from *Modern Love.* It is one of a series of love poems that creates an emotional scene through images which are not literally part of the picture. Analyze this poem for its effective use of the objective correlative.

*The Last Word*

When I saw your head bow, I knew I had beaten you.
You shed no tears—not near me—but held your neck
Bare for the blow I had been too frightened
Ever to deliver, even in words. And now,
In spite of me, plummeting it came.
Frozen we both waited for its fall.

Most of what you gave me I have forgotten
With my mind but taken into my body,
But this I remember well: the bones of your neck
And the strain in my shoulders as I heaved up that huge
Double blade and snapped my wrists to swing
The handle down and hear the axe's edge
Nick through your flesh and creak into the block.

Peter Davison (1928– )

## *Imagery and Selectivity*

Since no poem can include every sensory detail for even the most limited subject, the poet selects the imagery consistent with his mood. Confronted with the same objective experience, two poets will inevitably "see" it with their emotions as well as their eyes. Their descriptions of the experience will not only reveal their attitudes, but will in turn create attitudes, for in accepting a poem, a reader sees and hears with the poet's eyes and ears.

In attempting to record his most memorable thoughts fully so that nothing escapes when he transforms the experience into words, the poet's selection of images is more influential than his comprehensiveness.

The two poems that follow present disturbing views of the violence in American life. The emotions elicited by the poets are quite different, however, because of the selection and arrangement of detail. One is more strictly regular in structure and more generalized in detail. Despite their great differences in treating a similar subject, both poems are technically very admirable.

### *The Frontier*

The Pioneers, the Cat Men, and the Wolves,
    Leaning together under a hissing light,
In argot plan their conduct through the streets,
    Their violence upon the easy night.

Their studded belts, their leather jackets show
    Their wish to be alike and to be led,
Whether on motorcycles in a pack
    Or each in turn upon a single bed.

They crowd the highways with their mortal skill,
    The litter of their deaths, their games of speed;
In love with death, and loving nothing else,
    Their only conversation is the deed.

The wilder ones are made unique in print
    When it is only killing which delights,
But tiny fretful crimes for most of them
    Are adequate to glut their appetites.

Their small aggressions aggregate a war.
    Their random conduct signifies attack.
The Pioneers, the Cat Men, and the Wolves
    Gather within the cities they will sack.

Donald Hall (1928–     )

## *Picture of the Usual Murderer in the Usual Magazine*

Along with the victims' graduation portraits,
upholstery stains, weapons, etc.,
    a twenty-five-cent machine snapshot
    of him, at the amusement park:

You recognize the unbuttoned shirt and rolled-up sleeves,
shine of oil and sweat under slick-back hair,
    his liquid eyes
    evading you, although

you can track his steps: getting gas, pack of rubbers
fucking hot night clang slam squall of tires
    picking up a half-pint,
    his excitement picking up.

At the park, a marksman, he bangs the clattering ducks
for a perfect score, two times, and wants to bet
    he can do it again but
    everybody's chicken-shit.

Later, the arc-lights scouring the emptied spaces,
roller-coasters clanking, he's drunk, sullen, and *clunk*
    the machine presents him to us,
    eyes sliding out of focus

into the spread-out night of diners, bars, fields—
America's big tits pumped full for him,
    for him, ready to be
    sucked and punctured.

Robert S. Hahn

QUESTIONS

1. How does Donald Hall create a sense of distance between the speaker and the subject? What words in the first stanza would not be part of the gang members' vocabulary? Are the details presented from the point of view of an observer or of a participant? Why?

2. Why does Robert Hahn abandon "polite" diction in his poem? Do you think most readers react to the imagery as the poet intends for them to react?

3. How do the different approaches to the selection of imagery account for the individual appeal of each poem?

4. Neither poem presents sexual degeneracy in an appealing light, but Hahn's presentation is more likely to be questioned. How would you defend it?

## *The Imagists*

When a number of poets are attracted to some new theory or some new slant of literary activity, their work is said to comprise a *movement*. One such movement grew out of a theory about imagery, and the poets attracted to the theory are called *imagists*. Their main objective was to stimulate the imagintion by presenting a sharp, even harsh, image. To them compression, not fullness of detail, was the mark of true poetry, and hence they shunned elaborate statements of ideas in favor of the open suggestibility of a compact image. Their diction is simple, purged of all clichés and poeticisms, and their rhythms seek to produce ever changing moods rather than to imitate traditional "poetic" moods. Though their first surge of vitality came in the years just before and after World War I, their influence is still central. The imagists themselves were much affected by oriental poetry, particularly haiku, which concentrates on one striking image. Best known among the American imagists are Ezra Pound, "H. D.," Carl Sandburg, William Carlos Williams, and Amy Lowell, whose *Tendencies in Modern American Poetry* examines in detail the theory and practice of the imagists.

When readers find themselves perplexed by poems which are striking but unintelligible, their reactions may be exactly those which the poet intended. Many imagist poems and poems indebted to imagist theory are not idea oriented. This is not to say that imagist poetry is meaningless, but that it is unlikely to make some thematic proposition. Many contemporary poets in the imagist vein, unwilling to limit themselves to a *single* image, assemble a series of images which speak for themselves apart from any overt statement of theme.

Perhaps the most hauntingly compact of the imagist poems is this one by Ezra Pound:

*In a Station of the Metro*

The apparition of these faces in the crowd;
Petals on a wet, black bough.

Ezra Pound (1885–1972)

The poem grew out of an experience Pound had as he left a "metro" (subway) train in Paris and suddenly saw beautiful faces of women and children passing one after another. The sight moved him so that he tried for over a year to translate it into a poem. His first attempt turned into a thirty-line poem which he rejected, as he did a second, shorter, version. Finally he produced the sentence above which he admits can have meaning only to one who "has drifted into a certain vein of thought." In this poem he was trying to capture the exact moment when some external object suddenly becomes transformed into a highly personal thing.

*Night Clouds*

The white mares of the moon rush along the sky
Beating their golden hoofs upon the glass Heavens;
The white mares of the moon are all standing on their hind legs
Pawing at the green porcelain doors of the remote Heavens.
Fly, Mares!

Strain your utmost,
Scatter the milky dust of stars,
Or the tiger sun will leap upon you and destroy you
With one lick of his vermilion tongue.

Amy Lowell (1874–1925)

## QUESTIONS

1. Describe the actual scene which this poem fancifully calls to mind.
2. Is auditory imagery involved in the actual picture?
3. "Clouds," "moon," "sky," and "sun" are the only real things mentioned. Where does the poem's vivid imagery come from? How is the picture in the poet's eye related to the picture in her mind?

## *Upon Julia's Clothes*

Whenas in silks my Julia goes,
Then, then, methinks, how sweetly flows
That liquefaction of her clothes.

Next, when I cast mine eyes and see
That brave vibration each way free,
O how that glittering taketh me!

Robert Herrick (1591–1671)

## QUESTIONS

1. The mingling of sight and motion imagery accounts for much of this poem's success. Which two words in the poem capture this effect most strikingly?
2. Does the flow of the words enhance their meaning? Do you see any contrast between rough and smooth sounding lines? Are the rough ones intended to make the smooth stand out?
3. Is touch imagery involved in the poem?
4. What does "next" mean in line 4?
5. How does this poem measure up to the imagist's ideal, considering that it was written almost 300 years ago?

### *Splinter*

The voice of the last cricket
across the first frost
is one kind of good-by.
It is so thin a splinter of singing.

Carl Sandburg (1878–1967)

QUESTIONS

1. What is surprising about the word "splinter" in the last line?
2. Why should the poem be titled "Splinter" rather than "Cricket" or "First Frost"?

The poem that follows has that quality much admired in contemporary poetry by which the beauty of the poem does not depend on the exclusion of rough or ugly detail, but on the truthful blending of all kinds of sense impression.

### *Fishing Harbour Towards Evening*

Slashed clouds leak gold. Along the slurping wharf
The snugged boats creak and seesaw. Round the masts

Abrasive squalls flake seagulls off the sky:
Choppy with wings the rapids of shrill sound.

Wrapt in spliced airs of fish and tar,
Light wincing on their knives, the clockwork men

Incise and scoop the oily pouches, flip
The soft guts overboard with blood-wet fingers.

Among three rhythms the slapping silver turns
To polished icy marble upon the deck.

Richard Kell (1927– )

QUESTIONS

1. Do you think this poem was intended to create an idea, an attitude, or an uninterpreted picture? Can you have the picture without some emotional response to it?

2. The poet uses imagery of sight, sound, motion, smell, and touch. Describe the mood which the poem evokes in you. Point out the most effective example of each type.

3. Which of the images have unfavorable connotations? Do these impose upon the poem its dominant impression, or do they qualify a mood that is basically pleasant?

## *Imagery in Our Day*

Several factors have come to give imagery special importance in modern poetry. In times when poetry was the medium for long narrative compositions, plays, and extended verse essays, imagery functioned in support of story and theme. This is not to belittle imagery's role, for one of the most remarkable elements in such works as *The Faerie Queene, Paradise Lost, Macbeth,* or *The Prelude* is the way in which imagery is brought to bear on plot and theme. At times, as in the description of Cleopatra's barge, in Shakespeare's *Anthony and Cleopatra,* the spectacle of drama is more indebted to imagery than to scenery. Still, the medium of imagery was rarely the message as it is in some contemporary works.

As poems have diminished in length, the proportion of imagery has grown. The limit has been reached now that a single, sharp image may actually *be* a poem. Much of the supportive imagery has passed over into fiction where it continues to vivify storytelling by heightening the feeling of life through sense impressions.

The importance of imagery in modern poetry is accented by the twentieth century's faith in objectivity and its resistance to sermonizing. If the objective picture is vivid enough, the need to draw a moral from it fades.

### *Night Patrol*
### *(Washington)*

The wolf's cousin,
then gentled to clown for us,
paces now, forbidden
to be trusted, or trust—
paces the pavement.

The black shoes and the furry toes
pace together on the wide
street; from the raw light pace
into the shadows' jungle.
The wolf blood courses under hide.
The feet echo; silent go the paws.

A clock strikes winter.
Hunters are cold as hunted.
The dog teaches the man to listen—
something waits in the shadows' center.
The wolf heart knows what is wanted,
called back from a dream unnatural and human.

They walked like mutant friends in a season's sun.
Now they walk like wolves, and know their own.
Their own move toward them; empty, the street
moves toward them where in this bitter season
cold wolf and wolf meet.

Josephine Jacobsen (1908– )

## QUESTIONS

1. This poem implies some judgment about the quality of life in our cities. What is it?

2. Does your understanding of what the poem says come in any degree from a feeling that the poem instills? If so, how does sound and thermal imagery contribute to this understanding?

3. Nowhere in the poem does the poet mention policemen or police dogs. How does the poet bring your mind to focus on isolated images which suggest a fuller picture?

*Chapter 6*

# Allusion and Myth

### *Belshazzar had a Letter*

Belshazzar had a Letter—
He never had but one—
Belshazzar's Correspondent
Concluded and begun
In that immortal Copy
The Conscience of us all
Can read without its Glasses
On Revelation's Wall—

Emily Dickinson (1830–1886)

THIS poem may puzzle anyone who does not know about Belshazzar. When a poet through direct or indirect reference to some fact in history or literature requires his reader to have prior knowledge in order to respond to a poem, he is using *allusion.* At first glance the disadvantages of this literary device seem severe, since all is lost if the reader does not happen to have a very specific kind of information. Whereas a writer may expect everyone to have the same basic sensory experience, he can rarely depend on everyone's sharing the same cultural background. And yet poets have always been willing to run this risk.

The poem above alludes to the biblical story (Daniel 5) of Belshazzar, last King of Babylon, who used the sacred vessels stolen from the temple in Jerusalem at a great feast. His lords and their wives and concubines drank wine from the vessels and "praised the gods of silver, bronze, iron, wood, and stone." The fingers of a man's hand appeared and wrote a cryptic message on the king's wall. The court sent for Daniel, a wise Israelite, who interpreted the signs as a prophecy of Belshazzar's death and the fall of his kingdom.

The tone of Emily Dickinson's poem is altogether different from that of the apocalyptic story in the Old Testament. In fact, since the moral of the story is "beware of sacrilege," the poem's whimsical tone is a kind of challenge. Is it proper or sacrilegious, one might ask, to refer to the Bible in such a casual way? The mixture of seriousness and levity produces a surprising and pleasing effect. Though the miraculous message is called a mere "letter," though God is referred to as a "correspondent," and though the prophet is, by implication, one who reads with "glasses," there is no doubt about and no nonsense in Miss Dickinson's faith in revealed truth. The poem alludes not only to the story, but to a whole assortment of attitudes.

Allusion at its best is never mere name-dropping; rather, it assists in making poetry the most compressed form of language. With a word, a poet may considerably enlarge the scope of his work by letting in a mass of mental associations. He may reinforce the emotional impact he wishes to make by mentioning some work which he knows has already caused a similar emotional impact. Since poetry has been part of Western culture for thousands of years, it is very difficult to develop any thought without some degree of reference to what already exists.

Allusion is, in essence, a refined application of connotation. Where connotative imagery refers one mentally to his own primary experience, allusion refers one to the secondary experience of art and history. In some ways, allusion is very predictable since the mention of, say, Macbeth's guilty conscience or of Michelangelo's fresco of Adam's creation will call forth similar responses from people who have had similar cultural experience. In principle, allusion works like other connotative language. Because people react to what words suggest as well as to what they stipulate, poets exercise control over their subjects by using detail whose range of suggestion is, if not limited, at least partially predictable. One kind of control may come with such sensory detail as the mention of the sights and sounds of the seaside by night, as in Arnold's "Dover Beach." Another kind of control results from the mention of John the Baptist's head on a platter, as in Eliot's "The Love Song of J. Alfred Prufrock."

In the poem below, the emotional impact will be different for the reader who recognizes the allusion in the final lines. The reader who does not recognize it may have an intense realization of the sensory reality in the poem, yet if he does not see the something which the poet put there to be recognized, an important aspect of the literary pleasure will be lost.

*The U.S. Sailor with the Japanese Skull*

Bald-bare, bone-bare, and ivory yellow: skull
Carried by a thus two-headed U.S. sailor
Who got it from a Japanese soldier killed
At Guadalcanal in the ever-present war: our

Bluejacket, I mean, aged 20, in August strolled
Among the little bodies on the sand and hunted
Souvenirs: teeth, tags, diaries, boots; but bolder still
Hacked off this head and under a Ginkgo tree skinned it:

Peeled with a lifting knife the jaw and cheeks, bared
The nose, ripped off the black-haired scalp and gutted
The dead eyes to these thoughtful hollows: a scarred
But bloodless job, unless it be said brains bleed.

Then, his ship underway, dragged this aft in a net
Many days and nights—the cold bone tumbling
Beneath the foaming wake, weed-worn and salt-cut
Rolling safe among fish and washed with Pacific;

Till on a warm and level-keeled day hauled in
Held to the sun and the sailor, back to a gun-rest,
Scrubbed the cured skull with lye, perfecting this:
Not foreign as he saw it first: death's familiar cast.

Bodiless, fleshless, nameless, it and the sun
Offend each other in strange fascination
As though one of the two were mocked; but nothing is in
This head, or it fills with what another imagines

As: here were love and hate and the will to deal
Death or to kneel before it, death emperor,

Recorded orders without reasons, bomb-blast, still
A child's morning, remembered moonlight on Fujiyama:

All scoured out now by the keeper of this skull
Made elemental, historic, parentless by our
Sailor boy who thinks of home, voyages laden, will
Not say, "Alas! I did not know him at all."

Winfield Townley Scott (1910–1968)

The last line of this poem echoes a speech from Act V, scene 1, of Shakespeare's *Hamlet*. The allusion is not even a direct quotation, and yet for anyone who has seen or read the play, the mere echo calls up the whole assemblage of Hamlet's emotions and reflections on death. In reading Scott's poem one may, in a flash of recognition, see the insensitive American sailor vividly contrasted with one of the most sensitive characters in all literature. In the play, when Hamlet and his friend, Horatio, meet a gravedigger who has just exhumed a skull, Hamlet asks whose it was. He is told that it was the skull of Yorick, the king's jester.

Hamlet: Let me see. *Takes the skull.* Alas, poor Yorick! I knew him, Horatio: a fellow of infinite jest, of most excellent fancy: he hath born me on his back a thousand times; and now, how abhorred in my imagination it is! my gorge rises at it. Here hung those lips that I have kissed I know not how oft. Where are your gibes now? your gambols? your songs? your flashes of merriment, that were wont to set the table on a roar? Not one now, to mock your own grinning? quite chap-fallen? Now get you to my Lady's chamber, and tell her, let her paint an inch thick, to this favor she must come; make her laugh at that. Prithee, Horatio, tell me one thing:

Horatio: What's that, my Lord?

Hamlet: Dost thou think Alexander looked o' this fashion i' the earth?

Horatio: E'en so.

Hamlet: And smelt so? pah! *Puts down the skull.*

This allusion has great vitality partly because of the life which Shakespeare's play has in the minds of virtually all readers of English literature. Scott is able to appropriate the emotional impact of the play for his own purposes in a poem which, even without the allusion, has considerable force. Had he chosen to refer to some other skull in literature, say, Byron's "Lines Inscribed upon a Cup Formed from a Skull," the effect would have been entirely different, and, probably, lost.

All allusions are not so organically necessary. Many allusions appear almost incidental; they may be remarks in passing which tend to compress speech, as when Shylock in *The Merchant of Venice,* pleased to hear Portia's interpretation of the law, calls her "a Daniel come to judgment." Daniel is the wise judge mentioned in the apocryphal Book of Susannah who saves Susannah from evil men who have unjustly accused her. Everyday speech is full of this kind of allusion, which involves an implied comparison between one character and another. A "Judas," an "Iago," or a "Benedict Arnold" is treacherous; an "Uncle Tom" is a servile black. Such references, even when they have grown stale through overuse, make a great many shortcuts in speech possible.

The next poem uses the names of characters from literature in a different way. The names are not merely decorative, but are essential to the thematic and emotional content. More remarkable than the idea is the poet's formality and epigrammatic control. Like many love poems, this one promises a woman immortality in verse. Some students have difficulty with this work because they mistakenly think Ianthe has some significance as allusion. Actually this is simply the name of the woman being addressed—she is the one to whom the immortality is promised.

### *Past Ruined Ilion Helen Lives*

Past ruined Ilion Helen lives,
    Alcestis rises from the shades;
Verse calls them forth; 'tis verse that gives
    Immortal youth to mortal maids.

Soon shall Oblivion's deepening veil
    Hide all the peopled hills you see,

The gay, the proud, while lovers hail
In distant ages you and me.

The tear for fading beauty check,
For passing glory cease to sigh;
One form shall rise above the wreck,
One name, Ianthe, shall not die.

Walter Savage Landor (1775–1864)

## NOTES AND QUESTIONS

Helen of Troy (Ilion) is the Spartan queen of Homer's *Iliad,* the most beautiful woman in the world for whom the Greeks fought a ten-year war against Troy.

Alcestis (line 2) was the wife of Admetus, whose life she saved by dying in his place; but Hercules brought her back from Hades. Alcestis had earlier killed her father, Pelias, according to Medea's instructions, in order to restore his youth.

1. What is particularly fitting about the choice of Helen and Alcestis?
2. Why would Landor have chosen to allude to the relatively obscure Alcestis over some better known legendary character, since his poem is intended to make Ianthe's name live on?
3. Do you think the generalized picture of living persons which Landor gives in the second stanza is deliberately vague? Why or why not?
4. In line 5, does "oblivion" refer to death or to forgetfulness? Explain the appropriateness of the expression "Oblivion's deepening veil."
5. What is the "wreck" referred to in line 11? What connection does this have with the first line?

Allusion may be used decoratively, but it may develop into what Gerard Manley Hopkins amusingly called "Parnassian diction"—the kind of artificial speech poets use to gain elevated effects when their natural creative powers are sluggish. Parnassus is the mountain in Greece sacred to Apollo and the Muses. In legend, to become a poet, one had only to sleep there.

In reading older poems, one may find allusion used conventionally as decoration. When the writers of a given time accept some device, form, or style as a suitable trait in literary expression, those traits are called *conventions.* In reading Thomas Gray's verse, one expects to find certain poetic conventions which would probably be objectionable if seen in a later writer's work. William Wordsworth objected strenuously to the diction of Gray's "Sonnet on the Death of Mr. Richard West." Notice how allusion is an aspect of the poem's ornateness.

### *Sonnet on the Death of Mr. Richard West*

In vain to me the smiling mornings shine,
    And reddening Phoebus lifts his golden fire:
The birds in vain their amorous descant join,
    Or cheerful fields resume their green attire:
These ears, alas! for other notes repine,
    A different object do these eyes require.
My lonely anguish melts no heart but mine;
    And in my breast the imperfect joys expire.
Yet morning smiles the busy race to cheer,
    And new-born pleasure brings to happier men:
The fields to all their wonted tribute bear:
    To warm their little loves the birds complain:
I fruitless mourn to him that cannot hear,
    And weep the more because I weep in vain.

Thomas Gray (1716–1771)

QUESTIONS

1. Wordsworth claimed that all but lines 5, 6, 7, 13, and 14 were without value. He remarked also that the word "fruitless" for "fruitlessly" in line 13 is a defect. What can you deduce about Wordsworth's theory of diction after studying the word choice in this poem?

2. Why do you think Gray thought the allusion to Phoebus would be effective?

## *The Sublime and the Ridiculous*

As might be expected, allusion can become sheer mannerism —a means by which the writer can mechanically avoid literal statements, or a decorative way of raising the tone. At times what was intended to be elevated may come crashing down.

### from *Eonchs of Ruby. A Gift of Love.*

The Apollo Belvedere was adorning
    The chamber where Eulalie lay,
While Aurora, the Rose of the Morning,
    Smiled full in the face of the Day.

All around stood the beautiful Graces
Bathing Venus—some combing her hair—
While she lay in her husband's embraces
A-moulding my Lily Adair—
Of my fawn-like Lily Adair—
Of my dove-like Lily Adair—
Of my beautiful, dutiful Lily Adair.

Thomas Holley Chivers (1809–1858)

The picture that comes to mind after reading this has Venus being embraced by her husband while the Graces comb her hair —at dawn, in the Vatican.

### *A Chronological Sampling*

You can almost tell what preoccupies people by the things they allude to. In the Renaissance and the eighteenth century, when virtually every educated person was absorbed by Greek and Roman literature, writers took their inspiration from and filled their poems with details from it. The seventeenth century, with its religious quarreling, produced a literature full of biblical allusion. So did the Victorians, who were tormented by doubts brought about by science and scholarship. Since then, religion and the classics are less evident in allusion than psychology and sociology. In the years following World War I, there developed a trend toward highly allusive poetry of great obscurity. Poets such as Ezra Pound and T. S. Eliot made no attempt to screen references to the most eccentric reading, whether it be in Chinese philosophy, little-read Jacobean plays or contemporary anthropology. Works such as Eliot's "The Waste Land" and Pound's *Cantos,* for all their difficulty, show that the stream of modern man's consciousness is fed by innumerable tributaries of cultural influence. Lately, however, poets seem less attracted to bookish obscurity, and allusiveness in modern poetry can only be described as "diverse." One recent inclination seems to be a greater attention to graphic art in allusion. There is still a wealth of biblical, historical, and literary reference with a noticeable tendency away from ostentatious display of learning.

The next series of poems will show something of the durability and variety of allusion in poetry. It is just as attractive to poets today as it was hundreds of years ago, and it can be used to create every range of tone—from pious to irreverent, from dead serious to comic.

The first example, with its purely secular use of Greek legend, is from Elizabethan times. Like so many lyrics of the day, this one is an elaborate compliment paid to a lady by a speaker who is very aware that his is the voice of an artist. He is also aware that a great many of his fellow poets stole their lines from the classics.

### from *Astrophel and Stella*

I never drank of Aganippe well,
Nor ever did in shade of Tempe sit,
And Muses scorn with vulgar brains to dwell;
Poor layman I, for sacred rites unfit.
Some do I hear of poets' fury tell,
But, God wot, wot not what they mean by it;
And this I swear by blackest brook of hell,
I am no pick-purse of another's wit.
How falls it then that with so smooth an ease
My thoughts I speak; and what I speak doth flow
In verse, and that my verse best wits doth please?
Guess we the cause. What, is it thus? Fie, no.
Or so? Much less. How then? Sure thus it is:
My lips are sweet, inspired with Stella's kiss.

Sir Philip Sidney (1554–1586)

### NOTES AND QUESTIONS

Aganippe (line 1), the Muses' sacred well at the foot of Mt. Helicon. Tempe (line 2), a valley favored by the god of poetry, Apollo. Blackest brook of hell (line 7), the river Styx.

1. Does Sidney seem to be criticizing the use of classical allusions?
2. Is Sidney being facetious in swearing "by blackest brook of hell"? Consider lines 5, 6, and 7 before answering.

The poem that follows shares both the eighteenth century's love of elegance and the highly personal emotion of the romantic period. Keats's tone of sustained seriousness, his love of the classics, and his technical skill in the use of word music and imagery became the chief legacy of the Victorians. The form used is that of the ode. Originally a Greek lyric form, the *ode* is a poem of considerable length, dignified manner, and elevated theme. Keats's great odes are homostrophic, that is, they have strophes, or stanzas, of like structure in meter and rhyme.

### *Ode to a Nightingale*

1

My heart aches, and a drowsy numbness pains
  My sense, as though of hemlock I had drunk,
Or emptied some dull opiate to the drains
  One minute past, and Lethe-wards had sunk:
'Tis not through envy of thy happy lot,
  But being too happy in thine happiness—
    That thou, light-wingèd Dryad of the trees,
      In some melodious plot
  Of beechen green, and shadows numberless,
    Singest of summer in full-throated ease.

2

O, for a draught of vintage! that hath been
  Cooled a long age in the deep-delvèd earth,
Tasting of Flora and the country green,
  Dance, and Provençal song, and sunburnt mirth!
O for a beaker full of the warm South,
  Full of the true, the blushful Hippocrene,
    With beaded bubbles winking at the brim,
      And purple-stainèd mouth;
  That I might drink, and leave the world unseen,
    And with thee fade away into the forest dim:

3

Fade far away, dissolve, and quite forget
  What thou among the leaves hast never known,
The weariness, the fever, and the fret
  Here, where men sit and hear each other groan;
Where palsy shakes a few, sad, last gray hairs,
  Where youth grows pale, and specter-thin, and dies;
    Where but to think is to be full of sorrow
      And leaden-eyed despairs,
  Where Beauty cannot keep her lustrous eyes,
    Or new Love pine at them beyond tomorrow.

4

Away! away! for I will fly to thee,
Not charioted by Bacchus and his pards,
But on the viewless wings of Poesy,
Though the dull brain perplexes and retards:
Already with thee! tender is the night,
And haply the Queen-Moon is on her throne,
Clustered around by all her starry fays;
But here there is no light,
Save what from heaven is with the breezes blown
Through verdurous glooms and winding mossy ways.

5

I cannot see what flowers are at my feet,
Nor what soft incense hangs upon the boughs,
But, in embalmèd darkness, guess each sweet
Wherewith the seasonable month endows
The grass, the thicket, and the fruit tree wild;
White hawthorn, and the pastoral eglantine;
Fast-fading violets covered up in leaves;
And mid-May's eldest child,
The coming musk-rose, full of dewy wine,
The murmurous haunt of flies on summer eves.

6

Darkling I listen; and, for many a time
I have been half in love with easeful Death,
Called him soft names in many a musèd rhyme,
To take into the air my quiet breath;
Now more than ever seems it rich to die,
To cease upon the midnight with no pain,
While thou art pouring forth thy soul abroad
In such an ecstasy!
Still wouldst thou sing, and I have ears in vain—
To thy high requiem become a sod.

7

Thou wast not born for death, immortal Bird!
No hungry generations tread thee down;
The voice I hear this passing night was heard
In ancient days by emperor and clown:

Perhaps the self-same song that found a path
Through the sad heart of Ruth, when, sick for home,
She stood in tears amid the alien corn;
The same that oft-times hath
Charmed magic casements, opening on the foam
Of perilous seas, in faery lands forlorn.

8

Forlorn! the very word is like a bell
To toll me back from thee to my sole self!
Adieu! the fancy cannot cheat so well
As she is famed to do, deceiving elf.
Adieu! adieu! thy plaintive anthem fades
Past the near meadows, over the still stream
Up the hill-side; and now 'tis buried deep
In the next valley-glades:
Was it a vision, or a waking dream?
Fled is that music:—Do I wake or sleep?

John Keats (1795–1821)

## NOTES AND QUESTIONS

Hemlock (line 2), a poisonous plant or the drink made from this plant used by the Athenians as a means of execution.

Lethe-wards (line 4), the river of forgetfulness in Hades, the underworld.

Dryad (line 7), wood nymph.

Provençal song (line 14), love song from southern France, where the troubadours of the 12th and 13th centuries flourished.

Hippocrene (line 16), a fountain on Mt. Helicon whose waters were the source of poetic inspiration.

Bacchus and his pards (line 32), the god of wine and the leopards that drew his chariot.

Ruth (line 66), the young Moabite widow who followed her mother-in-law Naomi to Israel where she became a gleaner in the fields; see Ruth 2.

1. Assess the effectiveness of Keats's classical allusions. In the assessment, consider the theme and purpose of the poem as a whole. (One major theme is the superiority of the joy conveyed by great art over the transient pleasure derived from real life and nature.)

2. Note that the first two strophes contrast with the third. What role does allusion play in developing tension between the ideal world of the bird and the grimly real world of men?

3. The allusions are, of course, only one aspect of the stylized diction of

this poem. What effects disappear when you translate the poetic diction of the second strophe (including the allusions) into plain spoken English?

4. This poem follows the speaker through several states of mind, arriving at an emotional climax in strophe 7. The progress, roughly, is: from enchantment on hearing the bird, 1; to yearning for the trance of poetic intoxication, 2; to recognition of human misery unknown to the bird, 3; to yearning for escape through poetry, 4; sensation, 5; and death, 6; to wonder at the immortality of song which unifies all time and space in enchantment, 7; and, finally, back to consciousness as the bird departs.

How does the allusion to Ruth in strophe 7 contribute to the emotional and thematic climax?

5. It is said that this, like all of Keats's odes, achieves a unity of impression by resolving such opposites as those between pleasure and pain, melancholy and joy, illusion and reality, and art and nature. Do you find these sources of tension in the poem? How do imagery, connotation, and allusion play a role in this?

Allusion in contemporary works is often as likely to be an instrument of deflation as one for heightening the tone. In the poem that follows, the poet develops an impression of the bankruptcy of hope among those men who must haunt the penny arcades for a moment's relief from reality. Notice the way in which the poet uses contrasts of imagery, connotation, and allusion to give form and emphasis to his thought and to bring out a unified impression of unfulfilled lives.

### *Penny Arcade*

This pale and dusty palace under the El
The ragged bankers of one coin frequent,
Beggars of joy, and in a box of glass
Control the destiny of some bright event.
Men black and bitter shuffle, grin like boys,
Recovering Christmas and elaborate toys.

The clerk controls the air gun's poodle puff
Or briefly the blue excalibur of a Colt,
Sweeps alien raiders from a painted sky,
And sees supreme the tin flotilla bolt.
Hard lightning in his eye, the hero smiles,
Steady MacArthur of the doodad isles.

The trucker arrogant for his Sunday gal
Clouts the machine, is clocked as "Superman!"
The stunted negro makes the mauler whirl
Toy iron limbs; his wizen features plan
The lunge of Louis, or, no longer black,
Send to the Pampas battering Firpo back.

Some for a penny in the slot of love
Fondle the bosom of aluminum whores,
Through hollow eye of lenses dryly suck
Beatitude of blondes and fallen drawers.
For this Cithaeron wailed and Tempe sighed,
David was doomed, and young Actaeon died.

Who gather here will never move the stars,
Give law to nations, track the atom down.
For lack of love or vitamins or cash
All the red robins of their year have gone.
Here heaven ticks: the weariest tramp can buy
Glass mansions in the juke-seraphic sky.

John Frederick Nims (1914– )

## NOTES AND QUESTIONS

The El (line 1), elevated railroad, common to many large cities.

Box of glass (line 3), coin-operated game.

Excalibur (line 8), King Arthur's sword, which could be wielded only through magical power.

Colt (line 8), pistol associated with the "winning of the West."

MacArthur (line 12), General Douglas MacArthur, hero of the Pacific in World War II, who said, when he left the Philippines, "I shall return," and who, on his retirement, used the expression, "Old Soldiers never die—they just fade away."

The mauler (line 15), Jack Dempsey, heavyweight champion, called the "Manassa Mauler."

Louis (line 17), Joe Louis, heavyweight champion, called the "Brown Bomber."

Firpo (line 18), Louis Firpo, heavyweight champion, called "The Wild Bull of the Pampas."

Cithaeron (line 23), the mountain where Actaeon died.

Tempe (line 23), a valley in Thessaly, said to have mourned Actaeon's death.

David (line 24), biblical king (Samuel 2) who "displeased the Lord" when he watched Bathsheba bathe. He later married her after sending her husband to his death in battle.

Actaeon (line 23), mythical Greek huntsman who, when he watched the goddess and her attendants bathing, was turned into a stag and eaten by his dogs.

Red robins (line 28), allusion to the song, "When the Red, Red Robin Comes Bob, Bob, Bobbin' Along." One phrase in the song goes, "I'm just a kid again, doin' what I did again. . . ."

1. It is said that allusions expand the total meaning of a poem without adding to its size. Is this so of "Penny Arcade"? Explain.

2. How do the allusions figure in the contrast between illusion and reality in this poem?

3. Notice that the second, third, and fourth stanzas treat three different kinds of fantasies involving military glory, masculinity, and sexuality. Do you notice in the second stanza any language drawn from low-grade adventure stories?

4. What effect does the poet gain by contrasting in the fourth stanza the voyeurs of the arcade with classical and biblical characters? How does the language of lines 23 and 24 conflict with the language in the rest of the stanza?

5. Many word combinations seem mutually contradictory, for example, "ragged bankers." How many such combinations do you see, and what is their effect on the total emotional impression made by the poem?

6. Many details taken by themselves are comic, for example, "MacArthur in the doodad isles," or "blondes and fallen drawers." Why isn't the total impression comic?

The great variety and interplay of allusions give Nims's poem its force. By contrast, the next poem owes its impact to the vivid elaboration of a single allusion.

## *The Prodigal*

The brown enormous odor he lived by
was too close, with its breathing and thick hair,
for him to judge. The floor was rotten; the sty
was plastered halfway up with glass-smooth dung.
Light-lashed, self-righteous, above moving snouts,
the pigs' eyes followed him, a cheerful stare—
even to the sow that always ate her young—
till, sickening, he leaned to scratch her head.
But sometimes mornings after drinking bouts
(he hid the pints behind a two-by-four),
the sunrise glazed the barnyard mud with red;
the burning puddles seemed to reassure.

And then he thought he almost might endure
his exile yet another year or more.

But evenings the first star came to warn.
The farmer whom he worked for came at dark
to shut the cows and horses in the barn
beneath their overhanging clouds of hay,
with pitchforks, faint forked lightnings, catching light,
safe and companionable as in the Ark.
The pigs stuck out their little feet and snored.
The lantern—like the sun, going away—
laid on the mud a pacing aureole.
Carrying a bucket along a slimy board,
he felt the bats' uncertain staggering flight,
his shuddering insights, beyond his control,
touching him. But it took him a long time
finally to make his mind up to go home.

Elizabeth Bishop (1911–    )

QUESTIONS

1. Read Luke 15: 11–32. What details from the Bible does the poet omit? What does she add? How does her focus differ from that of Luke?

2. Does "The Prodigal" have a moral of its own? If there is one, is it the same as Luke's? If there is not, what is the appeal of the poem?

Matthew Arnold's "Dover Beach," you will recall, appeared in our discussion of imagery. The poem below is an allusion to that poem as well as to Arnold's idea that poetry is "the criticism of life by gifted men, alive and active with extraordinary power at an unusual number of points."

*The Dover Bitch*

A Criticism of Life

*for Andrews Wanning*

So there stood Matthew Arnold and this girl
With the cliffs of England crumbling away behind them,
And he said to her, "Try to be true to me,
And I'll do the same for you, for things are bad
All over, etc., etc."

Well now, I knew this girl. It's true she had read
Sophocles in a fairly good translation
And caught that bitter allusion to the sea,
But all the time he was talking she had in mind
The notion of what his whiskers would feel like
On the back of her neck. She told me later on
That after a while she got to looking out
At the lights across the channel, and really felt sad,
Thinking of all the wine and enormous beds
And blandishments in French and the perfumes.
And then she got really angry. To have been brought
All the way down from London, and then be addressed
As a sort of mournful cosmic last resort
Is really tough on a girl, and she was pretty.
Anyway, she watched him pace the room
And finger his watch-chain and seem to sweat a bit,
And then she said one or two unprintable things.
But you mustn't judge her by that. What I mean to say is,
She's really all right. I still see her once in a while
And she always treats me right. We have a drink
And I give her a good time, and perhaps it's a year
Before I see her again, but there she is,
Running to fat, but dependable as they come.
And sometimes I bring her a bottle of *Nuit d'Amour*.

Anthony Hecht (1923– )

QUESTIONS

1. Review Arnold's poem, paying attention to the level of diction, the imagery, and the speaker's attitude toward the subject. How does Hecht's poem use "Dover Beach" to build up tension?

2. What implications of meaning do you notice in Hecht's subtitle?

3. Judging from these two poems, contrast Hecht's idea of what poetry should be like with Arnold's idea.

4. If you admire Arnold's poem, does the irreverent allusion offend you? Does Hecht's poem alter the way you respond to Arnold's?

5. Contrast Archibald MacLeish's attitude toward Arnold's poem with Hecht's. (See " 'Dover Beach'—A note to that poem," page 94.)

## *Myth*

So many literary allusions are to mythological characters that some discussion of myth seems an appropriate sequel to allusion.

Mythology, a constant source of reference in the history of modern literature, is no mere source of remote and ornamental detail, but a most immediate influence on continuing art. Myth puts us in contact with human origins in an interesting way, perhaps because, as Northrop Frye has observed, its characters behave on a level "near or at the conceivable limits of desire."

A reference to Tiresias, for example, alludes to more than antiquity. He was already a legendary figure when Sophocles wrote *Oedipus Rex,* and he may be found in scores of works since by such poets as Matthew Arnold and T. S. Eliot. Any contemporary reference to Tiresias may owe as much to relatively recent work as it does to the writing of the remotest past.

The fact is that myth makes interesting allusion. Tiresias spent part of his life as a man and part as a woman. He was thereafter called on by the gods to tell whether men or women found greatest pleasure in the opposite sex. Small wonder that he is referred to in matters concerning the endless battle of the sexes. A character such as Tiresias need not be historically real in order to be an important aspect of humanity.

The opposite of "myth" in many contexts is "reality." This is so because myth gives way to reality as the mysteries of life fade one by one in the light of science and reason. Primitive societies, noticing that the tides flow according to the phases of the moon, invented stories that explain the attraction of sea and moon. Recognizing a force operating outside themselves, and feeling the awe inspired by it, they made the characters in their tales gods and goddesses. The stories were not only imaginative interpretations of unexplained phenomena, but they were also acts of reverence toward the mysteries of creation. When men learned that gravitational pull, rather than a love affair of the gods, caused the tides, they no longer needed the imaginative explanation, though the wonder and admiration remained. The opposite of "myth" may be "reality," but one can hardly say that reality is myth's replacement, or that myth is a lie.

*Myth* should not be thought of as a series of disconnected fables through which the beliefs of a people gain piecemeal expression, but as a structure of many narratives which, when woven together, embody a cosmic religious view. Myth tends to be concerned with religious issues—the nature of divinity, the creation, sacrifice, death, and the meaning of existence Studies in comparative myth and religion reveal a remarkable resemblance among myths in their cast of characters and their exploits. All true myths, which are anonymous, had their origins in oral traditions long before they were written. The resemblance among myths of peoples who have had no actual contact is offered as strong evidence that human concerns are universal and suggest that myth emerges from man's primeval and, perhaps, even his pre-human existence. According to Carl Jung, myths, like dreams, are dramatizations stemming from the collective unconscious, that is, the blocked-off remains of our racial past. Myths, like dreams, contain those elemental or archetypal images whose origins lie in the remotest experience of our ancestors.

It is difficult to say with certainty just how deep was the belief of ancient peoples in their myths. The Greeks and Romans were scientists and philosophers as well as ancient. Though Ovid clearly doubted the stories in his *Metamorphoses* as facts, there is no reason to suspect that the people of his day who did believe were any more credulous than modern people of religious faith. When we speak of the Christian Myth or the Myth of Islam, there is no intent to imply that they are either true or untrue. It is possible for Christians to accept and believe that God created the world, that the Ten Commandments are of divine origin, and that Christ shared a human and divine nature. To accept scripture as truth without concern that, in purely physical terms, some of it is impossible presents no insuperable difficulty for modern Christians. Why should not the ancients have been able to tolerate similar ambiguities?

William Wordsworth, disturbed by his own observation that people had given themselves over to the rush for wealth and power, called for a return to natural piety by which men could see the hand of God in nature.

### *The World Is Too Much with Us*

The world is too much with us; late and soon,
Getting and spending, we lay waste our powers:

Little we see in Nature that is ours;
We have given our hearts away, a sordid boon!
The sea that bares her bosom to the moon;
The winds that will be howling at all hours,
And are up-gathered now like sleeping flowers;
For this, for everything, we are out of tune;
It moves us not.—Great God! I'd rather be
A pagan suckled in a creed outworn;
So might I, standing on this pleasant lea,
Have glimpses that would make me less forlorn;
Have sight of Proteus rising from the sea;
Or hear old Triton blow his wreathéd horn.

William Wordsworth (1770–1850)

## NOTES AND QUESTIONS

Proteus (line 13), the old man of the sea, was the son of Neptune in Greek legend. He could assume various shapes to avoid those he did not wish to see, and he had the gift of prophecy.

Triton (line 14), another son of Neptune. He was said to live with him in a golden palace beneath the sea.

1. Does Wordsworth literally think that he could see the gods of the sea if he believed in them? Would you prefer to interpret this as saying that modern materialism keeps men from seeing God in nature?

2. Notice the references to the relationship between the sea and the moon (line 5) and to the winds which "*will be* howling," but which are, for now, held in check (line 6). What characters from mythology may be suggested here? How do these references prepare the way for the allusions in the last two lines?

3. The central contrast here is between modern man's and the ancients' response to nature. What do the allusions add to the poem's effect?

4. Why does Wordsworth shift from the pronoun "we" in the first eight lines, to "I" in the last six?

Proteus figures in the next poem, as in the last, but with a somewhat more detailed use of the myth. Besides being able to assume various shapes and to see into the future, Proteus would not tell the truth unless he was hopelessly trapped. Since he could turn into a dragon or a flood or a fire, he was hard to pin down. Ted Hughes's hero, Crow, does his best.

*Truth Kills Everybody*

So Crow found Proteus—steaming in the sun.
Stinking with sea-bottom growths
Like the plug of the earth's sump-outlet.
There he lay—belching quakily.

Crow pounced and buried his talons—

And it was the famous bulging Achilles—but he held him
The oesophagus of a staring shark—but he held it
A wreath of lashing mambas—but he held it

It was a naked powerline, 2000 volts—
He stood aside, watching his body go blue
As he held it and held it

It was a screeching woman and he had her by the throat—
He held it

A gone steering wheel bouncing towards a cliff edge—
He held it

A trunk of jewels dragging into a black depth—he held it

The ankle of a rising, fiery angel—he held it

Christ's hot pounding heart—he held it

The earth, shrunk to the size of a hand grenade

And he held it he held it and held it and

BANG!

He was blasted to nothing.

Ted Hughes (1930– )

## *Myth Making*

We have said that true myth is anonymous. Perhaps it would be truer to say that traditional myths are. Artistic systems, complete with supernatural personages, and attempting to explain one author's imaginative conception of the universe, have been designed. Thomas Hardy, finding traditional myth no longer workable, cast his great epic-drama, *The Dynasts,* with spirits representative of modern thought. As Hardy saw it, modern belief does not conceive that supernatural power is interested in the human scene, and accordingly he refused to let his spirit personages influence human events. Instead, with such names as "The Immanent Will," "The Spirit of the Pities," and "The Spirit Sinister," they represent slants of philosophical thought. William Blake's "Prophetic Books" develop his private view of a cosmos in which spirits of his own invention mingle with biblical and historical characters in scenes indebted to Platonic and Rosecrucian lore. Perhaps more successful and equally eclectic is William Butler Yeats's system which joins many myths into one vision of humanity without denying to any era its element of the truth. More recently, Robert Graves's mythology, based on worship of the White Goddess, claims to revive the most ancient of myths which is rooted in a prehistoric matriarchal society.

Of these private myths, only Hardy's is fully intelligible to a reader who has not informed himself in advance of the supernatural mechanics. Yeats's is no doubt the most widely acclaimed. With him, it is not the cast of characters which produces obscurity, for they are drawn from classic and Celtic lore, for the most part. Neither do his ideas about personal and historical cycles present any great obstacle. It is the complex system of connections which Yeats uses as the background for many poems that causes the difficulty, and even this does not much diminish the powerful effects.

The following poem uses a tale from Greek mythology which obliquely suggests the Christian belief of the unity of human and divine nature in Christ when Mary became pregnant by the Holy Spirit.

### *Leda and the Swan*

A sudden blow: the great wings beating still
Above the staggering girl, her thighs caressed
By the dark webs, her nape caught in his bill,
He holds her helpless breast upon his breast.

How can those terrified vague fingers push
The feathered glory from her loosening thighs?
And how can body, laid in that white rush,
But feel the strange heart beating where it lies?

A shudder in the loins engenders there
The broken wall, the burning roof and tower
And Agamemnon dead.
Being so caught up,
So mastered by the brute blood of the air,
Did she put on his knowledge with his power
Before the indifferent beak could let her drop?

William Butler Yeats (1865–1939)

## NOTES AND QUESTIONS

Leda, in Greek mythology, was loved by Zeus in the form of a swan. From this union she bore two eggs, one to be Helen of Troy and Pollux, the other to be Clytemnestra and Castor. Indirectly, then, Zeus's love for Leda brought about a chain of disaster including the fall of Troy and the murder of the Greek king Agamemnon (line 11) by his wife Clytemnestra. This poem first appeared in Yeats's book, *The Vision*, in a section entitled "Dove or Swan." In Christian tradition the Holy Spirit visited Mary in the form of a dove.

1. What might be Yeats's purpose in vivifying the rape of Leda? Why does the contrast between the human and the bird come across more vividly than a contrast between the human and some abstract personage?
2. What emotional response does the poet attempt to arouse in the reader? Do you regard this as a possible aspect of religious experience?
3. How does the telling of the union between God and a woman differ in Christian doctrine? Did this union have disastrous effects?
4. Is there any answer to the question which ends the poem?

For a verbally exciting and highly unusual example of mythological allusion, read the next poem aloud and try to get in step with the poet's quick beat. Don't worry too much about meaning the first time through. Afterwards, study the notes and check your dictionary; then go on to the discussion questions.

## *I Am a Cowboy in the Boat of Ra*

"The devil must be fórced to reveal any such physical evil (potions, charms, fetishes, etc.) still outside the body and these must be burned."
—*Rituale Romanum*, published 1947, endorsed by the coat of arms and introduction letter from Francis Cardinal Spellman

I am a cowboy in the boat of Ra,
sidewinders in the saloons of fools
bit my forehead like O
the untrustworthiness of Egyptologists
Who do not know their trips. Who was that
dog-faced man? they asked, the day I rode
from town.

School marms with halitosis cannot see
the Nefertiti fake chipped on the run by slick
germans, the hawk behind Sonny Rollins' head or
the ritual beard of his axe; a longhorn winding
its bells thru the Field of Reeds.

I am a cowboy in the boat of Ra. I bedded
down with Isis, Lady of the Boogaloo, dove
down deep in her horny, stuck up her Wells-Far-ago
in daring midday get away. "Start grabbing the
blue," i said from top of my double crown.

I am a cowboy in the boat of Ra. Ezzard Charles
of the Chisholm Trail. Took up the bass but they
blew off my thumb. Alchemist in ringmanship but a
sucker for the right cross.

I am a cowboy in the boat of Ra. Vamoosed from
the temple i bide my time. The price on the wanted
poster was a-going down, outlaw alias copped my stance
and moody greenhorns were making me dance; while my
mouth's
shooting iron got its chambers jammed.

I am a cowboy in the boat of Ra. Boning-up in
the ol West i bide my time. You should see
me pick off these tin cans whippersnappers. I
write the motown long plays for the comeback of
Osiris. Make them up when stars stare at sleeping
steer out here near the campfire. Women arrive
on the backs of goats and throw themselves on
my Bowie.

I am a cowboy in the boat of Ra. Lord of the lash,
the Loup Garou Kid. Half breed son of Pisces and
Aquarius. I hold the souls of men in my pot. I do
the dirty boogie with scorpions. I make the bulls
keep still and was the first swinger to grape the taste.

I am a cowboy in his boat. Pope Joan of the
Ptah Ra. C/mere a minute willya doll?
Be a good girl and
Bring me my Buffalo horn of black powder
Bring me my headdress of black feathers
Bring me my bones of Ju-Ju snake
Go get my eyelids of red paint.
Hand me my shadow
I'm going into town after Set

I am a cowboy in the boat of Ra
look out Set          here i come Set
to get Set          to sunset Set
to unseat Set          to Set down Set
                    usurper of the Royal couch
                    imposter RAdio of Moses' bush
                    party pooper O hater of dance
                    vampire outlaw of the milky way

Ishmael Reed (1938–        )

## NOTES AND QUESTIONS

Ra (line 1), Sun god of ancient Egypt, creator and protector of man and enemy of evil.

O (line 3), a solar disc, symbol of Ra. Apis, the sacred black bull of Memphis, carried the disc between his horns.

Dog-faced man (line 6), Anubis, the guardian deity, portrayed as having the head of a dog or jackal; he took the dead to judgment.

Nefertiti (line 9), beautiful Egyptian queen, wife of Akenaton, who tried to change the religion of Egypt. A painted limestone carving of her head is in a German museum.

Sonny Rollins (line 10), jazz musician and composer.

Field of Reeds (line 12), in the myth of Osiris, the god's coffin becomes caught in reeds, but the supernatural power in the body of Osiris changed the reeds to a mighty tree. This may be a play of words on the poet's name.

Isis (line 14), goddess of fertility; sister and wife of Osiris, often pictured with a cow's horns.

Ezzard Charles (line 18), former heavyweight boxing champion.

Motown (line 31), a record company.

Osiris (line 31), god of the underworld, patron of immortality and self-renewal, was murdered by his brother Set. Ra's boat sails across the sky by day, and by night Osiris guides the boat across the underworld to its starting place in the East. His soul inhabits the black bull, Apis.

Loup Garou (line 36), "werewolf" in French.

Pope Joan (line 40), the girl who, disguised as a man, is elected pope in E. Rhoidès's novel. The pope wears a triple crown.

Ptah Ra (line 41), master craftsman and artist.

Ju-Ju snake (line 45), magic charm or amulet in West Africa.

Set (line 48), the wicked brother and murderer of Osiris. He is evil personified—the spirit of death and drought. Like Osiris, he considers himself a protector of Ra's boat.

1. Think of the characters in this poem as if they were the players in a typical Western movie. What happens in the plot? Does the intermingling of the Western imagery and the Egyptian mythology give the poem a coherent internal structure?

2. How might this poem be interpreted as a song of black pride?

3. Among the many patterns of repetition in the poem is the frequent mention of horns. How does this help to pull the two basic elements (Western and Egyptian) together? What other patterns of repetition and allusion do you see?

## *The Myth of Icarus in Three Poems*

Each of the following poems alludes to the myth of Daedalus and his son Icarus. Daedalus, the master artisan of Athens and inventor of the axe, the wedge, and the sail, was summoned to Crete by King Minos to design a labyrinth. When Daedalus angered Minos, however, he and Icarus were confined in the labyrinth. They fled the island on wings of feathers and wax contrived by Daedalus. But Icarus flew too close to the sun which melted the wax, and he fell into the sea.

Notice how each poet's use of the allusion fits his distinct purpose. The story of Icarus may be obliquely mentioned to key some emotional response, or it may be the central metaphor and symbol.

### *Smoke*

Light-winged Smoke, Icarian bird,
Melting thy pinions in thy upward flight,
Lark without song, and messenger of dawn,
Circling above the hamlets as thy nest;
Or else, departing dream, and shadowy form
Of midnight vision, gathering up thy skirts;

By night star-veiling, and by day
Darkening the light and blotting out the sun;
Go thou my incense upward from this hearth,
And ask the gods to pardon this clear flame.

Henry David Thoreau (1817–1862)

QUESTIONS

1. What does the mention of Icarus contribute to the mood of this poem?

2. By what logic of comparisons does the adjective "Icarian" apply to smoke?

3. Reread the poem, substituting "Daedalian" for "Icarian." How is the dominant impression altered?

## *On the Death of a Metaphysician*

Unhappy dreamer, who outwinged in flight
The pleasant region of the things I love,
And soared beyond the sunshine, and above
The golden cornfields and the dear and bright
Warmth of the hearth,—blasphemer of delight,
Was your proud bosom not at peace with Jove,
That you sought, thankless for his guarded grove,
The empty horror of abysmal night?
Ah, the thin air is cold above the moon!
I stood and saw your fall, befooled in death,
As, in your numbed spirit's fatal swoon,
You cried you were a god, or were to be;
I heard with feeble moan your boastful breath
Bubble from depths of the Icarian sea.

George Santayana (1863–1952)

QUESTIONS

1. Look up the meaning of "metaphysician." How does a metaphysician's flight (of thought) resemble that of Icarus?

2. The speaker in the poem contrasts his own view of reality with the dead man's. How do their general viewpoints differ? Specifically, how do their attitudes about death conflict?

3. When the speaker asks, "Was your proud bosom not at peace with Jove,"

is this the same as saying "were you not at peace with God"? What difference does the allusion make?

4. What effect is gained by reserving explicit reference to Icarus until the last line?

## *Musée des Beaux Arts*

About suffering they were never wrong,
The Old Masters: how well they understood
Its human position; how it takes place
While someone else is eating or opening a window or just
walking dully along;
How, when the aged are reverently, passionately waiting
For the miraculous birth, there always must be
Children who did not specially want it to happen, skating
On a pond at the edge of the wood:
They never forgot
That even the dreadful martyrdom must run its course
Anyhow in a corner, some untidy spot
Where the dogs go on with their doggy life and the torturer's
horse
Scratches its innocent behind on a tree.

In Brueghel's *Icarus,* for instance: how everything turns away
Quite leisurely from the disaster; the ploughman may
Have heard the splash, the forsaken cry,
But for him it was not an important failure; the sun shone
As it had to on the white legs disappearing into the green
Water; and the expensive delicate ship that must have seen
Something amazing, a boy falling out of the sky,
Had somewhere to get to and sailed calmly on.

W. H. Auden (1907–1973)

### QUESTIONS

1. The title means "Museum of Fine Arts." Peter Breughel's (1564–1638) painting "Icarus" hangs in the Brussels museum. Does the use of the French phrase enlarge the suggestibility of the title more than the English translation? How? What does the word "musée" call to mind?

2. In the first thirteen lines, does the detail about pictures in the museum

become more or less concrete? What might be the reason for this, and why does Auden not give us the names of the artists and their paintings?

3. How does Breughel's painting of Icarus illustrate the theme?

4. Suppose that Auden had Daedalus in mind as the first "old master"; how does this influence your reading of the poem?

*Chapter 7*

# Figurative Language

OFTEN in the course of using language, speakers and writers attempt to express themselves through likenesses. Objects, ideas, and events remind us of other parts of our experience, and the mental associations which we make help us to convey what we mean vividly. With some speakers, the results of the habit of mind that makes frequent use of associative language pass without notice or with little notice. In referring to a difficult situation, one might say, "That's like playing with dynamite," or "That's dynamite," or perhaps, "That's an explosive situation." The situation might in fact be as remote from dynamite as one in which an art critic and a painter whose work he has ridiculed meet accidentally at a party. If asked to explain what the expression, "He's got a short fuse" means, one might answer with another figure of speech and say, "That means he blows up easily." What is meant literally is that he becomes angry easily. Even such a seemingly literal expression as "He lost his temper" is figurative, though through the years the definition of "temper" as a verb meaning to blend or mix in due proportion has been lost. The very idea of temper as a thing (an evenly balanced state of mind) that can be lost or found is figurative—that is, expresses an idea through an implied likeness. Figurative language, then, is a means of expression which is far from being peculiar only to poetry.

The ordinary person's supply of expressions which help him to convey his meaning with appropriate mental pictures includes many common phrases: "neat as a pin," "warm as toast," "cold as ice," "swears like a trooper," "sings like a bird," and "drinks like a fish." These are explicitly stated likenesses and would be called similes, though no careful writer would use them since they have, through overuse, lost their effectiveness. Many trite expressions like "straight from the shoulder," "on the beam," and "behind the eight ball" are uttered by people who have no idea of the intended meaning in the associative imagery they have employed.

All figures of speech occurring in everyday language are not, of course, clichés as are the ones above. These are metaphors because they imply a likeness even though they do not use "as" or "like." The metaphor as cliché survives perhaps because it is more easily managed than the literal equivalent. People may more readily manage the words: "I gave it to him straight from the shoulder, without beating around the bush, or mincing my words," than, "I told him directly, without trying to soften the impact of the words with circumlocution or euphemism." Ironically, the brace of clichés may be more generally understood than the literal statement, even though the likenesses implicit in the three clichés may remain a mystery to both the common speaker and listener. These are "dead" metaphors. The first is based on the similarity between delivering news and delivering a punch, as in boxing; the second, on the similarity between talking around a subject and trying cautiously to get an animal to come out of hiding, as in a hunt; and the last, on the similarity between making words sound inoffensive and making food more manageable and appealing by cutting it up into little bits, as in cooking.

The literary figure of speech, on the other hand, is always intentional, and always represents an attempt by the writer to engage the reader's imagination by forcing him to see an experience as *he* sees it. The writer uses likenesses to qualify and construct a thought by attaching it to the common sensory experience of humanity. In the poem below, Robert Frost records an experience that is more than just sensory, but it succeeds in achieving its ulterior goal—that is, in creating an emotional and intellectual response—by supplying sense impressions drawn from very simple human experience. All the sense impressions may not seem logically to have anything to do with the experience in its simplest form, yet with a system of likenesses, he qualifies the basic experience in such a way as to force the reader to see things as he saw them, and consequently to get a definite feeling and idea.

## *Design*

I found a dimpled spider, fat and white,
On a white heal-all, holding up a moth
Like a white piece of rigid satin cloth—
Assorted characters of death and blight
Mixed ready to begin the morning right,
Like the ingredients of a witches' broth—
A snow-drop spider, a flower like froth,
And dead wings carried like a paper kite.

What had that flower to do with being white,
The wayside blue and innocent heal-all?
What brought the kindred spider to that height,
Then steered the white moth thither in the night?
What but design of darkness to appall?—
If design govern in a thing so small.

Robert Frost (1874–1963)

### QUESTIONS

1. Frost seems to be saying that nature, if you look at her in a certain way, is a sign that some malevolent creator is responsible for the scheme of things. What words in the poem have a normally happy connotation?
2. What effect arises out of placing the gay words with the disturbing ones?
3. How many details in the poem are introduced by means of figurative, that is, non-literal statements? Can you summarize the first eight lines without saying anything figurative?

The very expression "figurative language" might suggest that the use of figures is a kind of decoration, a frill, and yet there is no element of poetry that bears a larger share of the burden of meaning. Earlier, we made the point that figures of speech are actually more straightforward than literal speech. (It is simpler, for example, to say a writer's prose is knotty or twisted, than to give a literal description.) They are also more memorable, because they involve our sense perceptions, and more compact because they suggest more than they state. In "Auto Wreck"

(p. 376), when Karl Shapiro says "Our throats were tight as tourniquets," or "one ruby flare/Pulsing out red light like an artery," he is not just describing the scene of an accident. He is involving the reader's senses and setting in motion a chain of thought and emotion. He does not say that arteries were actually severed and a tourniquet applied. Rather, he lets the reader infer these details. The literal equivalents (we could not swallow, and the flare burned in surges of red light) simply do not say enough.

In prose, one of the commonest uses for figurative language is to clarify a thought. To explain the idea that people change their vocabulary to fit the situation, a writer might say that language is like protective coloration in the animal world. The arctic hare is white in winter and brown in summer, and a man's words are shaded differently for his employee and for the policeman who stops him for speeding. Poets, too, may use figures of speech this way. But figurative language can do more than pin a thought down in definition; it can also set a thought loose by opening up possibilities of interpretation. Archibald MacLeish does something like this when he says (p. 94),

> A poem should be motionless in time
> As the moon climbs.

Almost any prose equivalent of this comparison will fail to include all the implications. Surely, to say that a poem should create a sense of permanence is not enough.

Some poets, particularly those of the eighteenth century, used figures of speech to illustrate their thoughts in much the same way a prose writer might. Their figures of speech tend to define rather than to invite speculation. The quotation below, from Alexander Pope's *An Essay on Man* will illustrate:

> Vice is a monster of so frightful mein,
> As, to be hated, needs but to be seen;
> Yet seen too often, familiar with her face,
> We first endure, then pity, then embrace.

The following quotation from Byron's *Don Juan* makes a similar but somewhat more elaborate use of the figure of speech.

In these lines the poet illustrates through comparison a clear-cut, yet subtle idea about passion.

But passion most dissembles, yet betrays
 Even by its darkness; as the blackest sky
Fortells the heaviest tempest, it displays
 Its workings through the vainly guarded eye,
And in whatever aspect it arrays
 Itself, 'tis still the same hypocrisy:
Coldness or anger, even disdain or hate,
 Are masks it often wears, and still too late.

Canto I, stanza 73

Byron's figurative lines are much less definitive than Pope's, though probably no less satisfying, for figures of speech do more than explain. They also *explore* meaning, and the poet may use them to set loose images which may help to reveal, both to the poet and the reader, some meaning that is held within the indefiniteness of much experience. The two poems by Emily Dickinson that follow may help to demonstrate the wide range of thought—from the clearly reasoned to the almost indistinct —which figures of speech help to recreate.

*There is no Frigate like a Book*

There is no Frigate like a Book
To take us Lands away
Nor any Coursers like a Page
Of prancing Poetry—
This Travel may the poorest take
Without offence of Toll—
How frugal is the Chariot
That bears the Human soul.

The idea in this poem is clarified and intensified by means of the images supplied through the figures of speech. Miss Dickinson not only creates images here, but also shapes the reader's attitude with such richly connotative words as "frigate," "coursers," and "lands." Any substitution of synonyms for these words will quickly demonstrate the original words' effectiveness. Moreover, the first stanza does not rely solely on the two expressed comparisons, "frigate like a book," and "coursers like a page," for the words "prancing poetry," imply a further comparison between horses and poetry. In the second stanza, the poet does more than make the bland statement that reading is cheaper than travel; she suggests that the human spirit may be moved without using up or wasting spiritual resources. The thought of the poem above is not so pleasing or surprising as the statement; the figurative language vitalizes and decorates a relatively clear idea. Often the poems of Emily Dickinson are more difficult. In the poem below she attempts to supply us with a reference point in sensory experience in order to convey an emotional experience.

*After great pain, a formal feeling comes*

After great pain, a formal feeling comes—
The Nerves sit ceremonious, like Tombs—
The stiff Heart questions was it He, that bore,
And Yesterday, or Centuries before?

The Feet, mechanical, go round—
Of Ground, or Air, or Ought—
A Wooden way
Regardless grown,
A Quartz contentment, like a stone—

This is the Hour of Lead—
Remembered, if outlived,
As Freezing persons, recollect the Snow—
First—Chill—then Stupor—then the letting go—

No substitution of synonyms will clarify the poem, which seeks with words to lure into the open a part of life that is wordless—the numbing aftermath of great physical or emotional suffering. Since there is no vocabulary to explain the feeling, the poet explores it with metaphor, comparing it with insensate objects and with situations associated with lack of sensation. The problem of conveying a feeling that is characterized by no feeling is probed in each stanza with a different set of images. First, the still, funereal stiffness of formality; then the moving stiffness of things mechanical; and finally, the creeping stiffness of anesthesia, in which pain is the anesthetic removing pain. With such words as "tombs," "ground," "quartz," "stone," and "lead," the poet links the subject with unfeeling objects. "Quartz" suggests a mingling of motion and rigidity, of liquid turned stone, of flux and stasis congealed. The first stanza, with its veiled allusion to Christ's suffering—"was it He, that bore,/And Yesterday, or Centuries before?"—gives the work a potential religious significance, suggesting perhaps, with its hesitation, the tentative mental search for meaning in suffering.

This poem exists as metaphor. Since it derives its life from metaphor, figurative language is the essence, not a decorative ingredient.

## *Simile and Metaphor*

The most widely known figures of speech, the simile and metaphor, occupy a prominent place not only in poetry, but in everyday language. The *simile,* with some word to indicate likening (as, like, than, etc.), explicitly compares objects belonging to different classes. A simile might compare people with animals: "Susan eats like a bird," "waddles like a duck," or "sleeps like a bear." To say "Susan eats like her sister," "walks like her father," or "sleeps longer than most girls," would be to use a literal, stated comparison, not a simile. A poet's simile, to be effective, must never be stale or distracting. It should blend with the rest of the work to assist in developing an overall unified effect. The next poem uses simile to make a statement about the mind and its use of comparisons for developing insight. The poem takes into account not only the likeness of the object compared, but also the difference.

## *Mind*

Mind in its purest play is like some bat
That beats about in caverns all alone,
Contriving by a kind of senseless wit
Not to conclude against a wall of stone.

It has no need to falter or explore;
Darkly it knows what obstacles are there,
And so may weave and flitter, dip and soar
In perfect courses through the blackest air.

And has this simile a like perfection?
The mind is like a bat. Precisely. Save
That in the very happiest intellection
A graceful error may correct the cave.

Richard Wilbur (1921– )

### QUESTIONS

1. Read this poem again. What effect does the poet gain through the simile? Does imagery make the thought vivid; does the simile give you some real thing to illustrate the thought with sensory perceptions?

2. Why do you think the poet deliberately blurs the vivid picture created in the first stanza? Does this blurring lead you on to explore the idea further?

The following poems use similes extensively. Point out all the similes and explain how the poet uses them to provide vivid detail and to advance thoughts or evoke emotions.

## *The Mind is an Enchanting Thing*

is an enchanted thing
    like the glaze on a
katydid-wing
        subdivided by sun
        till the nettings are legion.
Like Gieseking playing Scarlatti;

like the apteryx-awl
    as a beak, or the
kiwi's rain-shawl
        of haired feathers, the mind
        feeling its way as though blind,
walks along with its eyes on the ground.

It has memory's ear
        that can hear without
having to hear.
                Like the gyroscope's fall,
                truly unequivocal
because trued by regnant certainty,

it is a power of
        strong enchantment. It
is like the dove-
                neck animated by
                sun; it is memory's eye;
it's conscientious inconsistency.

It tears off the veil; tears
        the temptation, the
mist the heart wears,
                from its eyes,—if the heart
                has a face; it takes apart
dejection. It's fire in the dove-neck's

iridescence; in the
        inconsistencies
of Scarlatti.
                Unconfusion submits
                its confusion to proof; it's
not a Herod's oath that cannot change.

Marianne Moore (1887–1972)

## QUESTIONS

1. Is the poet attempting to explain exactly what the mind is like, or do you get the impression that she is searching her mind for similes to explore the magic of thought?

2. What main impression do the images introduced through the similes create?

3. Why did the poet choose so many far-fetched images, such as the close-up view of a katydid's wing reflecting sunlight—Gieseking playing Scarlatti—the apteryx-awl?

4. If the similes do not produce a more definite understanding than a literal explanation, what might be the use of them?

## *A Valediction: Forbidding Mourning*

As virtuous men pass mildly away,
　　And whisper to their souls to go,
While some of their sad friends do say,
　　The breath goes now, and some say, no:

So let us melt, and make no noise,
　　No tear-floods, nor sigh-tempests move,
'Twere profanation of our joys
　　To tell the laity our love.

Moving of th' earth brings harms and fears,
　　Men reckon what it did and meant,
But trepidation of the spheres,
　　Though greater far, is innocent.

Dull sublunary lovers' love
　　(Whose soul is sense) cannot admit
Absence, because it doth remove
　　Those things which elemented it.

But we by a love so much refined,
　　That ourselves know not what it is,
Inter-assured of the mind,
　　Care less, eyes, lips, and hands to miss.

Our two souls therefore, which are one,
　　Though I must go, endure not yet
A breach, but an expansion,
　　Like gold to airy thinness beat.

If they be two, they are two so
　　As stiff twin compasses are two,
Thy soul the fixed foot, makes no show
　　To move, but doth, if th' other do.

And though it in the center sit,
　　Yet when the other far doth roam,
It leans, and hearkens after it,
　　And grows erect, as that comes home.

Such wilt thou be to me, who must
　　Like th' other foot, obliquely run;
Thy firmness makes my circle just,
　　And makes me end, where I begun.

John Donne (1572–1631)

A summary of this poem might go as follows: the speaker, who is saying good-bye to his wife, asks her not to be emotional about the parting, because emotionalism is for ordinary, merely physical lovers. Since their love is spiritual, he says, even when they are apart they are together.

QUESTIONS

1. How do you know the speaker is not saying good-bye *forever?* Does the first simile help you to understand this? What poetic logic links the first three stanzas?

2. The simile in stanza six introduces the favorable associations of finely beaten gold. Why does the poet not end here?

3. Can you think of any reason why the poet ends matter-of-factly with a simile based on geometry rather than on some more conventionally romantic image?

A *metaphor* is a figure of speech that implies a comparison between two subjects which belong to different classes. In the poem below, Randall Jarrell implies that there is a horrible similarity between the human fetus and the ball turret gunner. By implying the similarity rather than stating it, Jarrell gives the poem a sense of eerie immediacy.

*The Death of the Ball Turret Gunner*

From my mother's sleep I fell into the State,
And I hunched in its belly till my wet fur froze.
Six miles from earth, loosed from its dream of life,
I woke to black flak and the nightmare fighters.
When I died they washed me out of the turret with a hose.

Randall Jarrell (1914–1965)

QUESTIONS

1. Obviously, the poem is about death in war. What does it gain by the introduction of the imagery of birth?

2. Does the poem gain any positive effect through the indefiniteness of the opening line?

3. Does the metaphor add to the complexity of the thought? Does it keep the poem from being read as violence for its own sake?

Sometimes the metaphor may be extended so that more than one point of similarity becomes important. Through the *extended metaphor* the poet may explore thought by elaborating on a network of similarities existing between unlike objects. In the first eight lines of the poem given below, two kinds of activity are implicitly compared; what are they?

### *On First Looking into Chapman's Homer*

Much have I travelled in the realms of gold,
And many goodly states and kingdoms seen;
Round many western islands have I been
Which bards in fealty to Apollo hold.
Oft of one wide expanse had I been told
That deep-browed Homer ruled as his demesne;
Yet did I never breathe its pure serene
Till I heard Chapman speak out loud and bold:
Then felt I like some watcher of the skies
When a new planet swims into his ken;
Or like stout Cortez when with eagle eyes
He stared at the Pacific—and all his men
Looked at each other with a wild surmise—
Silent, upon a peak in Darien.

John Keats (1795–1821)

QUESTIONS

1. In the last six lines Keats shifts to the use of two similes. How do these contribute to the thought of the first part of the poem?
2. What effect is gained by the connotation of the images introduced through figurative language?
3. Why would a literal statement about the effects of reading Chapman's translation of Homer's works be less appealing?

The poet depends on the reader's sense of poetic logic to make the necessary connections between figures of speech. The coherence may exist as strongly between what is implied by metaphor as between what is stated. In the following sonnet the poet establishes several points of contact between himself and objects in nature that share with him the fact that they are coming to an end. Notice how each progressive set of four lines is unified by one dominant metaphor.

### *Sonnet 73*

That time of year thou mayst in me behold
When yellow leaves, or none, or few, do hang
Upon those boughs which shake against the cold,
Bare ruined choirs, where late the sweet birds sang.
In me thou see'st the twilight of such day
As after sunset fadeth in the west,
Which by and by black night doth take away,
Death's second self, that seals up all in rest.
In me thou see'st the glowing of such fire
That on the ashes of his youth doth lie,
As the death-bed whereon it must expire,
Consumed with that which it was nourished by.
　　This thou perceiv'st, which makes thy love more strong,
　　To love that well which thou must leave ere long.

William Shakespeare (1564–1616)

QUESTIONS

1. What examples of thermal imagery can you find? Are these images drawn together by means of the shifting metaphors?
2. Is anything gained by speaking of death indirectly?

## *Personification, Apostrophe, Pathetic Fallacy*

A form of metaphor which is among the most widely used and easily recognized is *personification,* a figure of speech that ascribes to inanimate objects the qualities of living things. When Denise Levertov says, ". . . white clouds loiter arm-in-arm," she speaks of the clouds as if they had personality. A thousand years before, the old English poet who wrote "The Wanderer" used the same device:

Beaten by storms are these rock hills,
Subdued by driving snow this earth,
By winter's horror, smothering warmth
In the night's shadow.

The commonest use of personification involves *apostrophe,* in which the poet speaks directly to some abstract idea or nonhuman object as if it were a person. John Donne uses this device in his sonnet 10 of *The Holy Sonnets,* saying:

> Death, be not proud, though some have called thee
> Mighty and Dreadful, for thou art not so;

Walt Whitman's use of personification and apostrophe may also exemplify the *pathetic fallacy,* which implies an unconvincing use of personification. Addressing the thrush in "When Lilacs Last in the Dooryard Bloom'd," he says:

> Sing on dearest brother, warble your reedy song,
> Loud human song, with voice of uttermost woe.

If you do not find yourself able to accept the idea that the thrush's song expresses uttermost woe, you might call these lines an example of the pathetic fallacy. But, convincing or otherwise, personification and apostrophe have been widely used in every poetic era.

In its least exclusive sense, personification often is understood as a means of attributing to a subject, animate or not, the qualities of creatures of a higher order. Thus expressions such as "the howling wind," "the weeping clouds," "smiling flowers," and "mournful bird" are all in some sense personification. A common kind of comparison by which animate objects, particularly human beings, are given the qualities of the lower orders of creation does not have a commonly known name. To say "the cackling wife," then, though it implies a comparison between a hen and a woman, is not, properly speaking, personification.

Many poems rely on personification and apostrophe as their organizing principle. In these, with such familiar titles as "To A Mouse," "To a Skylark," and "To Autumn," the poet strikes a pose and uses the address to some nonhuman being as a means of delving into the mind. The object addressed acts as a crutch to help the speaker reflect on his thoughts. The personified object assumes a symbolic role the moment it begins to signify complex ideas in the speaker's mind. Edmund Waller's "Song" illustrates this use of personification and apostrophe.

### *Song*

Go, lovely rose!
Tell her that wastes her time and me
That now she knows,
When I resemble her to thee,
How sweet and fair she seems to be.

Tell her that's young,
And shuns to have her graces spied,
That hadst thou sprung
In deserts, where no men abide,
Thou must have uncommended died.

Small is the worth
Of beauty from the light retired;
Bid her come forth,
Suffer herself to be desired,
And not blush so to be admired.

Then die, that she
The common fate of all things rare
May read in thee;
How small a part of time they share,
That are so wondrous sweet and fair.

Edmund Waller (1606–1687)

QUESTIONS

1. Why is/is not the personification in this poem convincing?

2. How does the speaker's attitude differ from the conventional attitude of a lover who sends roses?

3. The poet never says outright what the attitude of the speaker is, yet he manages to suggest a complex state of mind and a complex relationship. Is the speaker a naïve admirer? Is he embittered? Sarcastic?

4. Why is/is not this poem remarkable for its striking imagery, its surprising metaphor?

5. Why does Waller make the poem move so slowly and deliberately, though the speaker is apparently eager to have the woman's love?

## *Metonymy and Synecdoche*

No less important, but much less readily recognizable than personification, are two closely related sub-types of metaphor

—*metonymy* and *synecdoche*. Comparisons of unlike objects implicit in these devices often pass without notice because one part of the comparison remains unspoken. Metonymy demands an understanding on the part of the reader of ideas and objects that are closely and commonly related. Here are a few such related pairs:

| | |
|---|---|
| spinning and weaving | storytelling |
| eye | sight-light |
| sweat | work |
| red coats | British soldiers |
| White House | presidency |
| heart | love-emotion |
| salt | sailors-tears |
| dice, cards | chance |

In *metonymy* a speaker uses the name of one thing (e.g., sweat) in the place of the name of some closely related idea or thing (e.g., work). *Synecdoche* most often involves the use of the part for the whole (e.g., wheels for cars), or the whole for the part (e.g., the law for the policeman). But other kinds of quantitative relationships may be the basis for synecdoche, too. The genus may be used for the species (e.g., creature for man), or the species for the genus (e.g., bread for food), the container for the thing contained (e.g., purse for money), or the material for the product (e.g., hardwood for basketball court).

One advantage of metonymy and synecdoche is that they may substitute an image-making word in place of a less vivid word. Also, they often add an element of surprise to speech. This manner of speaking is not merely indirect for the sake of evasiveness; it creates greater condensation and sharper imagery. To say "stay away from cards," even in everyday speech is more forceful than "do not gamble." Much of the inventiveness in slang comes from metonymy, as in "shrink" for psychiatrist.

Determining whether metonymy or synecdoche is present in a poem matters less than recognizing that a poet is using words inventively. Read the following poem and try to notice how Shelley has compressed his meaning through the use of these figures of speech.

### *Ozymandias*°

*Ramses II, 1300 BC*

I met a traveller from an antique land
Who said: Two vast and trunkless legs of stone
Stand in the desert . . . Near them, on the sand,
Half sunk, a shattered visage lies, whose frown,
And wrinkled lip, and sneer of cold command,
Tell that its sculptor well those passions read
Which yet survive, stamped on these lifeless things,
The hand that mocked them, and the heart that fed:
And on the pedestal these words appear:
"My name is Ozymandias, king of kings:
Look on my works, ye Mighty, and despair!"
Nothing beside remains. Round the decay
Of that colossal wreck, boundless and bare
The lone and level sands stretch far away.

Percy Bysshe Shelley (1792–1822)

Our useful vocabulary for speaking of figurative language is too limited to be of much help in showing how a poet's language really works. Some of the words we have, "metonymy" and "synecdoche," for example, to distinguish between types of figurative expression are of doubtful use. Yet being able to specify the distinctions may afford a certain intellectual pleasure, like distinguishing between sub-types of roses. The total appreciation of a poet's work may even be enriched by analyzing an occasional passage for its density of figurative devices, some of which may be difficult to label, but which are nonetheless not literal.

In the broadest sense, any comparison which is not explicit and which associates objects of different classes is metaphorical. Of the three statements below, one uses simile, one metaphor, and another the metaphorical use of an adjective.

1. The lids of her eyes were as soft and blue as the sky.
2. Her closed eyelids were a soft, blue sky as she slept.
3. And still she slept an azure-lidded sleep.

The third statement, from Keats's "The Eve of St. Agnes," surprises the reader with the manner of speech and suggests more than the two preceding statements. No doubt the sound effects account for some of this impression, but the surprise and compression of Keats's line shows that a comparison need not be drawn out—"azure-lidded sleep" not only says what the eyes were like, but what the sleep was like as well.

The process involved here is often used but little noticed perhaps because it does not call attention to itself as a simile or metaphor does. It is called the *transferred epithet,* in which an adjective modifies a noun which it might not literally be associated with. "Smiling" might literally describe only a person. Yet, a wide variety of effects may be gained by placing the word beside other nouns:

smiling eyes
smiling blue
smiling forest
smiling day
smiling flowers

You can test the adaptability of this device by substituting nouns and modifiers. Try "smirking," "laughing," "grinning," "chilling," "chiding," "hospitable," "tangled," "raven," "dewy."

The point is that poets consciously use figurative language as the most efficient way to create a definite impression. The fullest appreciation of their art demands an understanding of how they make figurative language both concise and effective.

### *Some Functions of Figurative Language*

Since poets constantly surprise us with the uses they find for figures of speech, any attempt to define their functions would be futile. In order to begin analyzing poetry with some basic theories on what metaphorical speech can do, however, it might be well to review some of its more obvious possibilities.

1. It provides shortcuts in speech and writing, often aiding in communication of ideas when literal vocabulary is inadequate.
2. It provides a way of introducing imagery into writing and speech.

3. It supplies a means by which connotative and symbolic language may be introduced and controlled.
4. It helps clarify and intensify thought through analogy, and thus becomes a rhetorical tool.
5. It becomes a means of *exploring* thought, especially those indefinite regions of thought-emotion which do not readily submit to explanation.

## *Poems for Study*

Analyze the following poems, trying to ascertain what the poet tried to accomplish through figurative devices. When you feel reasonably certain that you understand what is being undertaken in each poem, make some estimate of the effectiveness of the work.

The first two poems express strong reactions to the sense of awe and power in nature. Both use figurative devices to heighten the effect, but one does so very clearly, while the other offers some resistance. Try not to make any hasty value judgments about either until you have a good idea what the poets are trying to accomplish.

### *God's Grandeur*

The world is charged with the grandeur of God.
    It will flame out, like shining from shook foil;
    It gathers to a greatness, like the ooze of oil
Crushed. Why do men then now not reck his rod?
Generations have trod, have trod, have trod;
    And all is seared with trade; bleared, smeared with toil;
    And wears man's smudge and shares man's smell: the soil
Is bare now, nor can foot feel, being shod.

And for all this, nature is never spent;
    There lives the dearest freshness deep down things;
And though the last lights off the black West went
    Oh, morning, at the brown brink eastward, springs—
Because the Holy Ghost over the bent
    World broods with warm breast and with ah! bright wings.

Gerard Manley Hopkins (1844–1889)

QUESTIONS

1. What figurative devices does the poet use in the first four lines? How do the two similes in lines 2 and 3 serve to contrast the ways in which the grandeur of God manifests itself in nature?

2. How does Hopkins build an unfavorable connotation about man's effect on nature? Are figurative devices involved here?

3. What aim is served by the use of synecdoche in line 8? Judging from this, is the speaker concerned about man and his predicament?

4. The Holy Ghost is usually portrayed in the form of a dove. In what ways does the Holy Ghost "brood" over the world?

5. Does the poet convey a clear impression about the religious experience? Is it necessary to share his faith in order to share in his experience?

## *God's World*

O world, I cannot hold thee close enough!
　　Thy winds, thy wide grey skies!
　　Thy mists, that roll and rise!
Thy woods, this autumn day, that ache and sag
And all but cry with colour! That gaunt crag
To crush! To lift the lean of that black bluff!
World, World, I cannot get thee close enough!

Long have I known a glory in it all,
　　But never knew I this:
　　Here such a passion is
As stretcheth me apart, —Lord, I do fear
Thou'st made the world too beautiful this year;
My soul is all but out of me, —let fall
No burning leaf; prithee, let no bird call.

Edna St. Vincent Millay (1892–1950)

QUESTIONS

1. The speaker in this poem addresses the world as if it were a person. What is it about the personified world that is lovable?

2. Would you call the personification in lines 4 and 5 an example of the pathetic fallacy?

3. When a poet uses the idiom of religious worship to write a love poem he may gain the effect of elevating the human situation to spiritual heights. Do you think this idiom achieves its intended purpose here? Consider such

expressions as, "Thy winds, thy wide grey skies!"; "Here such a passion is/ As stretcheth me apart, —Lord, I do fear/Thou'st made the world too beautiful this year. . . ."

4. Does the poet convince you that the response to nature is a religious experience? If so, does the experience have any significance beyond itself, that is, does it seem to be a part of a coherent view of life?

5. What figure of speech do you see in, "To lift the lean of that black bluff!" Does this help you to get a vivid conception of the poet's emotion?

## *Years-End*

Now winter downs the dying of the year,
And night is all a settlement of snow;
From the soft street the rooms of houses show
A gathered light, a shapen atmosphere,
Like frozen-over lakes whose ice is thin
And still allows some stirring down within.

I've known the wind by water banks to shake
The late leaves down, which frozen where they fell
And held in ice as dancers in a spell
Fluttered all winter long into a lake;
Graved on the dark in gestures of descent,
They seemed their own most perfect monument.

There was perfection in the death of ferns
Which laid their fragile cheeks against the stone
A million years. Great mammoths overthrown
Composedly have made their long sojourns,
Like palaces of patience, in the gray
And changeless lands of ice. And at Pompeii

The little dog lay curled and did not rise
But slept the deeper as the ashes rose
And found the people incomplete, and froze
The random hands, the loose unready eyes
Of men expecting yet another sun
To do the shapely thing they had not done.

These sudden ends of time must give us pause.
We fray into the future, rarely wrought
Save in the tapestries of afterthought.

More time, more time. Barrages of applause
Come muffled from a buried radio.
The New-year bells are wrangling with the snow.

Richard Wilbur (1921– )

QUESTIONS

1. Find examples of personification, metaphor, and simile in the first stanza.

2. How does Wilbur use images of suspended animation to tie the first four stanzas together?

3. The poet repeatedly mentions the shapeliness of artistic creations, things that are "composed." Is the poet using metaphorical language to make a statement about art?

4. How does the poet use figurative devices to introduce imagery of hardness and softness, heat and cold, stillness and motion? What is the effect of this on the emotion of the reader?

5. The conflict mentioned in the last line uses auditory imagery. Do you think the contrast of this with the relative silence of the poem makes an effectively emphatic closing?

## *The Heavy Bear Who Goes with Me*

*the withness of the body*—Whitehead

The heavy bear who goes with me,
A manifold honey to smear his face,
Clumsy and lumbering here and there,
The central ton of every place,
The hungry beating brutish one
In love with candy, anger, and sleep,
Crazy factotum, dishevelling all,
Climbs the building, kicks the football,
Boxes his brother in the hate-ridden city.

Breathing at my side, that heavy animal,
That heavy bear who sleeps with me,
Howls in his sleep for a world of sugar,
A sweetness intimate as the water's clasp,
Howls in his sleep because the tight-rope
Trembles and shows the darkness beneath.
—The strutting show-off is terrified,
Dressed in his dress-suit, bulging his pants,

Trembles to think that his quivering meat
Must finally wince to nothing at all.

That inescapable animal walks with me,
Has followed me since the black womb held,
Moves where I move, distorting my gesture,
A caricature, a swollen shadow,
A stupid clown of the spirit's motive,
Perplexes and affronts with his own darkness,
The secret life of belly and bone,
Opaque, too near, my private, yet unknown,
Stretches to embrace the very dear
With whom I would walk without him near,
Touches her grossly, although a word
Would bare my heart and make me clear,
Stumbles, flounders, and strives to be fed
Dragging me with him in his mouthing care,
Amid the hundred million of his kind,
The scrimmage of appetite everywhere.

Delmore Schwartz (1913–1966)

## QUESTIONS

1. Why did the poet choose to use a bear to personify the physical side of his being? Why not an ape?

2. What variety of imagery has the poet been able to introduce by selecting the bear? How does imagery of motion figure in his plan?

3. Is the poet saying that the body is an absurd thing for the human spirit to dwell in? Is the tone of the poem pessimistic?

4. Classify the figurative device in line 26. How many words do you need to explain the meaning of this line?

5. By its nature personification tends to simplify, at times to oversimplify. In lines 28–30, the poet ignores the fact that "his dear" has a physical nature, too. Is this naïve or not?

*Chapter 8*

# Symbols

SINCE, loosely speaking, a symbol is something that stands for something else, all words, spoken or written, are symbols; they are auditory and graphic signals of meaning. Communication and order itself depends on a regular way of saying what we mean. Where safety on the highways is concerned, every driver must realize that a round sign indicates an approaching railroad crossing and that a green light indicates "go." In musical compositions, the time signature 3/4, for example, tells the musician how to read and play the notes. In short, some signs give directions or point out facts. But the poetic artist finds his task in expanding and deepening meaning; for him words are more than signs.

A rose is more than a type of flower; red is more than a color; and a worm is more than a soft-bodied animal. Consider this poem by William Blake:

*The Sick Rose*

O Rose, thou art sick!
The invisible worm
That flies in the night,
In the howling storm,

Has found out thy bed
Of crimson joy,
And his dark secret love
Does thy life destroy.

William Blake (1757–1827)

Virtually every important word in this poem is symbolic, for no single interpretation of the words exhausts the possibilities of meaning. Is the poem about beauty, virtue, or sexual love? Clearly, whatever the meaning, it is not a literal statement about a rose. Analyze the poem to discover if it makes an intelligible statement about virtue and evil—about beauty and death—about innocence and sexual experience. What emotional effect does the poet gain by leaving the possibilities of interpretation open?

### *Symbols*

The *symbol* itself, then, is any object that bears some significance beyond itself. Symbolic words most often name some object, action, or quality which has taken on dimensions of meaning not simply literal. Some objects often mentioned to suggest meaning not explicitly stated might include chains, butterflies, pistols, waterfowl, bridges, stars. The list could, of course, be so endless as to include the names of all things. But the word is not symbolic unless it is intended to be more than literal. For example, in telling the story of a factory worker who is ambitious to advance himself in the world, the storyteller might include the details that the man wore filter goggles to protect his eyes as he helped in the process of making chains. The goggles and the chains have a literal meaning beyond which many readers may never need to see in order to enjoy the story. But if the writer intends that the tinted goggles should suggest that the man's work keeps him from seeing life fully and clearly, and if he intends the chains to emphasize the idea of bondage for the worker, he is using the terms symbolically. In modern poetry the use of symbols tends to be less transparent and more freely suggestive than the simplified example given above. One of the marks of modern art is, in fact, its willingness to depart from the literal through the less restrained use of symbolism.

### *Symbolism*

One of the most haunting aspects of poetry is the element of symbolism. It is haunting because it often refuses to come clear, and because, as in life's experience, significance is never static.

The meaning of things constantly grows, changes, and drifts, while the mind, reflecting, may rarely be able to say, "this is it!" Yet the problem of meaning keeps coming back. In poetic symbolism, a writer may create for us the satisfying experience of aspiring to a clear understanding that may never be final. The poem below may be read as both an explanation and illustration of the tantalizing obscurity in clarity which so often characterizes poetic symbolism.

### *Man Carrying Thing*

The poem must resist the intelligence
Almost successfully. Illustration:

A brune° figure in winter evening resists — *shadowy*
Identity. The thing he carries resists

The most necessitous sense. Accept them, then,
As secondary (parts not quite perceived

Of the obvious whole, uncertain particles
Of the certain solid, the primary free from doubt,

Things floating like the first hundred flakes of snow
Out of a storm we must endure all night,

Out of a storm of secondary things),
A horror of thoughts that suddenly are real.

We must endure our thoughts all night, until
The bright obvious stands motionless in cold.

Wallace Stevens (1879–1955)

This poem begins much like a piece of expository prose, clearly stating a generalization about poetry that is to be illustrated. If the illustration were in prose, we might easily judge it a failure, for it does not make a clear and coherent explanation. Stevens wishes his example to resist intelligence, but to give in to it, at last, as a poem must. Let us consider some questions which may help, realizing as we proceed that absolute certainties are unlikely to be the answers.

### QUESTIONS

1. Notice the title. It is ambiguous, possibly meaning a man carrying a thing, but possibly also, a thing that carries a man. Why does the poet not make the title more definite?
2. What might the man and the thing suggest or represent?
3. Other images in the poem are as important for what they suggest as for what they mean. For example, the poet speaks of a storm (line 10), yet the poem is about poetry. How does the storm figure into the thought being illustrated?
4. What does the night (lines 10, 13) mean? Suggest? What connection do you make between the "floating . . . snow" (line 9) and the last line?
5. What abstract words in this poem contribute to the sense of indefiniteness? Do these abstract words affect the image-making words? How?
6. Do you think this poem successfully illustrates the theory stated in the first two lines?

The foregoing poem may be called symbolic because its images carry more than one meaning. We have already seen how the image may be literal or part of a figurative comparison; now it is time to consider the image in another of its roles. A writer might build a mood or mental picture through the image in its denotative and connotative meanings as follows: "The storm dashed the droplets of rain against the window pane. They clung to the smooth surface of the glass for a moment, then slipped, joined together, and ran off." Figuratively, he might say, "Our lives, like drops upon the pane, slip, and join, and go." Symbolically, he could use the image of the drops of water without limiting the meaning to any single idea; the image might suggest time, life, glory, work, or any other notion consistent with the context in which the image appeared.

The object in studying symbolism as an element of poetry is to direct attention to the poet's use of one of his resources. The experienced reader of poetry is not only affected by the symbolism, but he notices how the writer causes the effect. At the outset, it should be clear that symbolism is not an element apart from imagery, connotation, and figurative language, but one which merges with these and other elements to make the total impression.

*Symbolism and Connotation*

Because connotative language and symbols both suggest more than what is explicitly stated, the two terms should be treated together. Through connotation, a writer chooses words that create the associated impressions he wishes to make on the reader's mind. By means of his word choice, the writer may create a vivid mental picture or evoke a dominant mood without attempting to suggest an underlying meaning. Connotation may be used to induce a sense of pleasure or discomfort—advertisements that encourage people to buy one product in preference to others of equal quality, for example, depend almost entirely on their ability to build an appealing connotation. But the worker in symbols, always aware of connotation, must make the detail do more than call forth selected responses in the reader's attitudes and emotions. In general, connotations are instantaneous and, given an understanding of the audience, predictable. The symbol may cause a similarly instantaneous response, but it may very well demand some analytical thought. Many stories by Kafka or Chekhov, for example, leave a definite mood created through the connotation of the diction, yet keep the reader, however clear or dim his understanding of meaning may be, troubled by symbolic undercurrents of meaning which persist in remaining obscure. At the risk of oversimplifying, let us say that connotation suggests emotional responses while symbols go on to suggest thought or conceptual responses. Most symbols are connotative, but connotative words need not be symbols.

The following poem makes vivid use of connotation to portray a farmer's sensation of the weariness that comes after the hard work of a harvest. Since all the details are so accurately observed, some readers may feel no need to go beyond the literal level to have pleasure in the poem. The experience builds a mood, makes plain sense, and seems complete in itself. Yet, other readers will find the poet's questioning of his sleep in the last six lines an irresistible invitation to view the poem as a network of symbols.

*After Apple-Picking*

My long two-pointed ladder's sticking through a tree
Toward heaven still,
And there's a barrel that I didn't fill
Beside it, and there may be two or three
Apples I didn't pick upon some bough.
But I am done with apple-picking now.
Essence of winter sleep is on the night,
The scent of apples: I am drowsing off.
I cannot rub the strangeness from my sight
I got from looking through a pane of glass
I skimmed this morning from the drinking trough
And held against the world of hoary grass.
It melted, and I let it fall and break.
But I was well
Upon my way to sleep before it fell,
And I could tell
What form my dreaming was about to take.
Magnified apples appear and disappear,
Stem end and blossom end,
And every fleck of russet showing clear.
My instep arch not only keeps the ache,
It keeps the pressure of a ladder-round.
I feel the ladder sway as the boughs bend.
And I keep hearing from the cellar bin
The rumbling sound
Of load on load of apples coming in.
For I have had too much
Of apple-picking: I am overtired
Of the great harvest I myself desired.
There were ten thousand thousand fruit to touch,
Cherish in hand, lift down, and not let fall.
For all
That struck the earth,
No matter if not bruised or spiked with stubble,
Went surely to the cider-apple heap
As of no worth.
One can see what will trouble
This sleep of mine, whatever sleep it is.
Were he not gone,

The woodchuck could say whether it's like his
Long sleep, as I describe its coming on,
Or just some human sleep.

Robert Frost (1874–1963)

QUESTIONS

1. What mythological or biblical associations do "apples" bring to mind? Does Frost mean "heaven" as a literal word for sky? Could the ladder's pointing towards heaven be reminiscent of the biblical story of Jacob's ladder, and could the parable of the Lord's harvest be hinted at by the poem as a whole? Does the judgment of good and worthless fruit suggest some other kind of judgment?

2. Why does the poet make no mention of death? Does the woodchuck's long sleep mean more than literal hibernation? If you read the poem symbolically, must you conclude that Frost means to say that death is temporary, like sleep?

## *Symbolism and Imagery*

What has been said of connotation and symbolism holds true largely with respect to imagery. Since literary symbols are usually names of things, actions, and qualities, they are images, and hence create sense impressions which contribute to the impression of life. Incense, bread and wine, green and purple, burning and flying, blood and salt are all image-making words which not only create sense impressions and evoke connotative associations, but are used symbolically as well. The winding river or twisting flame may be literally representative in a descriptive passage, but they may mean more and thus become literary symbols. Obviously, some images lend themselves to symbolic undertones more readily than others. The image tries to impart a feeling of sensual life, the symbol adds concept, and the two contribute to the completeness of poetry as a repository of experience.

In this piece by William Carlos Williams, the images may be quite enough to make a poem. Still the subject of forbidden fruit can hardly be mentioned without sounding some undertones of symbolic meaning. How should this poem be read? The answer must be left to the individual reader to decide.

*This Is Just to Say*

I have eaten
the plums
that were in
the icebox

and which
you were probably
saving
for breakfast

Forgive me
they were delicious
so sweet
and so cold

William Carlos Williams (1883–1963)

### *Symbolism and Figurative Language*

Figurative language uses the image to say what may be too difficult or too dull to express literally. Symbolism, it would seem, does the same, but with this difference: the symbol has a literal meaning *plus* the unexpressed meaning. The figure of speech, though founded on something literal, uses that literal thing, usually an image, to comment on a related but different thought. The image in a figure of speech is a tool for vivifying or exploring an idea. To say that one eats like a bird is to use "bird" as illustration. But the bird in Hardy's "The Darkling Thrush" is not only an image, but a symbol of hope.

The two examples above do not suggest that symbols and figures of speech are somehow mutually exclusive; they indicate that the image may appear in the figure of speech without necessarily standing for more than an illustrative object. Shelley's comparison of life to a dome of many-colored glass would easily illustrate how the image in a figure of speech may carry a multitude of underlying meanings.

In the stanza from Shelley's "Adonais," quoted below, the dome may be considered not only as the image in the metaphor, but as a symbol that also lures the reader's mind into exploratory thought.

*52*

The One remains, the many change and pass;
Heaven's light forever shines, Earth's shadows fly;
Life, like a dome of many-colored glass,
Stains the white radiance of Eternity,
Until Death tramples it to fragments. —Die,
If thou wouldst be with that which thou dost seek!
Follow where all are fled! —Rome's azure sky,
Flowers, ruins, statues, music, words, are weak
The glory they transfuse with fitting truth to speak.

Percy Bysshe Shelley (1792–1822)

QUESTIONS

1. An idea implied here is the Platonic view of reality. It says that the finite universe and our perceptions of it conceal from human beings higher perceptions of the infinite. If you know the story of Plato's cave, do you think the dome in this passage might act as a symbolic reminder of the cave? Why?
2. Does the azure sky (dome-shaped) have any symbolic meaning?
3. Does the "dome of many-colored glass" suggest anything about art?

The two poems that follow use trees as central images which are both figurative and symbolic. Consider how figure and symbol overlap here:

*Tree at My Window*

Tree at my window, window tree,
My sash is lowered when night comes on;
But let there never be curtain drawn
Between you and me.

Vague dream-head lifted out of the ground,
And thing next most diffuse to cloud,
Not all your light tongues talking aloud
Could be profound.

But, tree, I have seen you taken and tossed,
And if you have seen me when I slept,
You have seen me when I was taken and swept
And all but lost.

That day she put our heads together,
Fate had her imagination about her,
Your head so much concerned with outer,
Mine with inner, weather.

Robert Frost (1874–1963)

## QUESTIONS

1. "Tree" is more than the thing that grows. What qualities of the tree does the poet single out for elaboration?

2. What does "tree" mean literally? How many ideas can you think of which have become associated with the tree?

3. In this poem the tree comes to be compared metaphorically with someing abstract. What is that something and what are the points of comparison?

4. Objects come to symbolize those qualities which they most vividly call to mind. In this way, the name of the thing comes to remind us of a set of qualities. Is Frost content here to let "tree" be symbolic in the ordinary way?

5. What other details of this poem may be potential symbols?

Read Joyce Kilmer's poem "Trees" and compare the poet's use of trees as symbols with Frost's.

### *Trees*

I think that I shall never see
A poem lovely as a tree.

A tree whose hungry mouth is pressed
Against the earth's sweet flowing breast;

A tree that looks to God all day,
And lifts her leafy arms to pray;

A tree that may in Summer wear
A nest of robins in her hair;

Upon whose bosom snow has lain;
Who intimately lives with rain.

Poems are made by fools like me,
But only God can make a tree.

Joyce Kilmer (1886–1918)

QUESTIONS

1. In analyzing the two foregoing poems, consider which of the poems makes the more clear statement. What does the tree symbolize to Frost? To Kilmer?

2. Both poems invite the reader to make certain comparisons between human beings and trees. Which poem makes the more satisfying use of these comparisons?

3. Those who admire Kilmer's poem are not troubled by the fact that "Trees" advances from one comparison in which the tree is regarded as a sucking babe to one in which it is compared to a young woman. Does this keep the poem from being an integrated whole?

4. Do you think it a valid criticism to say that Kilmer's "Trees" is weak because it is illogical? Do you think that poems which set out to make plain sense should be judged by different standards than those which do not?

## *Symbols: Central and Incidental*

Symbols may be central or incidental. Poems addressed to an inanimate object or to some object in nature make us think about that object as the concrete representative of the abstract qualities it possesses. Flowers come to stand for beauty that must die; tigers for strength, violence, and terrible beauty; clay for the still, lifeless stuff to which all living things turn, and so forth. The poet, if his attention is focused on the object, most often tries to see the symbol with greater complexity than a passing glance will reveal. Once a central symbol is placed in the context of a poem, any of the details surrounding it may become subsidiary symbols or may elaborate on the central symbol. The poems that follow illustrate this.

## *The Tiger*

Tiger! Tiger! burning bright
In the forests of the night,
What immortal hand or eye
Could frame thy fearful symmetry?

In what distant deeps or skies
Burnt the fire of thine eyes?
On what wings dare he aspire?
What the hand dare seize the fire?

And what shoulder, and what art,
Could twist the sinews of thy heart?
And when thy heart began to beat,
What dread hand forged thy dread feet?

What the hammer? what the chain?
In what furnace was thy brain?
What the anvil? what dread grasp
Dare its deadly terrors clasp?

When the stars threw down their spears,
And watered heaven with their tears,
Did he smile his work to see?
Did he who made the Lamb make thee?

Tiger! Tiger! burning bright
In the forests of the night,
What immortal hand or eye
Dare frame thy fearful symmetry?

William Blake (1757–1827)

### QUESTIONS

1. Does Blake intend the tiger to stand for more than the savagery of animal life? Since it is the nature of tigers to be killers, by what logic might the tiger symbolize evil?

2. Once you treat the tiger more than literally, other details in the poem assume symbolic meanings. Consider "forests," "night," "stars," and "spears."

3. If the tiger symbolizes the mystery of evil in a world made by a creator, is it inconsistent of the poet to call attention to the beauty of the thing—its symmetry?

## *In Waste Places*

As a naked man I go
Through the desert, sore afraid;
Holding high my head, although
I'm as frightened as a maid.

The lion crouches there! I saw
In barren rocks his amber eye!
He parts the cactus with his paw!
He stares at me, as I go by!

He would pad upon my trace
If he thought I was afraid!
If he knew my hardy face
Veils the terrors of a maid.

He rises in the night-time, and
He stretches forth! He snuffs the air!
He roars! He leaps along the sand!
He creeps! He watches everywhere!

His burning eyes, his eyes of bale
Through the darkness I can see!
He lashes fiercely with his tail!
He makes again to spring at me!

I am the lion, and his lair!
I am the fear that frightens me!
I am the desert of despair!
And the night of agony!

Night or day, whate'er befall,
I must walk that desert land,
Until I dare my fear, and call
The lion out to lick my hand!

James Stephens (1882–1950)

### QUESTIONS

1. To some extent James Stephens uses the lion as Blake does the tiger. What are the similarities?

2. If the sixth stanza were deleted, could you interpret the poem? Why does Stephens deliberately remind us of Blake's poem, then steer us away from reading supernatural symbolism into his poem?

3. Do the subsidiary details, for example, the desert, the rock, and the cactus, have any symbolic meaning, or do they merely make the image of the lion more vivid?

## *Symbols: Natural and Contrived*

Certain objects and the names for them carry special and even identical meanings with them beyond the usual cultural boundaries. A skull means "death" to any cultural group. Much the same might be said of fire, water, lambs, fish, and other items in a lengthy list. Notice how the poet identifies the meaning of the two main symbols in this poem; these might be called "natural" symbols.

### *Fire and Ice*

Some say the world will end in fire,
Some say in ice.
From what I've tasted of desire
I hold with those who favor fire.
But if it had to perish twice,
I think I know enough of hate
To say that for destruction ice
Is also great
And would suffice.

Robert Frost (1874–1963)

But certain symbols grow out of cultural circumstances. Religion and politics supply some of the symbols, and occult societies, social classes and heraldry have given others. Though the cultural symbols may borrow from the natural, there is an essential difference. For the cultural symbol, some group must come together to agree that the *fleur de lis* or star of David, for example, stand for France or Judaism, yet no one needs to explain that skulls stand for death.

In studying poetry, there is no special advantage in making the distinction between natural and cultural symbols. Yet certain culture-linked symbols, such as the deities of ancient Greece, Rome, Egypt, and Scandinavia may have lost any ability they once had to stir emotion. Therefore the student must inform himself about some dated symbols to read certain older poems. Experience with reading poetry and good editorial notes help most students over this obstacle.

Here is a poem with symbolism drawn from Christian writings and tradition. The poet allows his reader the pleasure of recognizing and interpreting the symbols which the speaker in the poem, one of the wise men from the Christmas story, might be unaware of.

*Journey of the Magi*

'A cold coming we had of it,
Just the worst time of the year
For a journey, and such a long journey:
The ways deep and the weather sharp,
The very dead of winter.'
And the camels galled, sore-footed, refractory,
Lying down in the melting snow.
There were times we regretted
The summer palaces on slopes, the terraces,
And the silken girls bringing sherbet.
Then the camel men cursing and grumbling
And running away, and wanting their liquor and women,
And the night-fires going out, and the lack of shelters,
And the cities hostile and the towns unfriendly
And the villages dirty and charging high prices:
A hard time we had of it.
At the end we preferred to travel all night,
Sleeping in snatches,
With the voices singing in our ears, saying
That this was all folly.

Then at dawn we came down to a temperate valley,
Wet, below the snow line, smelling of vegetation,
With a running stream and a water-mill beating the darkness,
And three trees on the low sky.

And an old white horse galloped away in the meadow.
Then we came to a tavern with vine-leaves over the lintel,
Six hands at an open door dicing for pieces of silver,
And feet kicking the empty wine-skins.
But there was no information, and so we continued
And arrived at evening, not a moment too soon
Finding the place; it was (you may say) satisfactory.

All this was a long time ago, I remember,
And I would do it again, but set down
This set down
This: were we led all that way for
Birth or Death? There was a Birth, certainly,
We had evidence and no doubt. I had seen birth and death,
But had thought they were different; this Birth was
Hard and bitter agony for us, like Death, our death.
We returned to our places, these Kingdoms,
But no longer at ease here, in the old dispensation,
With an alien people clutching their gods.
I should be glad of another death.

T. S. Eliot (1888–1965)

QUESTIONS

1. What details in the poem are directly or indirectly associated with the life and death of Jesus? Would direct reference to the last supper and the cross be more or less convincing as symbols than indirect references?

2. Remembering that the Magi knew about the birth of Christ from the reading of heavenly signs, explain how some detail associated with the death of Christ could be included in a statement made before the crucifixion.

3. The attitude of the speaker in this poem is less than joyous. What is it in the experience he has been through that accounts for his mood?

4. Are there any details in the poem which seem significant but which do not quite come clear? Consider, for example, the white horse (line 25). What might this symbolize? What purpose might the poet have in leaving the reader with a feeling of indefiniteness?

Some of the greatest poets have found that the symbols of already existing mythologies are inadequate and therefore go on to construct their own view of the universe with symbols of their own invention. These poets, Blake and Yeats, to name the two most important, put an extra burden on the reader because understanding of certain of their meanings is not likely without some specialized knowledge of their symbols. When these writers are unconventional or obscure, they are not trying to confuse us; they are trying to use symbols that are broadly suggestive.

The information given below, for example, summarizes a few of Yeats's ideas which may aid in the reading of the following poem. Try to estimate how your reaction to the poem is formed by any background information you may happen to have about Yeats's ideas.

1. Historical eras move in cycles of about 2,000 years, the last having begun at about the time of the birth of Christ.
2. Spiral or circular motion is symbolic of the cycles of change in nature, history, and personality development.
3. Humanity is bound together in part by a great repository of symbols drawn from a common past and stored in the collective but subconscious memory of the human race. The archetypal symbols of dreams and poetry are means by which the living maintain contact with the memory of the entire human race.
4. Two interpenetrating cones make a good geometrical symbol for all human interaction, be it sexual or historical.
5. The mythology of one era may be echoed and varied in the mythology of some other era.

### *The Second Coming*

Turning and turning in the widening gyre
The falcon cannot hear the falconer;
Things fall apart; the centre cannot hold;
Mere anarchy is loosed upon the world,
The blood-dimmed tide is loosed, and everywhere
The ceremony of innocence is drowned;
The best lack all conviction, while the worst
Are full of passionate intensity.

Surely some revelation is at hand;
Surely the Second Coming is at hand.

The Second Coming! Hardly are those words out
When a vast image out of *Spiritus Mundi*
Troubles my sight: somewhere in sands of the desert
A shape with lion body and the head of a man,
A gaze blank and pitiless as the sun,
Is moving its slow thighs, while all about it
Reel shadows of the indignant desert birds.
The darkness drops again; but now I know
That twenty centuries of stony sleep
Were vexed to nightmare by a rocking cradle,
And what rough beast, its hour come round at last,
Slouches towards Bethlehem to be born?

William Butler Yeats (1865–1939)

### *Symbols: Free and Assigned (Allegory)*

An *allegory* is any extended symbolic composition. It is often a narrative in which the scenes, characters, and actions make sense literally, but are open to interpretation for meanings below the surface. Once the reader begins to understand the underlying meaning, he can say with some confidence what the symbolic details represent. Since the context tells us how to interpret these symbols, we call them assigned. Though the allegorical work may have multiple layers of meaning, as in Spenser's *The Faerie Queene,* it may be so simple in its intention as "The Three Little Pigs," or so tantalizing as Swift's *Gulliver's Travels* or Golding's *The Lord of the Flies.* Such works provide the reader with the pleasure of contemplating important aspects of human relationships and institutions. It would be absurd to say that works of allegory do not stir the reader's emotional responses, but such uses of symbolism make a dominantly intellectual, problem-solving appeal. The folklore of good advice overflows with examples of assigned or allegorical symbols. We hear such expressions as: "You can lead a horse to water, but you can't make him drink," or "The grass is always greener on the other side of the fence," or "Never leave a goat in charge of a cabbage patch." These statements are not simply figures of speech, because they mean something literally as well as something unexpressed.

The free symbol, sometimes called the *romantic symbol,* seeks to imply added levels of meaning without limiting the ability of the symbol to suggest. The free symbol may deliberately leave the reader in doubt about intended meaning, while the assigned symbol probably should not. This is not to say that one type of use of symbol is preferable to another; they are simply different, and what is to be preferred in one instance may be inappropriate in another.

The poem by Emily Dickinson given below is an allegory in the sense that it uses a narrative structure to relate a sequence of symbolic details. Study the poem to determine if all the details in the story of the carriage ride are a coherently related set of details about the journey from time to eternity.

### *Because I could not stop for Death*

Because I could not stop for Death—
He kindly stopped for me—
The Carriage held but just Ourselves—
And Immortality.

We slowly drove—He knew no haste
And I had put away
My labor and my leisure too,
For His Civility—

We passed the School, where Children strove
At Recess—in the Ring—
We passed the Fields of Gazing Grain—
We passed the Setting Sun—

Or rather—He passed Us—
The Dews drew quivering and chill—
For only Gossamer, my Gown—
My Tippet—only Tulle—

We paused before a House that seemed
A Swelling of the Ground—
The Roof was scarcely visible—
The Cornice—in the Ground—

Since then—'tis Centuries—and yet
Feels shorter than the Day
I first surmised the Horses Heads
Were toward Eternity—

Emily Dickinson (1830–1886)

QUESTIONS

1. Does the use of the allegory help to clarify the attitude of the speaker towards Death? Is there a discrepancy between the light verbal atmosphere of the poem and the seriousness of the subject matter? What purpose might this serve?

2. Do you find any inconsistency in the idea that Death, Immortality, and a person should be the passengers in the same carriage? Explain.

3. Interpret the symbolism of the supporting details in the poem. Do you find any difficulty in being definite in your interpretation? If so, what does the poet gain through this indefiniteness?

The next poem certainly invites an allegorical interpretation. You may be reminded of Gloucester's words in Act IV, scene 1 of *King Lear:* "As flies to wanton boys, are we to the gods,/They kill us for their sport." Why does Eberhart avoid summing up his experience in a generalization like this?

## *New Hampshire, February*

Nature had made them hide in crevices,
Two wasps so cold they looked like bark.
Why I do not know, but I took them
And I put them
In a metal pan, both day and dark.

Like God touching his finger to Adam
I felt, and thought of Michaelangelo,
For whenever I breathed on them,
The slightest breath,
They leaped, and preened as if to go.

My breath controlled them always quite.
More sensitive than electric sparks
They came into life
Or they withdrew to ice,
While I watched, suspending remarks.

Then one in a blind career got out,
And fell to the kitchen floor. I
Crushed him with my cold ski boot,
By accident. The other
Had not the wit to try or die.

And so the other is still my pet.
The moral of this is plain.
But I will shirk it.
You will not like it. And
God does not live to explain.

Richard Eberhart (1904–     )

*The Symbolist Movement*

Much twentieth century poetry has been influenced by the symbolist movement which originated in France during the last half of the nineteenth century. The *symbolists,* such as Baudelaire, Rimbaud, and Valéry, sought to shift the focus of poetry away from physical reality and towards mental reality. For them, the fittest subjects for art were not persons and events as externally observed, but the deeply personal and emotional responses which are so unique that they almost defy description. Since the emotional experience is so nearly incommunicable, the symbolist must invent a private body of symbols in his attempt to recreate the impression of the emotion. Because he does not expect to find the precise meaning of his subject, the inner life, he bothers little with external preciseness and depends rather on musical effects and the evocative power of his symbols.

The symbolist poet uses effects that have always been known to poets, but he uses them with less concern over whether he will be understood. He is aware that the strictly rational approach to human experience is severely limited, and that the subconscious may at any moment upset the seeming order and reason on the surface. In order to transmit his knowledge of "felt" thought (as opposed to "understood" thought, such as factual knowledge and logical conclusions) he deliberately assumes the risk that many readers may not understand what he says. Even so, he relies on the notion that all men are affected by certain correspondences between things in nature and in the history of man, as well as fundamental emotional responses. For students of poetry in English these theories are especially relevant to the reading of such poets as Yeats, Pound, and Eliot. Few writers of the present day have escaped the influence of the symbolists.

### *Poems for Study*

The following poems, which span many years of literary history, illustrate the use of symbols in several modes, beginning with a medieval lyric, passing through the symbolist movement, and ending with a twentieth century work. All the works invite interpretation, but remain, somehow, slightly beyond a final grasp. Study these poems in detail, noticing how the symbols may provide the poem with:

1. A way to touch off emotional responses to images, or even abstract designs, for example, circles or spirals in Yeats.
2. A means of exploring thought beyond the reaches of literal explanation.
3. A means of compressing material that would ordinarily require elaboration.
4. A means of expanding the suggestiveness of images by releasing them in the poem without the strict guidance of ideas.

#### *Westron Winde When Will Thou Blow*

Westron winde, when will thou blow,
The smalle raine downe can raine?
Crist, if my love wer in my armis
And I in my bed againe.

Anonymous

In this medieval lyric, simplicity brings about the most stirring artistic effects. The speaker makes a perfectly spontaneous utterance, and the emotional force of his words is undiluted by any sense of artificiality. He asks for wind and rain in the first two lines, and for his love in his arms and in his bed in the second two. Yet the forthright appeal in the third and fourth lines does not limit the suggestibility of the first two. Is the call for spring—for the small rains and the wind—given any symbolic meaning by the call for love which follows?

### *They Flee from Me*

They flee from me, that sometime did me seek,
With naked foot stalking in my chamber.
I have seen them gentle, tame, and meek,
That now are wild, and do not remember
That sometime they put themselves in danger
To take bread at my hand; and now they range
Busily seeking with a continual change.

Thanked be fortune it hath been otherwise
Twenty times better; but once, in special,
In thin array, after a pleasant guise,
When her loose gown from her shoulders did fall,
And she me caught in her arms long and small,
Therewithal sweetly did me kiss,
And softly said, Dear heart, how like you this?

It was no dream; I lay broad waking:
But all is turned thorough my gentleness
Into a strange fashion of forsaking;
And I have leave to go of her goodness,
And she also to use newfangleness.
But since that I so kindely am served,
I fain would know what she hath deserved.

Sir Thomas Wyatt (1503–1542)

This poem, in its mood and method, resembles other love songs in the renaissance tradition of the *complaint*. The lover begins with an elaborate "conceit," or extended figure of speech, and laments his ill-treatment by a cold-hearted lady. But in this poem Wyatt keeps the identity of the creature indefinite, so that the image of the tame-wild thing takes on the suggestibility of the symbol. The combination of indefiniteness and plain sense makes the poem seem highly charged with emotion, and not at all a mannered exercise in Petrarchan love poetry.

*The Collar*

I Struck the board°, and cried, No more, *table*
I will abroad.
What? Shall I ever sigh and pine?
My lines and life are free; free as the road,
Loose as the wind, as large as store.
Shall I be still in suit?
Have I no harvest but a thorn
To let me blood, and not restore
What I have lost with cordial° fruit? *health restoring*
Sure there was wine
Before my sighs did dry it: there was corn° *wheat*
Before my tears did drown it.
Is the year only lost to me?
Have I no bays to crown it?
No flowers, no garlands gay? all blasted?
All Wasted?
Not so, my heart: but there is fruit,
And thou hast hands.
Recover all thy sigh-blown age
On double pleasures: leave thy cold dispute
Of what is fit and not; forsake thy cage,
Thy rope of sands,
Which petty thoughts have made, and made to thee
Good cable, to enforce and draw,
And be thy law,
While thou didst wink and would not see.
Away; take heed:
I will abroad.
Call in thy death's-head there: tie up thy fears.
He that forbears
To suit and serve his need,
Deserves his load.
But as I rav'd and grew more fierce and wild
At every word,
Methought I heard one calling, *Child;*
And I replied, *My Lord.*

George Herbert (1593–1633)

Typical of some poems of the seventeenth century called *emblems,* this selection has as its chief symbol its title. But in its ambiguity, the title is more than a sign or emblem; it is a symbol adding much to the enjoyable complexity of the piece. Consider the title in three lights: first, "collar" as the name of a neck ring, the symbol of servitude; second, as the last two lines suggest, "collar" (caller) is the symbol of Christ, who calls his own back to him; third, in the psychology of the seventeenth century, "collar" (choler) is the fluid in the body that governs anger and rage, hence "collar" is symbolic of the poem's dominant tone.

Consider also the symbolism of these words: "thorn" (line 7), "blood" (line 8), "cordial fruit" (line 10), "corn" (line 11), "rope of sand" (line 22). Do these words take on any conventionally symbolic meaning when you discover in the last lines of the poem that the subject is a religious one?

## *Kubla Khan*

In Xanadu did Kubla Khan
A stately pleasure-dome decree:
Where Alph, the sacred river, ran
Through caverns measureless to man
Down to a sunless sea.
So twice five miles of fertile ground
With walls and towers were girdled round:
And here were gardens bright with sinuous rills
Where blossomed many an incense-bearing tree;
And here were forests ancient as the hills,
Enfolding sunny spots of greenery.

But oh! that deep romantic chasm which slanted
Down the green hill athwart a cedarn cover!
A savage place! as holy and enchanted
As e'er beneath a waning moon was haunted
By woman wailing for her demon-lover!
And from this chasm, with ceaseless turmoil seething,
As if this earth in fast thick pants were breathing,
A mighty fountain momently was forced;
Amid whose swift half-intermitted burst
Huge fragments vaulted like rebounding hail,

Or chaffy grain beneath the thresher's flail:
And 'mid these dancing rocks at once and ever
It flung up momently the sacred river.
Five miles meandering with a mazy motion
Through wood and dale the sacred river ran,
Then reached the caverns measureless to man,
And sank in tumult to a lifeless ocean;
And 'mid this tumult Kubla heard from far
Ancestral voices prophesying war!

The shadow of the dome of pleasure
Floated midway on the waves;
Where was heard the mingled measure
From the fountain and the caves.
It was a miracle of rare device,
A sunny pleasure-dome with caves of ice!

A damsel with a dulcimer
In a vision once I saw:
It was an Abyssinian maid,
And on her dulcimer she played,
Singing of Mount Abora.
Could I revive within me
Her symphony and song,
To such a deep delight 'twould win me,
That with music loud and long,
I would build that dome in air,
That sunny dome! those caves of ice!
And all who heard should see them there,
And all should cry, "Beware! Beware!
His flashing eyes, his floating hair!
Weave a circle round him thrice,
And close your eyes with holy dread,
For he on honey-dew hath fed,
And drunk the milk of Paradise."

Samuel Taylor Coleridge (1772–1834)

"Kubla Khan" provides an ideal sample of romantic symbolism. Coleridge himself claimed that it is a record in verse of a vision he had in a dream. When he awoke from the dream, he tried to write down his vision but lost the train of his memory of the subconscious when the famous "man from Porlock" came to visit him on business. By Coleridge's account, then, the poem is a fragment, but many readers regard it as a complete work. In its shifting rhythms it relies, like the later work of the symbolists, on indefinable musical effects. It may be read as a stylized allegory of the alternating forces of life and death; of the conscious and the subconscious; or of the poetic imagination when controlled or uncontrolled. Coleridge has been able, in any case, to recreate in the mind of his reader the sense of awe and frustration in watching the fading vision which "had passed away like the images on the surface of a stream into which a stone had been cast, but, alas!"

*Metamorphoses of the Vampire*
*(Les Métamorphoses du Vampire)*

The woman, meanwhile, from strawberry lips,
Twisting and turning like a snake on coals,
And kneading her breasts against her corset stays,
Let flow these words, which seem infused with musk:
"My lips are moist, I know the science well
Of losing the old conscience deep in bed.
I dry all tears on my triumphant breasts
And set old men to laughing like young boys.
For those who see me naked and unveiled
I take the place of sun, and moon, and stars!
Dear scholar, I am so learned at this art
That when I smother a man in my smooth arms,
Or when I abandon to their teeth my bosom,
The timid man, the rake, the weak, the strong
Shiver these cushions so before they swoon
The impotent angels would damn themselves for me!"

When she had sucked the marrow from my bones,
And, languishing, I turned towards her to give
Her one more kiss of love, I only saw
Her sticky loins—a winesack filled with pus!
I shut my eyes in a cold fright, and when
I opened them again to the live light,
Beside me lay no mannequin whose power
Seemed to have come from drinking human blood:
There trembled a confusion of old bones

Which squeaked in turning like a weathervane,
Or like a signboard on an iron pole
Swung by the wind through the long winter nights.

Charles Baudelaire (1821–1867)
(translated by Donald Justice)

In this poem, the first twenty-four lines describe a sordid reality which prepare the reader for the last three lines which describe a situation in the speaker's mind. If the poem succeeds in these final lines, it succeeds as pure symbol, for the images named have completely shed all literal meaning. Baudelaire died in 1867, yet the poem is distinctly modern in subject and method. Works such as this prepared the way for the other symbolists and for twentieth century surrealism.

### *The Wild Swans at Coole*

The trees are in their autumn beauty,
The woodland paths are dry,
Under the October twilight the water
Mirrors a still sky;
Upon the brimming water among the stones
Are nine-and-fifty swans.

The nineteenth autumn has come upon me
Since I first made my count;
I saw, before I had well finished,
All suddenly mount
And scatter wheeling in great broken rings
Upon their clamorous wings.

I have looked upon those brilliant creatures,
And now my heart is sore.
All's changed since I, hearing at twilight,
The first time on this shore,
The bell-beat of their wings above my head,
Trod with a lighter tread.

Unwearied still, lover by lover,
They paddle in the cold
Companionable streams or climb the air;

Their hearts have not grown old;
Passion or conquest, wander where they will,
Attend upon them still.

But now they drift on the still water,
Mysterious, beautiful;
Among what rushes will they build,
By what lake's edge or pool
Delight men's eyes when I awake some day
To find they have flown away?

William Butler Yeats (1865–1939)

"Coole" in the title of this poem is the site of Lady Gregory's estate in Galway where Yeats spent several years and where he frequently visited. He was much attracted to the calm grace and ceremoniousness of the aristocracy, and it troubled him to find that in the changing political scene in Ireland, the aristocracy's influence would diminish. Swans, with their aloofness and grace, came to symbolize the aristocracy for Yeats, though the poem does not limit their symbolism to this. Notice the circular movement of their flight, which calls to mind Yeats's use of the gyre as a symbol. In some ways, Yeats uses the swan as a conventional symbol of permanence in flux, but his indefiniteness, particularly in the last two stanzas, releases the symbolism of the poem from stipulated limits.

### *Three Poems About Snakes*

For comparative study, analyze the poems that follow to see how the image of the snake may take on variations of symbolic meaning. The contexts and attitudes of the speakers are different from poem to poem, and, though some of the poems are old and some are new, there seems to be a constant factor in how people of all times have reacted to snakes, and how poets have chosen to use them to elicit predictable responses. For further study read Book IX of Milton's *Paradise Lost* and compare the treatment of serpents there with that of Keats in his allegorical narrative, *Lamia*.

### *To a Fair Lady, Playing with a Snake*

Strange! that such horror and such grace
Should dwell together in one place;
A fury's arm, an angel's face!

'Tis innocence, and youth, which makes
In Chloris' fancy such mistakes,
To start at love, and play with snakes.

By this and by her coldness barred,
Her servants have a task too hard;
The tyrant has a double guard!

Thrice happy snake! that in her sleeve
May boldly creep; we dare not give
Our thoughts so unconfined a leave.

Contented in that nest of snow
He lies, as he his bliss did know,
And to the wood no more would go.

Take heed, fair Eve! you do not make
Another tempter of this snake;
A marble one so warmed would speak.

Edmund Waller (1606–1687)

### *To the Snake*

Green Snake, when I hung you round my neck
and stroked your cold, pulsing throat
as you hissed to me, glinting
arrowy gold scales, and I felt
the weight of you on my shoulders,
and the whispering silver of your dryness
sounded close at my ears—

Green Snake—I swore to my companions that certainly
you were harmless! But truly
I had no certainty, and no hope, only desiring
to hold you, for that joy,

which left
a long wake of pleasure, as the leaves moved
and you faded into the pattern
of grass and shadows, and I returned
smiling and haunted, to a dark morning.

Denise Levertov (1923– )

## *Eurynome*

Come all old maids that are squeamish
And afraid to make mistakes,
Don't clutter your lives up with boyfriends:
The nicest girls marry snakes.

If you don't mind slime on your pillow
And caresses as gliding as ice
—Cold skin, warm heart, remember,
And besides, they keep down the mice—

If you're really serious-minded,
It's the best advice you can take:
No rumpling, no sweating, no nonsense,
Oh who would not sleep with a snake?

Jay Macpherson (1931– )

*Title.* Eurynome, *one of the many wives of Zeus. An earth goddess, she would be presumed to have snakes as her lovers.*

*Chapter 9*

# Irony, Paradox, and Satire

LIKE the other elements of poetry which have been defined and discussed, irony occurs first in spoken language, and only later in writing. *Irony* is not so tangible an element as imagery or figurative language, for it is a manner of expression; it is a way of saying something so that the meaning becomes the reverse of a literal statement. To achieve irony, one simply adds to an assertion the intention of having it mean its opposite. Words mean what people want them to mean, and clear communication depends upon some mutual agreement about definitions. The word "hot," for example, begins by describing anything that has a temperature higher than that of the human body. Through a variety of extensions it can describe strong feeling, excitability, a peppery taste, extreme desire, closeness to a goal, radioactivity, high voltage, and so on. When we use "hot" to mean the opposite of any of these meanings, we are using it ironically. In simple irony, the context and several possible signals, such as facial expressions or tonal inflection, will keep the statement from being misunderstood. A man in the midst of a blizzard who complains about the "hot" weather cannot easily be misinterpreted. If one were to say that Henry VIII could scarcely conceal his hot desire for Anne of Cleves, he would depend on his listener's knowing that Henry found Anne to be extremely homely. In speech the irony may be signaled by a heavy "laying on" of emphasis. But a speaker might speak as if what he says is a simple, literal truth and depend on the interpretive powers of his listener. Irony can be endlessly varied between the extremes of blatancy and subtlety.

Irony depends upon a doubleness of view. It allows the conventional usage of the words to set up a pattern of expectancy which might at any point be reversed. Without the original sense of fitness or congruity in language which makes accurate statements possible, there could be none of the added dimension of irony.

Like figurative language and symbolism, irony is a way to removing the limits of literalness. Like them, it changes the way a listener responds to a statement at the same time it alters his understanding. This is to say that irony changes the emotional as well as the intellectual content of a statement. But unlike figurative and symbolic language, irony does not depend upon imagery or upon stated and implied comparisons. It does not necessarily require the senses to assist in advancing thought. The system of opposites in irony does involve comparison and contrast, but not necessarily imagery.

Frequently the diction in a poem will guide a reader to see an apparent irony. Beware, as always, of any inclination to equate the speaker with the poet. In reading the following poem, remember that D. H. Lawrence was from the working class and had no sympathy for pretentiousness.

### *To Be Superior*

How nice it is to be superior!
Because really, it's no use pretending, one *is* superior, isn't one?
I mean people like you and me.—

Quite! I quite agree.
The trouble is, everybody thinks they're just as superior
as we are; just as superior.—

That's what's so boring! people are so boring.
But they can't really think it, do you think?
At the bottom, they must *know* we are really superior
don't you think?
Don't you think, *really,* they *know* we're their superiors?—
I couldn't say.
I've never got to the bottom of superiority.
I should like to.

D. H. Lawrence (1885–1930)

### QUESTIONS

1. What do you think is the poet's attitude to the speaker (or speakers)?
2. Experiment with quotation marks to make this into a dialogue. Can you arrange a conversation in which one speaker is humoring another?
3. Explain the irony of the next to last line.
4. Though there is no imagery in the usual sense here, how can you account for the vivid mental picture Lawrence has produced?
5. Can you judge the social class of the speaker from the diction?
6. What use does Lawrence make of the repetition of key words? Are there any concrete words in the poem? Why?

Up to this point the emphasis has been on statements that are intended to be ironical. When irony appears in poetry, such is usually the case. Irony is present because the poet put it there. But in life, people often discover irony which was never intended. Any kind of phenomenon which has a normal, original nature or usage can become involved in irony when its nature or usage is reversed. For example, an instrument of death used to bring life would be ironic. The crucifixion of Christ would illustrate this. When the cure for one disease happens to be another disease, we recognize the presence of irony. King Mithridates, for example, protected himself from assassins by taking poison. When we note a discrepancy between the intended result and the actual result of a process, we are noticing an irony, as when for example a bird is observed building his nest in a tree which is to be cut down. In all these cases there is a pattern of expectancy and a reversal. Poets often take situations such as this as subjects for their work. There need not be any ironic use of word meaning in poems which are ironic.

In the next poem the words sketch a scene, but there is no intention to make the words ironic—the irony is in the situation.

### *The 1st*

What I remember about that day
is boxes stacked across the walk
and couch springs curling through the air
and drawers and tables balanced on the curb
and us, hollering,

leaping up and around
happy to have a playground;

nothing about the emptied rooms
nothing about the emptied family

Lucille Clifton( 1935– )

QUESTIONS

1. What does the title mean? What happens on the 1st? What is ironic?

2. Notice that every detail in the poem is literal except for the last line. In what way has the family been "emptied," and what is the emotional impact of the repetition and variation in the last two lines?

One of the advantages of irony is that it has the effect of putting a listener on guard against misinterpretation. Once the signals of irony are recognized, the listener begins to translate. It is as if he were watching a film that suddenly went from positive to negative, and he would immediately have to read all the black images as white and all the white as black. Along with the possibility of heightening a reader's alertness goes the risk of being misunderstood. But the risk is well worth the possibly good outcome. One does not often decline to tell a humorous story on the grounds that the listener will not get the joke or may miss some subtle incongruity. What might be a fairly routine way of saying something may, with irony, produce a pleasurable result that gives a poem its particular effectiveness. Consider this poem, reading it first as if it were a literal statement, then as an ironic one. Can you be certain that irony is intended? The poem is one of Blake's *Songs of Innocence,* which were to be sung by children as yet unspoiled by worldly experience. In Blake's day, children were bought from poor families and used as chimney sweeps.

### *The Chimney Sweeper*

When my mother died I was very young,
And my father sold me while yet my tongue
Could scarcely cry " 'weep! 'weep! 'weep! 'weep!"
So your chimneys I sweep, and in soot I sleep.

There's little Tom Dacre, who cried when his head,
That curled like a lamb's back, was shaved: so I said,
"Hush, Tom! never mind it, for when your head's bare
You know that the soot cannot spoil your white hair."

And so he was quiet, and that very night,
As Tom was a-sleeping, he had such a sight!
That thousands of sweepers, Dick, Joe, Ned, and Jack,
Were all of them locked up in coffins of black.

And by came an Angel who had a bright key,
And he opened the coffins and set them all free;
Then down a green plain leaping, laughing, they run,
And wash in a river, and shine in the Sun.

Then naked and white, all their bags left behind,
They rise upon clouds and sport in the wind;
And the Angel told Tom, if he'd be a good boy,
He'd have God for his father, and never want joy.

And so Tom awoke; and we rose in the dark,
And got with our bags and our brushes to work.
Though the morning was cold, Tom was happy and warm;
So if all do their duty they need not fear harm.

William Blake (1757–1827)

QUESTIONS

1. What is your reaction to the child's words? What do you think the poet felt about the child's situation?

2. Does the child understand the double meaning of "'weep! 'weep! 'weep! 'weep!"?

3. Comment on the logic of the argument in the second stanza.

4. Does the child understand the full meaning of Tom's dream?

5. What is Blake's attitude toward the advice in the last line?

6. How does the rhythm of these lines affect the irony?

## *The Relationship of Irony and Humor*

There is something about incongruity that makes men smile, with or without pleasure. The incongruity may be ironic without being funny, but the recognition of the incongruity always arouses a sense of amusement, whether it be joyous or grim. Men have had to burn their most valuable possessions to keep warm, and men have used cream pies to throw at one another. Both situations involve incongruity but only the latter causes the agreeable response of humor. Irony always has a meaning. The spectacle of seeing furniture burned for warmth might lead us to say, "Human values are so surprising that what we may need to collect and build today might be as necessarily destroyed tomorrow." A pie in the face, however irresistibly funny, does not mean anything. Much humor does indeed have meaning, however, and it is frequently ironic.

*The Uses of Irony*

Although it would be impossible to catalog all the uses of irony as an element of poetry, a few of the more clear-cut uses might be set down. First, irony expands any statement's ability to be shaded. It allows a speaker to introduce degrees of meaning not easily managed literally. Second, irony alerts a reader to use his interpretive powers with greater attention to subtleties. Third, it helps the writer to manage his tone, that is, to convey his attitude toward his subject, his reader, and even toward himself. This is particularly effective in an age such as ours when the skeptical, objective outlook has put people on guard against unqualified statements. Fourth, irony helps the writer to maintain control over emotional subject matter which might lean toward the excesses of sentimentality. Finally, irony produces an intellectual pleasure in itself when the reader recognizes the complexities of ironic experience and ironic language.

In the analysis of literature, a full understanding of the poet's intention may require some classification of the kinds of irony. A single division can be made between ironies that are expressed verbally and those expressed not through words, but in actions and situations. Among verbal ironies, those which are intended by the speaker may be distinguished from those not intended. When the speaker in a work of literature is someone other than the author, he may be unaware of the ironic implications of what he says. A simple schematic of this classification might look like this:

| | Verbal | Nonverbal |
|---|---|---|
| Heard or seen by chance | 1. unintentional | 4. situation |
| Said or done deliberately | 2. intentional | 5. action |
| Portrayed | 3. dramatic speech | 6. dramatic action |

The examples listed below will briefly illustrate each of these types of irony. Note that the portrayed ironies can involve any combination of planned or inadvertent types.

1. A father who is unaware that his son smokes marijuana teases him about how old fashioned he is in the presence of young people who know how inaccurate the father's impression actually is. Here the irony as understood is not the irony intended by the speaker.
2. A man at a golf course meets his secretary, who has reported herself too ill to come to work. He says, "Glad to see you have recovered."
3. A poet portrays a character (e.g., the friar in Browning's "Soliloquy in a Spanish Cloister") who speaks of his great purity and faith. The reader sees through the talk, understanding that the speaker is lecherous and faithless.
4. A ship, reputedly unsinkable, even by God, strikes an iceberg and sinks on its first voyage.
5. A businessman hires his former commanding officer to work as a clerk.
6. A character in a play or story conducts an inquiry to discover who is guilty of some wrong, but surprisingly finds that he himself is the culprit (e.g., Sophocles's *Oedipus Rex*).

Situations which involve surprises, inadvertencies, reversals of role, overheard conversations, deceptions, and discoveries are the mark of exciting storytelling. Almost all of these situations use irony, and the writer who can construct a work which rings true without belabored or contrived ironies has a device that lends itself to interesting compositions. As with any literary element, irony is easier to understand than to write, and the most appreciative reader will enlarge the pleasure of literature by noticing the subtleties and complexities of irony.

Study the following poems, trying to understand as precisely as you can the nature of the ironies involved.

### *Yes; I Write Verses*

Yes; I write verses now and then,
But blunt and flaccid is my pen,
No longer talked of by young men
As rather clever;
In the last quarter are my eyes,
You see it by their form and size;
Is it not time then to be wise?
Or now or never.

Fairest that ever sprang from Eve!
While Time allows the short reprieve,
Just look at me! would you believe
'Twas once a lover?
I cannot clear the five-bar gate,
But, trying first its timbers' state,
Climb stiffly up, take breath, and wait
To trundle over.

Through gallopade I cannot swing
The entangling blooms of Beauty's spring;
I cannot say the tender thing,
Be't true or false,
And am beginning to opine
Those girls are only half-divine
Whose waists yon wicked boys entwine
In giddy waltz.

I fear that arm above that shoulder,
I wish them wiser, graver, older,
Sedater, and no harm if colder,
And panting less.
Ah! people were not half so wild
In former days, when, starchly mild,
Upon her high-heeled Essex smiled
The brave Queen Bess.

Walter Savage Landor (1775–1864)

## QUESTIONS

1. To what question might the speaker's opening "yes" be an answer? Describe the scene in which the speech is given. What differences are there between the speaker and the person he is addressing?

2. Does the speaker believe that wisdom comes with age? That "former days" were mild? What was the relationship between Elizabeth and Essex?

3. What attitude toward young girls does the speaker reveal in lines 22 and 23? Is "half-divine" an understatement or an overstatement? Explain the irony.

4. In line 9 the speaker addresses the girl as "Fairest that ever sprang from Eve!" How does this affect your reading of lines 19 and 20?

5. What effect does Landor achieve by having the speaker be literal at times and at other times ironic? Is the speaker amused, annoyed, jealous, worried, flirtatious, objective?

May Swenson takes up the theme of youth and age in the next poem, but she presents her irony in a very different tone and framework. Landor's speaker is an old man—the amused observer of young people at a dance. Swenson's speaker, though in less definite circumstances, represents the voice of experience.

### *How to Be Old*

It is easy to be young. (Everybody is,
at first.) It is not easy
to be old. It takes time.
Youth is given; age is achieved.
One must work a magic to mix with time
in order to become old.

Youth is given. One must put it away
like a doll in a closet,
take it out and play with it only
on holidays. One must have many dresses
and dress the doll impeccably
(but not to show the doll, to keep it hidden.)

It is necessary to adore the doll,
to remember it in the dark on the ordinary
days, and every day congratulate
one's aging face in the mirror.

In time one will be very old.
In time, one's life will be accomplished.
And in time, in time, the doll—
like new, though ancient—will be found.

May Swenson (1919– )

QUESTIONS

1. What is the speaker's attitude toward the listener? What irony, if any, do you see in the first stanza?
2. Does the speaker think that the young can understand what he is saying?
3. Who forces us to put youth away (stanza 2)? Does the speaker seem glad or resentful about youth? Explain your reply. Is there any criticism of America's youth worship implied here?
4. What sense do you make of the final stanza?

## *Overstatement and Understatement*

Irony in the form of *understatement* treats a subject as if it were less than it actually is. In speech one might say that an elderly person is "no teen-ager." When Swift says in his satirical elegy on the Duke of Marlborough that the Duke will wish to sleep a "little longer" when he hears the "last loud trump," he is being ironic, for the Duke will surely want to postpone the final reckoning indefinitely. The technical term for intentional understatement is *meiosis. Litotes* is a form of understatement which makes an affirmative statement by denying what is opposite. Tennyson uses this device when in "Ulysses" he says,

Some work of noble note may yet be done
Not unbecoming men that strove with gods.

*Overstatement,* called *"hyperbole,"* may also be used ironically, especially for the sake of deriding deliberate exaggerations which are not ironic. Alexander Pope's poem, "The Rape of the Lock," exemplifies this by using the inflated language of heroic tragedy to tell a story of a man stealing a lock of a girl's hair.

The Peer now spreads the glittering forfex wide,
To enclose the Lock; now joins it, to divide.
Even then, before the fatal engine closed,

A wretched Sylph too fondly interposed;
Fate urged the shears, and cut the Sylph in twain
(But airy substance soon unites again):
The meeting points the sacred hair dissever
From the fair head, forever, and forever!

The term applied to poetry such as this which treats an ordinary subject in the grand manner is *"mock heroic."*

Irony may be evident in a poem when the speaker's words do not seem consistent with his role. The speaker in a love poem might be expected to profess his devotion, loyalty, or passion, for example, but notice how often poems about love have an ironic element.

### *The Constant Lover*

Out upon it, I have loved
  Three whole days together!
And am like to love three more,
  If it prove fair weather.

Time shall moult away his wings
  Ere he shall discover
In the whole wide world again
  Such a constant lover.

But the spite on't is, no praise
  Is due at all to me:
Love with me had made no stays,
  Had it any been but she.

Had it any been but she,
  And that very face,
There had been at least ere this
  A dozen dozen in her place.

Sir John Suckling (1609–1642)

QUESTIONS

1. Does "constant" in the title have more than one meaning?
2. Where is the irony in line 4?
3. Comment on Suckling's use of the customary overstatement of love poetry.

This poem may remind you of Waller's "Go, Lovely Rose" in its irony, or of Lovelace's "To Lucasta, Going to the Wars" in its comparison of breast and convent. Notice that the seemingly elaborate compliment in the beginning is an ironic accusation. The overstatement of conventional love poetry finally becomes an ironic combination of overstatement and understatement in the conclusion. No doubt the poet's chiseled phrases are calculated to match the imagery of chilly marble in the final stanza.

*To Roses in the Bosom of Castara*

Ye blushing virgins happy are
In the chaste nunnery of her breasts,
For he'd profane so chaste a fair,
Whoe'er should call them Cupid's nests.

Transplanted thus how bright ye grow,
How rich a perfume do ye yield.
In some close garden, cowslips so
Are sweeter than in th'open field.

In those white cloisters live secure
From the rude blasts of wanton breath,
Each hour more innocent and pure,
Till you shall wither into death.

Then that which living gave you room
Your glorious sepulcher shall be;
There wants no marble for a tomb,
Whose breast hath marble been to me.

William Habington (1605–1654)

QUESTIONS

1. What hints of sensuality do you find in the poem? Do they produce a kind of ironic tension in contrast with the anti-sensualist detail?
2. Comment on the use of overstatement in the third stanza.
3. Castara's breasts are compared to several places; when, in your first reading of the poem, did you first notice the ironic drift?

## *Paradox*

*Paradox* is a state of affairs in which things which seem illogical actually make sense. When we recognize paradox in everyday experience our attention comes into sharper focus. Paradox always brings some revelation through some sudden and unexpected combination of fact. Since paradox is usually condensed, emphatic, and surprising, it is also memorable. The wisdom of proverbs often is expressed through paradox for this reason, and much good advice is stated in paradox. It is said that you have to spend money to make money—that the way to lose a friend is to lend him money—that it is best to make haste slowly—"He is not poor that hath little, but he that desireth much."

Good sense as expressed in paradox does not necessarily make good art, and yet it is the complexity of life as perceived in paradox that often challenges the artist to try his hand at illuminating it. Paradox makes a perfect symbol of the mysteriousness of life. It often figures into statements which call for belief (or disbelief) in some higher than human wisdom, for it is a repeated reminder that man's judgment has flaws, whether that judgment leads him towards or away from skepticism. This sonnet by Joseph Blanco White uses a paradox about natural perceptions in order to pose questions about possible supernatural perceptions:

### *To Night*

Mysterious Night! when our first parent knew
Thee from report divine, and heard thy name,
Did he not tremble for this lovely frame,
This glorious canopy of light and blue?
Yet 'neath the curtain of translucent dew,
Bathed in the rays of the great setting flame,
Hesperus with the host of heaven came,
And lo! creation widened on man's view.
Who could have thought such darkness lay concealed
Within thy beams, O Sun! or who could find,
While fly, and leaf, and insect stood revealed,
That to such countless orbs thou mad'st us blind!
  Why do we, then, shun Death with anxious strife?—
  If Light can thus deceive, wherefore not Life?

Joseph Blanco White (1775–1841)

Paradox and irony are closely related, but where an ironic statement implies a meaning opposite to that which is literally expressed, the paradox overtly asserts as true that which seems false. All paradoxes are ironic, but only ironies stated so as to seem self-contradictory are called paradox. We note the irony in a situation in which the United States sold its scrap iron to Japan, which used it to produce weapons. But the irony becomes recognizable as paradox when the terms involved are stated so as to seem self-contradictory: "Our best friend was our worst enemy." "The greatest profit made the greatest waste."

When the contradictory terms of a paradox are placed side by side, the result is called *oxymoron,* as in "profitable waste," or "best enemy." Henry Vaughan uses this when he speaks of the "deep but dazzling darkness" of death. Ben Jonson uses it in this song:

### *Still to Be Neat*

Still to be neat, still to be dressed,
As if you were going to a feast;
Still to be powdered, still perfumed;
Lady, it is to be presumed,
Though art's hid causes are not found,
All is not sweet, all is not sound.

Give me a look, give me a face
That makes simplicity a grace;
Robes loosely flowing, hair as free;
Such sweet neglect more taketh me
Than all th' adulteries of art.
They strike mine eyes, but not my heart.

Ben Jonson (1573–1637)

Paradox emerges when some configuration of facts leads in one direction for one kind of logic but in an opposite direction for another kind of logic. Most paradoxical statements dramatize the contradiction by emphasizing the unexpected conclusion. In such debatable statements as: "No one is more credulous than an infidel," the contradiction implies that nonbelievers have great difficulty in adhering to their disbelief, or, perhaps, that people who are on their guard against accepting belief in the supernatural tend to be relaxed about believing in other dubious "truths."

When in Vietnam, after the "Tet" offensive of 1968, an American officer claimed that the only way he could save a village was to destroy it, no one had difficulty in seeing the contradiction between military logic and humanitarian logic. This would be like the paradox in the statement: "The operation was a success, but the patient died."

The poet as ironist might choose to make an outright statement explaining the contradictions of human existence, or he might elect to show a character who is emotionally involved by trying to make sense of life's paradox. In the two poems below, two opposing views of experience are stated in two different ways. The first, from Alexander Pope's *An Essay on Man,* reflects the thought of the Age of Reason. Thomas Hardy's "Hap," written in 1867 in a time of troubled religious thought, dramatizes the concern of his day.

Cease then, nor Order imperfection name;
Our proper bliss depends on what we blame.
Know thy own point: this kind, this due degree
Of blindness, weakness, Heaven bestows on thee.
Submit. —In this, or any other sphere,
Secure to be as blessed as thou canst bear:
Safe in the hand of one disposing Power,
Or in the natal or the mortal hour.
All Nature is but Art, unknown to thee;
All Chance, Direction, which thou canst not see;
All Discord, Harmony not understood;
All partial Evil, universal Good:
And, spite of Pride, in erring Reason's spite,
One truth is clear, WHATEVER IS, IS RIGHT.

Alexander Pope (1688–1744)

## *Hap*

If but some vengeful god would call to me
From up the sky, and laugh: "Thou suffering thing,
Know that thy sorrow is my ecstasy,
That thy love's loss is my hate's profiting!"

Then would I bear it, clench myself, and die,
Steeled by the sense of ire unmerited;
Half-eased in that a Powerfuller than I
Had willed and meted me the tears I shed.

But not so. How arrives it joy lies slain,
And why unblooms the best hope ever sown?
—Crass Casualty obstructs the sun and rain,
And dicing Time for gladness casts a moan. . . .
These purblind Doomsters had as readily strown
Blisses about my pilgrimage as pain.

Thomas Hardy (1840–1928)

## QUESTIONS

1. Define the central paradox in each poem.
2. Pope mentions "bliss," "power," "submission," "spite," "blindness," and "chance." How many of these details appear in Hardy's poem? Does Hardy seem to be responding to Pope's point of view?
3. How do the movement and the form of Pope's poem reflect the idea he supports? How do Hardy's form and movement reflect the ideas of his speaker?
4. "Hap" is an old word meaning "chance." Which words pertaining to chance can you find in the poem? Do these words affect the poem's unity?
5. Does Pope's statement reflect any emotional involvement? Should it? Does his vocabulary contain any surprises? Should it?
6. Apply these questions to Hardy's poem, and try to decide whether one statement is more poetically successful than the other.

In the selection below, his thoughts about leaves lead the poet through paradox and into ambiguity. *Ambiguity* arises when some expression, having more than one meaning, leaves us in doubt about how to interpret the statement.

## *Old Leaves*

It's not wind that takes old leaves
From trees in autumn. It's the next
Year's leaf buds. The buds dream them off.
But this last rainless summer perplexed
The buds, and so this tree
Has gone into winter with its old leaves.
A weird dust-green, they are almost no
Color at all. In wind they do not wave
But twitch on stiff stems. Light dazes

Them, and ice riddles. Without the bud's wild
Dream they can only hang on for dear death
As if they fought against some lively
Disease that troubles the dead.

God save, send the destroying child.

Radcliffe Squires (1917– )

QUESTIONS

1. What is the central paradox? Is it true that the old die to make way for the young?
2. Does the poet suggest that what is true of leaves is also true of humans? If you answer "no," how do you account for the last word in the poem? If "yes," how far would you be willing to go with the analogy?
3. Explain the possible ambiguities in lines 10 and 14.
4. Point out and explain any examples of oxymoron.

## *Satire*

*Satire* is literature that ridicules human frailty. The ridicule may be kindly or ruthless, but it usually has as its objective the improvement of man's character and his institutions. Satire tends to be ironic, not only through the close relationship between irony and humor, but also because in its indirect way irony has the effect of making the reader a participant in the ridicule by involving his wit. Though satirical writing may laugh at an individual, its tendency is toward a more generalized scorn of vice and folly. It often employs the beast fable, allegory, or fiction and drama which use stereotyped characters. Some familiar examples of these forms could be Orwell's *Animal Farm,* G. B. Shaw's plays, or Samuel Butler's *Erewhon.*

Satire is often spoken of as being Juvenalian or Horatian, after the Roman satirists Juvenal and Horace. *Juvenalian satire,* with its angry view of corrupt men in a corrupt society, has a bitter and contemptuous tone, and may be very personal in its invective. *Horatian satire* is much more amiable in its amusement at people and hopeful about improving them through sympathetic humor.

These two characteristic tones are exemplified in the poems below.

from *A Beautiful Nymph Going to Bed*

Corinna, pride of Drury-Lane,
For whom no shepherd sighs in vain;
Never did Covent-Garden boast
So bright a battered, strolling toast;
No drunken rake to pick her up,
No cellar where on tick to sup;
Returning at the midnight hour,
Four stories climbing to her bower;
Then, seated on a three-legged chair,
Takes off her artificial hair;
Now picking out a crystal eye,
She wipes it clean, and lays it by.
Her eyebrows from a mouse's hide
Stuck on with art on either side,
Pulls off with care, and first displays 'em,
Then in a play-book smoothly lays 'em.
Now dext'rously her plumpers draws,
That serve to fill her hollow jaws,
Untwists a wire, and from her gums
A set of teeth completely comes;
Pulls out the rags contrived to prop
Her flabby dugs, and down they drop.
Proceeding on, the lovely goddess
Unlaces next her steel-ribbed bodice,
Which, by the operator's skill,
Press down the lumps, the hollows fill.
Up goes her hand, and off she slips
The bolsters that supply her hips:
With gentlest touch she next explores
Her chancres, issues, running sores;
Effects of many a sad disaster,
And then to each applies a plaster;
But must, before she goes to bed,
Rub off the daubs of white and red.

Jonathan Swift (1667–1745)

QUESTIONS

1. Most satire assumes that humans have flaws but that these may be remedied. Does this poem seem to hold any hope for improvement? Would you call this Juvenalian or Horatian?

2. One of the limits of satire is sheer fun, with no criticism implied; the other is flat criticism, with no laughter. What accounts for the humor in this selection?

## *Ego*

When I was on Night Line,
flying my hands to park
a big-bird B-29,
I used to command the dark:
four engines were mine

to jazz; I was ground-crew,
an unfledged pfc,
but when I waved planes through
that flight line in Tennessee,
my yonder was wild blue.

Warming up, I was hot
on the throttle, logging an hour
of combat, I was the pilot
who rogered the tower.
I used to take off a lot.

With a flat-hat for furlough
and tin wings to sleep on,
I fueled my high-octane ego:
I buzzed, I landed my jeep on
the ramp, I flew low.

When a cross-country hop
let down, I was the big deal
who signaled big wheels to stop.
That's how I used to feel.
I used to get all revved up.

Philip Booth (1925– )

### QUESTIONS

1. How can you tell from the word choice here that the speaker is being satirical? What is he making fun of?
2. What would be lost if the poem were written in the third person?

## *The Unknown Citizen*

*(To JS/07/M/378*
*This Marble Monument*
*Is Erected by the State)*

He was found by the Bureau of Statistics to be
One against whom there was no official complaint,
And all the reports on his conduct agree
That, in the modern sense of an old-fashioned word, he was a saint,
For his Union reports that he paid his dues,
Except for the War till the day he retired
He worked in a factory and never got fired,
But satisfied his employers, Fudge Motors Inc.
Yet he wasn't a scab or odd in his views,
For in everything he did he served the Greater Community.
(Our report on his Union shows it was sound)
And our Social Psychology workers found
That he was popular with his mates and liked a drink.
The Press are convinced that he bought a paper every day
And that his reactions to advertisements were normal in every way.
Policies taken out in his name prove that he was fully insured,
And his Health-card shows he was once in hospital but left it cured.
Both Producers Research and High-Grade Living declare
He was fully sensible to the advantages of the Instalment Plan
And had everything necessary to the Modern Man,
A phonograph, a radio, a car and a frigidaire.
Our researchers into Public Opinion are content
That he held the proper opinions for the time of year;
When there was peace, he was for peace; when there was war, he went.
He was married and added five children to the population,

Which our Eugenist says was the right number for a parent of
his generation,
And our teachers report that he never interfered with their
education.
Was he free? Was he happy? The question is absurd:
Had anything been wrong, we should certainly have heard.

W. H. Auden (1907–1973)

### QUESTIONS

1. What is the difference between a monument to a soldier and this monument to the unknown citizen?
2. Who might be the author of the eulogy?
3. What would be the values of the society that would choose J. S. as a hero?
4. How can you tell from the poet's word choice that he disapproves of the society that erected the monument?
5. Is the tone of the satire serious or lighthearted?

## *A True Maid*

"No, no; for my virginity,
When I lose that," says Rose, "I'll die!"
"Behind the elms last night," cried Dick,
"Rose, were you not extremely sick?"

Matthew Prior (1664–1721)

### QUESTIONS

1. What kind of behavior is being ridiculed here?
2. How does the word choice in this poem emphasize the comic effect?

## *"next to of course god america i*

"next to of course god america i
love you land of the pilgrims' and so forth oh
say can you see by the dawn's early my
country 'tis of centuries come and go
and are no more what of it we should worry
in every language even deafanddumb
thy sons acclaim your glorious name by gorry
by jingo by gee by gosh by gum

why talk of beauty what could be more beaut-
iful than these heroic happy dead
who rushed like lions to the roaring slaughter
they did not stop to think they died instead
then shall the voice of liberty be mute?"

He spoke. And drank rapidly a glass of water

E. E. Cummings (1894–1962)

## QUESTIONS

1. How many subjects are satirized here?
2. What effect does the medley of clichés have on the tone of the poem? Would you say the tone tends to be merry or serious? How would the effect change if the poem were a composite of complete sentences?
3. Do you notice any ironic discrepancy between the tone and the theme?
4. Why does Cummings set off the last line from the others and make it a coherent sentence?
5. What is ironic about the first sentence?

## *England in 1819*

An old, mad, blind, despised, and dying king, —
Princes, the dregs of their dull race, who flow
Through public scorn—mud from a muddy spring;
Rulers, who neither see, nor feel, nor know,
But leech-like to their fainting country cling,
Till they drop, blind in blood, without a blow;
A people starved and stabbed in the untilled field, —
An army, which liberticide and prey
Makes as a two-edged sword to all who wield—
Golden and sanguine laws which tempt and slay, —
Religion Christless, Godless—a book sealed;
A Senate, —Time's worst statute° unrepealed, — *laws disenfranchis*
Are graves, from which a glorious Phantom may *Catholics*
Burst, to illumine our tempestuous day.

Percy Bysshe Shelley (1792–1822)

## QUESTIONS

1. Shelley wrote this poem after the Peterloo Massacre, in which several people at a rally for parliamentary reform were killed by soldiers. King George III was literally old (81 years), blind, and mad. His heirs, particularly

the vain and ineffectual Prince of Wales, seemed not likely to improve matters. Considering the literal basis of all this, do you class this poem as a satire?

2. How does Shelley use sentence structure and punctuation to convey his anger and disgust? Do the sounds as well as the meanings of the words play a role here? What role does connotation play in unifying the impression of this poem?

## *The Latest Decalogue*

Thou shalt have one God only; who
Would be at the expense of two?
No graven images may be
Worshipped, except the currency.
Swear not at all; for, for thy curse
Thine enemy is none the worse.
At church on Sunday to attend
Will serve to keep the world thy friend.
Honor thy parents; that is, all
From whom advancement may befall.
Thou shalt not kill; but need'st not strive
Officiously to keep alive.
Do not adultery commit;
Advantage rarely comes of it.
Thou shalt not steal: an empty feat,
When it's so lucrative to cheat.
Bear not false witness; let the lie
Have time on its own wings to fly.
Thou shalt not covet, but tradition
Approves all forms of competition.

Arthur Hugh Clough (1819–1861)

### QUESTIONS

1. What is the effect of the word "latest" in the title?

2. What is Clough's attitude toward the value system of his day? Is Clough saying that the ten commandments are not being kept?

3. At times, the rhymed pairs of lines seem like a jingle. Point out a few. What effect does this have on the tone?

4. Does the poet seem cynical, that is, does he seem to have stopped believing in human beings' better nature? What, if any, is his hope? Contrast the tone of this poem with "Say Not the Struggle Naught Availeth," also by Clough.

*Chapter 10*

# From Rhythm to Meter

RHYTHM is any steady pattern of repetition, particularly that of a sequence of regularly recurring stressed and unstressed syllables. It is the basis for poetry's musical effect. No one needs to be told that the rhythm of "Taps" or "Reveille," or the drum beat of a marching band stirs an emotional response even apart from words and music. If you were to drum out the rhythm of the following quotations, you could probably guess at the mood of the speaker without even knowing what the words mean:

> I once was a maid, tho' I cannot tell when,
> And still my delight is in proper young men.
> Some one of a troop of dragoons was my daddy:
> No wonder I'm fond of a sodger laddie!

from *The Jolly Beggars*
Robert Burns (1759–1796)

Or:

> Weary of myself, and sick of asking
> What I am and what I ought to be,
> At this vessel's prow I stand, which bears me
> Forwards, forwards, o'er the starlit sea.

from "Self-Dependence"
Matthew Arnold (1822–1888)

It is self-evident that the pace or rhythm of a poem has a strong influence on the effect of the words. Take away the "bounce" from the selection by Burns, and you get something like this:

> I was formerly a maid, although I can't recall just when,
> Nevertheless, proper young men delight me.

> My daddy was a member of a troop of dragoons;
> Small wonder that I am attracted to a soldier.

Before introducing the uninviting terminology that has become a part of the study of poetry's musical basis, it is well to review what we already know about the subject from common sense and instinct. The inescapable response to rhythm is never consciously learned. Even before birth and before the rhythms of pulse and breath, of eating and sleeping, become a part of a person, the beat of the heart surrounds him in the womb. Rhythm comes to create a conditioned response. After the repeated experience of feeling great excitement or depression to the quickening or slowing of life's rhythms, people may have the feelings called forth by the rhythms alone. They are such an intimate part of every person's being that he reacts to them without necessarily realizing what he is doing. Some business offices, for example, play lively music throughout the workday to provide a quick pace for the workers who instinctively respond by making their motion match that of the music. Waiting rooms and doctors' offices are filled with slow, soothing music to help patients set aside their apprehensiveness.

Rhythm is a powerful tool, both preconscious in origin and subconscious in effect. A poet uses rhythm chiefly to construct a mood and to create a response suitable to the sense of his words and ideas. Sometimes, for the sake of comic or ironic effects, he will make the rhythm run counter to his sense. One need not have a detailed knowledge of a poet's techniques to notice the correspondences between rhythm and emotion, a few of which are tentatively given here:

| | |
|---|---|
| strong galloping rhythm | strenuous activity |
| quick, skipping rhythm | sprightly mood |
| quick, stacatto | anticipation, nervous apprehension |
| slow | solemn, serious |
| slow, stacatto | ominously serious |
| slow, regular | deliberate activity |
| halting, irregular | difficulty of expression, deep questioning |

In order to heighten your awareness of the close relationship between the rhythmical element and the other elements of poetry, read the poems below and answer the questions that follow.

## *His Elegy*

### *Written Before His Execution*

My prime of youth is but a frost of cares;
    My feast of joy is but a dish of pain;
My crop of corn is but a field of tares;
    And all my good is but vain hope of gain:
The day is past, and yet I saw no sun;
And now I live, and now my life is done.

My tale was heard, and yet it was not told;
    My fruit is fall'n, and yet my leaves are green;
My youth is spent, and yet I am not old;
    I saw the world, and yet I was not seen:
My thread is cut, and yet it is not spun;
And now I live, and now my life is done.

I sought my death, and found it in my womb;
    I looked for life, and saw it was a shade;
I trod the earth, and knew it was my tomb;
    And now I die, and now I was but made:
My glass is full, and now my glass is run;
And now I live, and now my life is done.

Chidiock Tichborne (1558–1586)

QUESTIONS

1. Tichborne was executed in 1586 for having conspired to assassinate Queen Elizabeth and to give the throne of England to Mary Stuart. He protested his innocence at first, but at last confessed to the crime. How does the series of balanced, yet contradictory statements convey his emotion?

2. The midsection of each line in the first two stanzas may be read quickly, but in the third stanza, a noticeable slowing occurs. Would anything be lost if the third stanza moved as the first two; if, for example, in lines 13, 14, and 15, "yet" were substituted for "found," "saw," and "knew"? Can you generalize that the more nouns and verbs a statement has the slower it will move?

3. How is the movement altered if the word "but" is removed from the first three lines?

4. This poem was put to music several times shortly after it was first published in a collection of poems celebrating Queen Elizabeth's escape from the "Babington" plot in which Tichborne confessed complicity. What qualities does it have which would lend it to musical accompaniment?

Tichborne's poem, however touched we may be by his personal tragedy, has not lasted all these years because of its autobiographical interest. He was a conscious artist working in a vein well known to the Tudor poets who went before. In some respects Tichborne's poem resembles one by Thomas Wyatt which is given below; it is an adaptation of one of Petrarch's sonnets, "*Pace non trovo et non ó da far guerra.*" Compare the rhythmical effects in Wyatt's poem with those of Tichborne. As another biographical note, Thomas Wyatt himself was twice imprisoned for capital offenses—once charged with adultery with Anne Boleyn and once charged with treason. Luckily for him, he was able on both occasions to regain his freedom and his favor with King Henry VIII.

### *I Find No Peace*

I find no peace and all my war is done,
  I fear and hope, I burn and freeze like ice,
  I fly above the wind, yet can I not arise,
  And naught I have and all the world I seize on;
That looseth nor locketh holdeth me in prison
  And holdeth me not, yet can I 'scape nowise;
  Nor letteth me live nor die at my devise°, *wish*
  And yet of death it giveth none occasion.
Without eyen, I see; and without tongue I plain°; *complain*
  I desire to perish, and yet I ask health;
  I love another, and thus I hate myself;
I feed me in sorrow, and laugh in all my pain.
  Likewise displeaseth me both death and life,
  And my delight is causer of this strife.

Sir Thomas Wyatt (1503–1542)

Part of the pleasure in reading poems comes with noticing how a writer will make his words go and pause in time with the subject at hand. Even the simplest observations have been sharpened with this kind of wit in rhythm and sound. The effect may be as comic as Armour's lines on catsup:

*Going to Extremes*

Shake and shake
  The catsup bottle.
None will come,
  And then a lot'll.

Richard Armour (1906– )

Or as serious as this poem by A. E. Housman:

*Eight O'Clock*

He stood, and heard the steeple
  Sprinkle the quarters on the morning town.
One, two, three, four, to market-place and people
  It tossed them down.

Strapped, noosed, nighing his hour,
  He stood and counted them and cursed his luck;
And then the clock collected in the tower
  Its strength, and struck.

A. E. Housman (1859–1936)

QUESTIONS

1. Clearly, this poem involves many verbal devices besides rhythm, but the emphatic closing owes much to this element. How often and why does Housman change his pace in this poem?

2. How does the poet's use of series and punctuation affect lines 3 and 5? Does a list tend to slow down or speed up a statement?

3. In the seventh line, Housman places the phrase "in the tower" out of its usual order; normally one would say, "The clock in the tower collected its strength." How can you tell the poet did not use this arrangement simply to make the rhyme come out?

4. Until the second stanza, with the word "noosed," the reader may not

know exactly what the situation in the poem is. Does the rhythm in the first stanza in any way help to prepare the mood?

5. In England, eight o'clock is the traditional time for executions. What is particularly apt in the use of the words "quarters," and "morning" in line 2?

## *Apparently with no surprise*

Apparently with no surprise
To any happy Flower
The Frost beheads it at it's play—
In accidental power—
The blonde Assassin passes on—
The Sun proceeds unmoved
To measure off another Day
For an Approving God.

Emily Dickinson (1830–1886)

### QUESTIONS

1. Why is the rhythm so regularly arranged in the first seven lines? Why should the last line break the rhythm?
2. Does the rhythm run with or against the sense in this poem? Why?

## *Meeting at Night*

The gray sea and the long black land;
And the yellow half-moon large and low;
And the startled little waves that leap
In fiery ringlets from their sleep,
As I gain the cove with pushing prow,
And quench its speed i' the slushy sand.

Then a mile of warm sea-scented beach;
Three fields to cross till a farm appears;
A tap at the pane, the quick sharp scratch
And blue spurt of a lighted match,
And a voice less loud, through its joys and fears,
Than the two hearts beating each to each!

Robert Browning (1812–1889)

### *Parting at Morning*

Round the cape of a sudden came the sea,
And the sun looked over the mountain's rim:
And straight was a path of gold for him,
And the need of a world of men for me.

Robert Browning (1812–1889)

## QUESTIONS

1. If you think these poems evoke the emotions which might precede and follow a secret meeting of lovers, how would you describe the dominant emotional impression left by the first poem? By the second poem?

2. Both stanzas in "Meeting at Night" are punctuated as complete sentences, yet, technically, neither is a complete sentence, since neither has a main verb. What effect comes with preparing the reader for a predicate that never comes?

3. How does punctuation and sentence structure affect "Parting at Morning"? Does the presence of three main verbs in this poem tend to make you read slower or more quickly? Do you seem to drop your voice more often in this poem?

4. For the fullest appreciation of these poems, analyze Browning's use of words evoking sense impressions. How are the rhythm and imagery dependent on each other in these poems?

We should not overlook the fact that poetry has more than just accentual rhythm, though this kind is perhaps most fundamental. There are other rhythms based on the repetition and variation of sound, though this variety may be more relevantly discussed later in connection with rhyme, alliteration, and consonance. In passing, however, we might notice the musical effects produced by the interflow of stress and sound rhythms. The first line of Coleridge's "Kubla Kahn" makes a good example:

In Xanadu did Kubla Kahn

We first notice the rocking of stress between alternate syllables, but a less obvious rhythm affects us simultaneously as the vowels in the stressed syllables go: "ah-oo-oo-ah."

Poets set up other rhythms by varying the length of their lines and by arranging resting places between groups of lines. Also, in passing, we should not overlook the rhythms inherent in any English sentence. Here, units of sound larger than the syllable come into play. Nouns, verbs, adjectives, and adverbs, in general, get more emphasis than articles, prepositions, and conjunctions. Short prepositional phrases gallop or skip, while parenthetical interruptions slow sentence movement. In prose writing as in speech we do not often take great pains to arrange for rhythmical effects. The spoken word, which allows less opportunity for revision than the written, may be given emphasis by raising or lowering the volume, and by altering the tone of the voice. Still, most sentences may be rearranged without undue distortion of the normal word order patterns. The rhythm of poetry evolves from the poet's arranging words carefully into the most appropriate rhythmical patterns.

### *Meter*

Here are parts of two poems; one is metrical, the other not, though the poem which is not measured is no less poetic:

Let me know, O Lord, my end
And what is the number of my days,
That I may know how frail I am.
A short span you have made my days,
And my life is nought before you;
Only a breath is any human existence.
A phantom only, man goes his ways;
Like vapour only are his restless pursuits;
He heaps up stores, and knows not who will use them.

Psalm 39: 5–8 (*c.* 150 B.C.)

Oh threats of Hell and Hopes of Paradise!
One thing at least is certain—This Life flies;
    One thing is certain and the rest is Lies—
The Flower that once has blown forever dies.

Strange, is it not? that of the myriads who
Before us passed the door of Darkness through,
    Not one returns to tell us of the Road,
Which to discover we must travel too.

from *The Rubáiyát of Omar Khayyám*
Edward FitzGerald (1809–1883)

Rhythm, equally important in both of these passages, is measured or counted out regularly in the second. Since the author of the second passage set rhythmical boundaries for himself when he decided to make each line ten syllables long and to give every other syllable an accent, we can understand his purpose and method if we have a few basic terms to work with. The Psalms of David, most often printed as prose, are printed above as verse, with indentations and the conventional capitalization of each line, in order to give some visual indication that they have a strong rhythmical quality. Between the relatively loose arrangement of the Psalms and the strict four line units of the Rubáiyát, lie many degrees of regularity, some of which may be analyzed for their meter.

Up to this point we have deliberately avoided mentioning most terms used in the discussion of meter. There are two main reasons for this. First, everyone reacts to rhythm and *knows* that he reacts, though it is only when he begins to pay attention to the "how" and "why" of his reaction that he starts to notice the poet's work with appreciation. Only then does he have much use for special terminology. Second, meter is not characteristic of all poetry. By definition, *meter* is the measurement and arrangement of rhythm in a poem. In free verse and in the more relaxed forms of recent poetry, the poet may work for greater spontaneity in verse by avoiding the confines of prearrangement in "metered" forms. Still, in many poems, including most older ones, the writer may rely less on rhythms he can improvise and more on a set pattern to which he provisionally commits himself, breaking away from it only when a sense of fitness requires. In studying poems written in this fashion a reader may arrive at a detailed understanding of the art of the work if he is familiar with the basics of metrical form which the poet had in mind.

The frequently proposed objection to studying metrics, that knowledge about them is irrelevant to appreciating poetry, would be difficult to justify. Nevertheless, one can quickly arrive at the point of diminishing returns, when a whole lot more of technical information returns but little in the way of enjoyment. Only the most doctrinaire rebel against this study would deny that rhythms are *controlled* and varied by the poet to suit subject mood and ideas. The mechanical ways through which the poet controls this rhythm may be studied by scansion.

*Scansion*

Scansion begins with discovering the standard of measure in a poem. The basic unit, called a *foot,* consists usually of one accented syllable, plus one or not more than three unaccented syllables. The customary arrangements, with stressed and unstressed syllables marked ( / and ⌣) are:

| | | |
|---|---|---|
| *Dupal* | *Iambic* | To tell / the truth, / I do. |
| | *Trochaic* | Go and / watch the / little / children. |
| *Triple* | *Anapestic* | There's a list / of the peo/ple who went. |
| | *Dactyllic* | Turn to the / left when you / feel like it. |

Five additional measures, useful mainly in describing irregular arrangements which occur along with the above are:

| | |
|---|---|
| *Spondaic* | Each day, / men die. |
| *Amphimacer* | Every man / tells his son / how to act. |
| *Amphibrach* | The truth of / the matter / of course is / a secret. |
| *Anapestic paeon* | In the begin/ning was the word. |
| *Dactyllic paeon* | Joyfully and / eagerly they / recognized his / masterliness. |

Statements in English do not lend themselves to sustained use of these measures, and they are of little use in all but the most technical discussions. A pair of unaccented syllables which do not appear to accompany an accented syllable are called a *pyrrhic.* In this line from Shelley, two unstressed sounds at the beginning of a line precede the start of the dominant rhythm:

As from / thy pre/sence showers / a rain / of mel/ody

In any of the examples given, the use of the two symbols (◡ and /) would be an oversimplification, if this usage were taken to mean that there are only two degrees of stress. In polysyllabic words like "romanticism" and "education," and in most sentences, all the stressed syllables are clearly not the same. But, since any sound is stressed or not, relative to the sounds immediately surrounding it, the use of two symbols conveniently serves the purpose of scanning. Much of the unusual effect of variation derives from this difference in degree. A reader who insists on seeing a statement in only one possible way will inevitably get into arguments about scansion which, though mechanical, does not operate with the regularity of a clock. Though any given word should be pronounced according to ordinary usage, the accents in any statement of more than one word may shift from word to word according to the emphasis intended. According to this, no one would say "poétry," stressing the middle syllable, yet the sentence: "I want to drive her to the station," might be said with greatest stress on any word except, perhaps, "to" or "the." The sense of the words in verse should always be the guide in assigning stress. Thus, in order to indicate in the above sentence that the speaker is not acting out a sense of duty, but on the basis of a sincere desire, he would say: "I *want* to take you to the station."

Once we agree what the poet's basic unit of rhythm is, the next step is to see how often he uses this unit in each line. The meter is classed according to the number of feet per line. Terms used to describe meter are as follows:

| | |
|---|---|
| *monometer* | one foot |
| *dimeter* | two feet |
| *trimeter* | three feet |
| *tetrameter* | four feet |
| *pentameter* | five feet |
| *hexameter* | six feet |
| *heptameter* | seven feet |
| *octometer* | eight feet |
| *nonometer* | nine feet |

The first five of these are illustrated in the following selection:

from *An Ode to Him*

(monometer) Ah Ben!
(dimeter) Say how, / or when /
Shall we / thy guests /
(trimeter) Meet at / those Lyr/ick Feasts /
(dimeter) Made / at the Sun,
(trimeter) The Dog, / the Tri/ple Tunne? /
Where we / such clus/ters had /
(tetrameter) As made / us nob/ly wild, / not mad; /
And yet / each verse / of thine /
(pentameter) Out-did / the meat, / out-did / the fro/lick wine. /

Robert Herrick (1591–1674)

The poem might be described as being mainly iambic, arranged in rhymed couplets with line length varying from monometer to pentameter. The alternation between long and short lines creates a rhythm within the rhythm. Herrick made the rhymes surprising by placing them at irregular intervals, and yet within an iambic pattern interrupted only once, in the fourth line. The interruption lightens the otherwise somber tone to fit the sense of the line.

Most poems do not contain the variety of this one by Herrick, but the process of scansion is the same. After reading through the poem several times, first, determine metrical foot; second, notice the line length; third, describe the rhyme scheme, if any; and fourth, account for any irregularities. Notice if lines are arranged in clusters which follow similar metrical patterns. Such groupings are called *stanzas*.

Lines longer than pentameter are scarce in English verse, though some successful poems have been done in hexameter and heptameter. When these long lines have three syllables to the foot, the galloping pace grows quickly wearisome. Algernon Swinburne's "Hymn of Man" goes on for 200 lines of anapestic hexameter, concluding with this statement on the theme of the death of God:

> Thou art smit/ten, thou God, / thou art smit/ten, //
>     thy death / is upon / thee, O Lord /
> And the love/-song of earth / as thou diest // resounds /
>     through the wind / of her wings — /
> Glory to Man / in the High/est! // For Man / is the mas/ter
>     of things. /
>
> Algernon Charles Swinburne (1834–1896)

The tendency in reading lines such as these is to pause after the third foot, so that the poem seems to be arranged in 400 sets of three rather than 200 sets of six. The strong pause within a line of poetry, punctuated or not, is called a *caesura,* and is marked //, as above. Hexameter more often occurs as a variation on pentameter, as in the *Spenserian stanza,* in which the ninth line is iambic hexameter, following eight of iambic pentameter.

Some types of lines have been given special names. Five iambic feet are called *blank verse,* if there is no rhyme. Lines of six iambic feet are called *alexandrines,* after the French poet, Alexander Paris. Iambic heptameter lines, called *"fourteeners,"* are, like alexandrines, rare. Whereas the alexandrines tend to break up into a set of trimeter lines, the "fourteeners" break up into phrases of four and three feet, since the caesura falls after the fourth accent, as a rule. George Chapman used fourteeners in his translation of Homer, perhaps in an attempt to preserve the oral tradition of the Greek epics by imitating the movement of the ballad, a folk poem. In general, the longer the line, the more weighty the effect; but the pentameter line has proven to be the longest manageable line in works of great length. Research has shown that the 1,000 most used words in English are predominantly from the largely monosyllabic Old English word stock. This means that a sequence of ten or twelve or fourteen syllables is likely to have more individual words than a line of equal length in a more polysyllabic tongue, and that the normal phrase groupings in English will, on the average, have fewer syllables.

In scanning a poem, as you look for some apparent norm, avoid making hasty conclusions based on a reading of the first line or so. In fact, the first line is the one most likely to be irregular. Preferably, you should go through the entire poem or read at least six or seven lines aloud in search of the dominant pattern or repetition. It is this dominant pattern that sets up a sense of expectancy in the mind; then, any departure from the norm produces an irresistible effect. The whole object of scanning is to discover to what end the poet uses repetitions and variations—to become aware of an effect which is subconscious. Psychologically, we are often awakened to attention by some break of rhythm, as when a dripping faucet, which may for a long time go unnoticed, alters its beat and becomes the most obvious of sounds. Shifts in the wind, in the chirping of insects, or the sound of an engine all have their psychological responses.

The effect of meter may be lost entirely on the reader who approaches the poem as some strange and remote language. If one is to catch the feel of a poem's basic movement, he must read it in the most normal way possible; the meter is in the arrangement, not in some superimposed and artificial system of accents. In all probability, the poet has tried to avoid the nursery rhyme, singsong effect; the reader should honor this intention. Finally, since the sound and not the appearance of a poem provides the rhythm, one must pronounce words as he knows them, not as he sees them. Thus "missed" is a word of one syllable, "partial," a word of two syllables. Since meter is based on syllabification, not word units, the reader should be more attuned for the segments of sound and not hesitate to see the metrical foot as being composed of parts of different words. Customarily, the rhyme scheme is noted in the scansion of rhymed verse.

The final step in scansion may be naming the stanzaic form, if, in fact, the poem uses one of the stanza patterns familiar enough to have been given a name. *Stanzas,* sometimes called *strophes,* are groups of two or more recurring line patterns. They are classed according to the number of lines, the meter, and the rhyme scheme. Beginning with the two-line stanza and proceeding to units of greater length, some of the best known patterns are as follows:

*couplet* Two rhymed lines of any length. If the couplet is a complete grammatical unit and can stand as an independent statement, it is called "closed." The heroic couplet is a closed couplet in iambic pentameter. Eight syllable couplets are called *Hudabristic verse.*

*tercet* Three rhyming lines of any length. Either one of the two sets of three lines which go to make up the sestet in an Italian sonnet may also be called a tercet.

*terza rima* Sets of three lines with the second line of any given three rhyming with the first and third lines in the following set: *a b a, b c b, c d c,* etc. Iambic tetrameter or pentameter are the most frequently used meters.

*quatrain* A stanza of four lines, with or without rhyme, and unrestricted in line length. The *ballad stanza,* one form of the quatrain, rhymes *a b c b,* with the first and third lines having four stressed syllables and the second and fourth having three.

Though there is no stanza of five lines which has been given a name, the *limerick* is a five-line unit in anapests. It rhymes *a a b b a,* with the first, second, and fifth lines consisting of three feet and the third and fourth having two.

*sestet* The six lines, usually of iambic pentameter, rhyming *c d e c d e,* which go to make up the second part of an Italian sonnet. Various other rhyme schemes are also used.

*rime royal* Seven lines of iambic pentameter rhyming *a b a b b c c.* The form was used by Chaucer and others, but named for King James I of Scotland who wrote in the form.

*octave* Any eight line stanza, but specifically the first eight lines of the Italian sonnet usually rhyming *a b b a a b b a.*

*ottava rima* Eight lines of iambic pentameter rhyming

*a b a b a b c c.* The form, borrowed from Italian poetry, is said to have been invented by Boccaccio.

*spencerian stanza* A stanza of nine lines, the first eight of which are in iambic pentameter, followed by a single alexandrine (iambic hexameter). The rhyme scheme is *a b a b b c b c c.* This form is named after the sixteenth-century poet, Edmund Spenser.

There should be little difficulty in hearing the basic pattern of meter and its variations in the following sonnet by Shakespeare, which we have previously analyzed for its figurative language.

That time / of year // thou mayst / in me / behold a
When yel/low leaves, // or none, // or few, / do hang b
Upon / those boughs // which shake / against / the cold, a
*Bare / ruin'd choirs,* // where late / the sweet / birds sang. b
In me // thou see'st / the twi/light of / such day c
As af/ter sun/set fad/eth in / the west, d
Which by / and by // *black night* / doth take / away, c
*Death's se*/cond self, // that seals / up all / in rest. d
In me / thou see'st // the glow/ing of / such fire, e
That on / the ash/es of / his youth / doth lie, b
As the *death-bed* // whereon / it must / expire, e
Consum'd / with that // which it / was nour/ish'd by. f
*This thou* / perceiv'st // which makes / thy love /
more strong g
To love / *that well* // which thou / must leave / ere long. g

No two readers will be likely to agree in every detail about how this poem should sound, but the main drift of the beat and the key variations on it will stir little debate. Shakespeare uses accented syllables in at least five or six places where the weak stress is expected. The first four (which I have italicized) focus the attention on the bleakness of the scene and on the subject of death. The final departures from the norm accompany a shift of tone which comes in the concluding set of two lines, or couplet. When Shakespeare wrote this poem speakers of English might or might not pronounce the verb endings, "eth," "est," and "ed," as separate syllables as they saw fit; but the poet, through his spelling in this case, indicated that he did not intend the endings to be pronounced separately. Historically, in fact, the first stage in the disappearance of such endings was in the loss of distinction as shown in this poem.

One does not need to be a specialist to use scansion to advantage, as an analysis of the Shakespearean sonnet given above or of almost any piece of traditional verse would illustrate. What happens in too many classrooms, however, is that not enough tolerance is exercised when the apparent "natural" reading rendered by one person seems less than natural to another. This is not to say that it is impossible to misread a poem through a misreading of the meter, just that room must be reserved for the differences that individual personalities make on the interpretation of any poem.

Since the first and most obvious difference between prose and poetry is that the latter is written in verse, that is, written with a systematic arrangement of rhythm, no one with a wish to appreciate poetry can afford to overlook the function of the verse. It is through verse that the poet gains control of the language. This control comes first, through the usefulness of verse in focusing the reader's attention; for the design of the meter, once we become accustomed to it, produces the expectation that the design will continue. Our expectations are constantly being fulfilled or frustrated by the regularity or irregularity of the meter. Secondly, and especially when used in conjunction with rhyme, verse is a keen instrument for tying the divisions of a poem together. Thus a subtle shift may be to the ear what the indentation is to the eye. Finally and perhaps most importantly, verse supports meaning in ways too numerous to list. As Coleridge has put it, verse acts "as a medicated atmosphere, or as a wine during animated conversation, [when] the anticipations set up by the meter act powerfully, though themselves unnoticed."

Sonnet 130 by Shakespeare is given below, as he wrote it, along with a version amended to disturb the rhythm without affecting the other poetic elements. Needless to say, the changes do not improve the poem. Read both versions and decide which one is authentic.

*A*

My mistress' eyes are nothing like the sun;
Her lips are not so red as coral's red:
If snow be white, why then her breasts are dun;
If hairs be wires, black wires do crown her head.
I've seen the damasked roses, red and white,
But no such roses see I in her cheeks;
And many perfumes give me more delight
Than all the breath that from my mistress reeks.
I love to hear her speak, yet well I know
That music hath a far more pleasing sound;
I grant I never saw a goddess go;
And when my mistress walks, she treads on ground:
  And yet, by Jove, I think my love as rare
  As any she belied with false compare.

*B*

My mistress' eyes are nothing like the sun:
Coral is far more red than her lips' red:
If snow be white, why then her breasts are dun;
If hairs be wires, black wires grow on her head.
I have seen roses damask'd red and white,
But no such roses see I in her cheeks;
And in some perfumes is there more delight
Than in the breath that from my mistress reeks.
I love to hear her speak, but well I know
That music hath a far more pleasing sound.
I grant I never saw a goddess go;
My mistress, when she walks, treads on the ground:
  And yet, by heaven, I think my love as rare
  As any she belied with false compare.

## QUESTIONS

1. Which poem more regularly conforms to the iambic pattern?
2. In the version which contains the irregularities, what idea is being expressed at any given point of departure from the pattern? Compare, for example, lines 5, 7, and 12 in "A" with 5, 7, and 12 in "B".
3. Which poem shows the greatest correlation between the idea expressed and the tone conveyed by the rhythm?
4. Do irregularities ever produce a pleasant effect in either of these poems?

Thomas Campion (1567–1620), who was a contemporary of Shakespeare's (1564–1616), wrote the following poem which represents a kind of attitude often struck in the love poems of the day. Shakespeare's sonnet 130 satirizes this kind of elaborate compliment-paying by reversing the much over-used imagery. Campion's poem makes the most of the conventional language; its success depends largely on its musical effects. Scan the poem and try to notice how the meter affects the emotional tone. Would you alter any of the irregularities?

### *There Is a Garden in Her Face*

There is a garden in her face,
Where roses and white lilies grow;
A heavenly paradise is that place,
Wherein all pleasant fruits do flow.
There cherries grow which none may buy,
Till "Cherry-ripe" themselves do cry.

Those cherries fairly do enclose
Of orient pearl a double row,
Which when her lovely laughter shows,
They look like rosebuds filled with snow.
Yet them nor peer nor prince can buy,
Till "Cherry-ripe" themselves do cry.

Her eyes like angels watch them still;
Her brows like bended bows do stand,
Threatening with piercing frowns to kill
All that attempt with eye or hand
Those sacred cherries to come nigh,
Till "Cherry-ripe" themselves do cry.

We will end this chapter with a modern poem that is both formal and free. It would also make a fine example of word play, imagery, and figurative language, so be sure not to scan the poem until you have enjoyed all its music and good humor. Just as Shakespeare's and Campion's praise of a woman are typically Elizabethan, Roethke's is perfectly modern.

*I Knew a Woman*

I knew a woman, lovely in her bones,
When small birds sighed, she would sigh back at them;
Ah, when she moved, she moved more ways than one:
The shapes a bright container can contain!
Of her choice virtues only gods should speak,
Or English poets who grew up on Greek
(I'd have them sing in chorus, cheek to cheek).

How well her wishes went! She stroked my chin,
She taught me Turn, and Counter-turn, and Stand;
She taught me Touch, that undulant white skin;
I nibbled meekly from her proffered hand;
She was the sickle; I, poor I, the rake,
Coming behind her for her pretty sake
(But what prodigious mowing we did make).

Love likes a gander, and adores a goose:
Her full lips pursed, the errant note to seize;
She played it quick, she played it light and loose;
My eyes, they dazzled at her flowing knees;
Her several parts could keep a pure repose,
Or one hip quiver with a mobile nose
(She moved in circles, and those circles moved).

Let seed be grass, and grass turn into hay:
I'm martyr to a motion not my own;
What's freedom for? To know eternity.
I swear she cast a shadow white as stone.
But who would count eternity in days?
These old bones live to learn her wanton ways:
(I measure time by how a body sways).

Theodore Roethke (1908–1963)

## QUESTIONS

1. Explain how timing or meter is thematically important in this work.
2. How does the imagery of motion bear upon the movement of the lines?
3. Notice the meter of each seventh line (the line in parentheses). Is there any purpose served in the regularity here? Would you say, after scanning the poem, that it is metrical?
4. Explain the puns in lines 12 and 15. What other signs of joking do you see? Does the poet's lighthearted tone influence the way you read, and therefore scan, the poem?

*Chapter 11*

# Patterns in Rhythm

THE primary aim of this chapter is to build upon the fundamentals of rhythm, meter, and scansion by introducing a few of the better known approaches to versification. Its secondary purpose is to show how, at given times in the development of poetry, definite trends become evident. Finally, since no survey of trends can reveal much about the rhythmical virtuosity of poets, the chapter ends with a series of works remarkable for their use of rhythm.

## *Free Verse*

Poets are constantly experimenting with rhythmical and metrical devices, though the one constant value always to be expected is rhythm. In the twentieth century the drift has tended to be away from the strict regularity of confining stanzaic forms and toward greater freedom from artificiality that may set in when a poet commits himself to a set format. This drift accounts for the widespread use of free verse by twentieth century poets who have sought to preserve the sense of vitality that crumbles when verse becomes too mechanical. *Free verse* is said to be polyrhythmical because it has no commitment to the foot as a unit of measure. In speaking of free verse, we find words such as tetrameter and dactyl all but useless since the thought or mood groupings guide the composition without much regard for line length. Stephen Crane (1871–1900) was writing this kind of verse well before it came into its present widespread usage. In the poem below, Crane uses free verse in presenting a sharp, puzzling, almost oriental image.

*The Heart*

In the desert
I saw a creature, naked, bestial,
Who, squatting upon the ground,
Held his heart in his hands,
And ate of it.
I said, "Is it good, friend?"
"It is bitter—bitter," he answered;
"But I like it
Because it is bitter
And because it is my heart."

Without presuming perfect agreement about the stress markings tentatively supplied for Crane's poem, we will find that about half of the syllables are stressed (29 of the 62 syllables) as in the dupal meters, which helps to support the steady seriousness of the poem. Little can be gained by pointing out that "he answered," is an amphibrach, or that the lines,

I said, "Is it good, friend?"
"It is bitter—bitter," he answered.

contain iambic, anapestic, pyrrhic, amphibrach, and monosyllabic feet. The likelihood of such a combination is always present when verse is polyrhythmic. What is worth noticing, however, is that the poet uses his stops and starts to great mood-evoking advantage, and that his use of "friend" which, as a single accented word, standing alone at the end of a line, calls emphatic attention to itself and is most effective.

Some free verse is rhymed, some is arranged in stanzas, and sometimes it appears in conjunction with measured verse. Hence any attempt to describe and exemplify it fully would be futile. This type of verse is one of the oldest forms, familiar to all in poems as ancient as the Psalms of the Old Testament. To the inexperienced reader and to those who would like to write poetry without troubling to learn about meter, free verse seems to be an "easy" form. In fact, it requires the greatest control on the part of the poet who must find the shaping rhythms within himself, constantly adapting form to content. It is no wonder that in past times poets have often found the stricter forms to be liberating.

Three short selections by Walt Whitman (1819–1892) should provide good examples of free verse in which the poet makes the rhythms adapt to the sense.

### *When I Heard the Learn'd Astronomer*

When I heard the learn'd astronomer,
When the proofs, the figures, were ranged in columns before me,
When I was shown the charts and diagrams, to add, divide, and measure them,
When I sitting heard the astronomer where he lectured with much applause in the lecture-room,
How soon unaccountable I became tired and sick,
Till rising and gliding out I wandered off by myself,
In the mystical moist night-air, and from time to time
Look'd up in perfect silence at the stars.

#### QUESTIONS

1. The sense of this poem is based on a simple contrast. Where does a change in the rhythm occur?
2. The poem is comprised of one sentence, beginning with four adverbial clauses in parallel construction. Do you notice any progression in length or complexity in the four clauses? To what purpose? Does the rhythm recreate Whitman's sense of growing discomfort?
3. In the fifth line, why doesn't Whitman say "unaccountably" instead of "unaccountable"?

### *The Dalliance of the Eagles*

Skirting the river road, (my forenoon walk, my rest,)
Skyward in air a sudden muffled sound, the dalliance of the eagles,
The rushing amorous contact high in space together,
The clinching interlocking claws, a living, fierce, gyrating wheel,
Four beating wings, two beaks, a swirling mass tight grappling,

In tumbling turning clustering loops, straight downward falling,
Till o'er the river pois'd, the twain yet one, a moment's lull,
A motionless still balance in the air, then parting, talons loosing,
Upward again on slow-firm pinions slanting, their separate
diverse flight,
She hers, he his, pursuing.

QUESTIONS

1. Here again Whitman paces his rhythms to fit the subject. What effect does he gain by using so many participles as modifiers for the nouns? Why is the poet so careful to avoid a clear-cut, independent clause?

2. Do you think the fact that so many of the nouns are associated with action is accidental? (See "contact," "claws," "wheels," "wings," "loops," etc.)

3. Where do you notice shifts in rhythm from rough to smooth? Would you call the poem polyrhythmic?

## *Cavalry Crossing a Ford*

A line in long array where they wind betwixt green islands,
They take a serpentine course, their arms flash in the sun—
hark to the musical clank,
Behold the silvery river, in it the splashing horses loitering stop
to drink,
Behold the brown-faced men, each group, each person a
picture, the negligent rest on the saddles,
Some emerge on the opposite bank, others are just entering the
ford—while,
Scarlet and blue and snowy white,
The guidon flags flutter gayly in the wind.

QUESTIONS

1. Like "The Dalliance of the Eagles," this poem seeks to create a mental image involving action, but unlike it, "Cavalry Crossing a Ford" vivifiies a different kind of movement. How does Whitman use the movement of words to evoke a sense of the moving cavalry?

2. Why does Whitman ignore the conventions of punctuation? How does this affect the rhythm?

3. Why does Whitman use so many finite verbs (verbs that could be the main verb in a sentence), whereas he used none in "The Dalliance of the Eagles"?

The great difficulty with reading free verse is that, before you can make a judgment about the rhythm, you must understand what the poet is trying to accomplish. In reading metered poetry, deviations from the metrical norm call attention to themselves, and the reader is in effect signaled to note and, if he wishes, evaluate the deviation.

### *Sprung Rhythm*

One further term which has come into use in analyzing verse is *"sprung rhythm,"* coined by Gerard Manley Hopkins to describe a kind of meter he used which maintained regularity of stressed syllables, but not of unstressed. A foot consists of one, two, three, or four syllables, and every foot begins with an accent. The effect of this kind of verse is greatly irregular meter which may be difficult to read unless accent marks are supplied by the poet. To Hopkins, sprung rhythm's appeal rests in its ability to follow the natural rhythms of speech. Though he coined the term, Hopkins did not regard sprung rhythm as new to English verse. In fact, verse based on the number of accents per line goes back to Anglo-Saxon poetry. The following poem has four stresses, with a variable number of unaccented syllables per line. The accents have been supplied by the poet to guide the reader. Though the strangeness of the rhythm makes the poem somewhat difficult to read correctly the first time through, the musical effects are especially appealing.

*Spring and Fall:*

*to a young child*

Márgarét, áre you gríeving
Over Goldengrove unleaving?
Leáves, líke the things of man, you
With your fresh thoughts care for, can you?
Áh! ás the heart grows older
It will come to such sights colder
By and by, nor spare a sigh
Though worlds of wanwood leafmeal lie;
And yet you wíll weep and know why.
Now no matter, child, the name:
Sórrow's spríngs áre the same.

Nor mouth had, no nor mind, expressed
What heart heard of, ghost guessed:
It ís the blight man was born for,
It is Margaret you mourn for.

Gerard Manley Hopkins (1844–1889)

QUESTIONS

1. The poet has taken great pains to keep the tone of this poem from becoming over-sentimental. The short rhymed lines could easily have become a singsong. How does the sprung rhythm give the poet control?

2. There is much latitude in spoken English about which words in a sentence get greatest stress, but almost none with the accentuation of syllables. Do you notice anything unusual about the accents supplied by Hopkins? What effect is gained by having the reader stress the first and third syllables of "Márgarét" (line 1), "líke" (line 3), "ás" (line 5)?

3. "Unleaving" (line 2) is formed by analogy with "undressing," and means, taking off its leaves; "leafmeal" (line 8), by analogy with "piecemeal," means leaf by leaf; "wanwood" (line 8), means dark woods. Do these coinages of Hopkins seem convincing in a poem addressed to a young child? Would they be any more appropriate if addressed to an adult? What is their purpose and effect?

4. The title of the poem suggests not only spring and fall of the year, but of youth and age, and the creation and fall of man in Christian lore. Can you interpret the poem to mean that there are intimations of death sensed, but not understood, even in childhood? Is the meaning broader than this?

5. How does the meter of this poem differ from free verse?

## *Quantitative Metrics Versus Accentualist Metrics*

Students of poetry have often been sidetracked in trying to understand metrics because of some basic disagreements about the essential nature of rhythm in English. As in most such debates, neither side is altogether satisfactory. The most ancient theory is *quantitative,* based on the notion that some syllables take longer to say than others, and that metrical feet may be classed on the basis of this principle. The crucial question is whether the pronunciation of English words should be guided by a sense of time or of stress. The *accentualist* argues that stress forms the basis, even though, for rhetorical purposes, words may be said slower or faster as befits the occasion. In fact, the syllables that would be called "long" by the advocate of quantitative metrics would be called "stressed" by the accentualist. For practical purposes, since all dictionary directions for pronunciation are based on the placement and degree of stress, the accentualist approach seems most usable. The ear which can distinguish time duration distinctions is a rare instrument. Moreover, being able to classify vowel sounds according to length helps little in the description of meter because those vowels traditionally described as "long" appear as often as not in unaccented positions. We can add to this the fact that the common usage of the terms "long" and "short" are largely inaccurate. The "a" in "hate," commonly called a "long a," is actually a diphthong. The so-called "long o" of "tote" takes no longer to say than the "short o" of "tot."

Poets who have taken a particular interest in metrical techniques, from Campion to Auden, have experimented successfully with quantitative metrics, often closely imitating highly complex forms. Thomas Campion, a musician, strongly favored quantitative verse as having the highest claim to musicality. When the sense of vowel length and timing is well-rendered, he held, the need for less subtle devices of sound such as rhyme become unnecessary. Below is a poem in which Campion puts his theory to the test. It has been called one of the most successful unrhymed lyrics in English poetry.

*Rose-cheeked Laura*

Rose-cheeked Laura, come,
Sing thou smoothly with thy beauty's
Silent music, either other
Sweetly gracing.

Lovely forms do flow
From concent divinely framed;
Heaven is music, and thy beauty's
Birth is heavenly.

These dull notes we sing
Discords need for helps to grace them;
Only beauty purely loving
Knows no discord.

But still moves delight,
Like clear springs renewed by flowing,
Ever perfect, ever in themselves
Eternal.

Thomas Campion (1567–1620)

QUESTIONS

1. Though this poem was written according to quantitative theory, scan it for its pattern of stress. What type of metrical foot occurs most frequently? Do you get a sense of lengthened sound accompanying the stressed syllables?

2. What effect does Campion gain by beginning each line with a stress? Can you hold the stressed syllables naturally, that is, without distorting the sense of the lines?

3. In the old sense of the word, a lyric is a poem intended to be sung. In singing, words are held or stopped in accord with the music. Do you think the reading of a poem without music can use this kind of movement? Try rereading this poem, slightly exaggerating the time used to say stressed syllables.

Regardless of how successful Campion's verse was, certain facts about English make the accentualist approach seem more manageable in the analysis of poetry. Most statements in English tend to accent every other syllable. This is because we stress words of one syllable according to whether we wish to emphasize them or not, and with polysyllabic words each syllable has a fixed accent which is usually distinct from syllables preceding or following. The student may well ask how it is possible to tell the difference between an iambic line and a trochaic line. Probably, it does not make much difference so long as one notices the alternation between stressed and unstressed words. Meters based on two syllable units are most widely used, for they make a steady foundation from which the poet may depart by adding extra stressed syllables to slow the beat or extra unstressed syllables to speed it up. Most poetry in English which has a serious tone has the basis of two syllables. The epic and the sonnet, for example, use iambic pentameter with each line composed of five iambs:

⌣ / | ⌣ / | ⌣ / | ⌣ / | ⌣ /

It is difficult to find long stretches of verse that are clearly trochaic, in which the stressed syllables seem to be exaggerated. Take the words from the familiar song, "Í Căn't Gíve Yŏu Ány̆-

thing but Love, Baby"; without the music it would be impossible to say exactly how the words should be stressed. Superimpose the music and you have an emphatic example of the trochee.

Of the feet based on three syllables, it is safe to say that the anapest is commonest, though one is unlikely to find many poems with an anapestic framework. The anapest occurs frequently in prepositional phrases and is less difficult to manage than the dactyl. In Latin however, to illustrate that the generalizations about meter in one language do not apply to another, the dactyl turns up frequently and is even the common unit in Latin epic poetry, which favors dactylic hexameter.

There is no recipe telling poets when to use one type of metrical foot over another, yet definite moods have come to be associated with the types of movement produced by each metrical foot. "Dupal" measures, which are made up of two syllables, particularly the iambus, trochee, and spondee, tend to move at a slower rate than the dactyl and anapest, called "triple" measures. The spondee creates the effect of a very deliberate, staccatto march. The iambus moves deliberately and seriously, but at a greater speed, while the trochee has a skipping effect though it does not actually move faster than the iambus. The movement of the anapest is associated with a free, galloping stride, and the dactyl with a more controlled but no less lively pace. These characteristics are both explained (in quantitative terms) and memorably illustrated in the following verses by Coleridge:

Trochee trips from long to short.
From long to long in solemn sort
Slow Spondee stalks; strong foot! yet ill able
Ever to come up with Dactyl trisyllable.
Iambics march from short to long;—
With a leap and a bound the swift Anapests throng.
One syllable long, with one short at each side,
Amphibrachys haste with a stately stride.

Metrical Feet: Lesson for a Boy
Samuel Taylor Coleridge (1772–1834)

The line length also has an influence on the sense of movement, with the long line tending toward slowness, the short toward speed. When the poet selects a rhythm suitable to his thought and mood, he makes an art of what is and has always been instinctive to humanity. Heightened states of emotion have found their most apt form of expression in rhythmical movement. In all languages and in all times, poetry has been inseparable from rhythmic speech in its attempt to recreate the emotional aspects of experience. The poet as artist has consistently striven to strike some harmony between mood and movement, form and content.

One does not need to be a linguist to realize that every language has a music of its own. The rhythms of Chinese, French, or Russian sound distinctly different even to the untrained ear. Yet, the vocabulary for speaking of English metrics is based on terms used to describe the poetry of the ancient Greeks and Romans whose verse had a quantitative basis. The fact that we have come to imitate the ancients is no accident, for just at the time when modern English was developing, that is, in the years when it was beginning to look more like the language of today and less like that of Chaucer's day, the most talented writers were devoted to the imitation of works by the classical masters, and to the introduction into English verse of French and Italian poetic forms. In this stage of the renaissance in England (during the sixteenth century), the English language was undergoing a radical change in pronunciation, particularly in the way words of more than one syllable should be accented. It is not surprising then that writers such as Wyatt and Surrey turned toward the continent and the steadying influence of Petrarch. More than this, the educated classes, particularly anyone who was likely to write poetry, read and wrote Latin. In their attempt to bring to English some of the excellence of the ancients, they tried in some cases to superimpose the standards of Latin on English grammar and criticism.

### *Metrical Trends*

The history of poetry in English may be viewed as a cycle in which poets who strive to gain control over language through rhythm and meter are followed by those who try to free themselves from the confinement of strict measures. Poetry, like any vital organism, thrives because it constantly renews itself without ever losing its identity. Constantly evolving, poetry like politics goes through periods of advancement, solidification, advancement, solidification. And as in politics, yesterday's rebel is today's conservative. Perhaps no poet illustrates this fact so well as William Wordsworth, who, though he helped bring about one of the most dramatic revolutions in English literary history, the romantic movement, strikes readers of today as a conventional poet, sharing more with the eighteenth century than with the twentieth. And Robert Browning, who seems old fashioned to readers who do not have a sense of historical perspective, did as much as any poet of his century to advance the art of his day by adapting metrical verse to the spoken language. The tendency of scholars in trying to trace literary developments is to see trends more distinctly than the poets acting out the history would willingly admit. So it is that today, though one can easily name modern poets who widely use and even favor traditional forms, one can also look into the strictly conventional eighteenth century and find many poets whose work is as clearly romantic as Byron's.

In outline the metrical trends can be summarized as follows:

Old English—Accentual meter, based on the number of stresses rather than on the number of syllables. The four beat line without rhyme typifies the era.

Medieval—Accentual meter with general regularity in the number of syllables to a line. Appearance of rhyme helps to disguise the often clumsy rhythms which result from irregularity of pronunciation. During this period the language was undergoing rapid changes in pronunciation, grammar, and vocabulary which made control through meter particularly troublesome.

Renaissance—Increasing control through stricter meters in imitation of French and Italian models. This new control and the leveling off of changes in the structure of the language assisted poets in the mastery of longer lines for the treatment of serious subject matter. Development of blank verse; high point of dramatic poetry.

Late Renaissance—Increase of experimentation in search of new and freer forms. Verse metrical, but with a slant toward irregularity and eccentric rhythms.

Eighteenth Century—Renewed insistence upon strict order and decorum. Heightened sense of propriety, widespread use of the heroic couplet.

Romantic Movement—General reaction against the stultifying limitation of the previous era. Renewal of the spirit of experimentation. Conventions of meter upheld, but with insistence on wider variety.

Victorian Period—Metrically, a time of solidification, with the major poets building on the theory of the romantics. Beginning of radical experimentation directed at loosening the restrictions of metered verse.

Modern Era—General decline of reverence for confining meters. Increased use of free verse. Experimentation uninterrupted by any inclination to resume stricter conventions, though traditional forms flourish side by side with the new.

### *The Current Scene*

The emphasis here has been on traditional prosody, taking stressed sounds as the basic source for rhythm and meter. But in fact, almost anything can be a source of rhythm, and if you measure it, a source of meter. For example, there are visual rhythms which, by the arrangement of the words on the page, force a rhythmical movement of the eyes of the reader.

#### *Constantly risking absurdity*

Constantly risking absurdity
and death
whenever he performs
above the heads
of his audience
the poet like an acrobat
climbs on rime
to a high wire of his own making
and balancing on eyebeams
above a sea of faces

paces his way
to the other side of day
performing entrechats
and sleight-of-foot tricks
and other high theatrics
and all without mistaking
any thing
for what it may not be

For he's the super realist
who must perforce perceive
taut truth
before the taking of each stance or step
in his supposed advance
toward that still higher perch
where Beauty stands and waits
with gravity
to start her death-defying leap

And he
a little charleychaplin man
who may or may not catch
her fair eternal form
spreadeagled in the empty air
of existence

Lawrence Ferlinghetti (1919– )

With meters, as with rhythms, you can have spatial measurements or verbal ones. Anytime a poet makes a line long or short because of the way it affects the eye, he is using spatial meter. Most "shape" poems are in this category. A *"shape" poem* is one in which the typography is related to the meaning—an hourglass shape for a poem about time, for example. A great many stanzaic poems depend more on the way they look than on any measurement of words, syllables, or stresses. Examine the following, for example:

### *No One to Blame*

Birds move from branch to branch
with so little emotion. I think it is easy for them.
They splash in puddles of air,

fold their wings and fall
without caring how far, and do not touch the bottom.
There are no accidents.

It has all been planned for them.
We suppose they mourn their dead, and are good at keeping
secrets. It is not a matter

of kindness. The beaks are cruel.
It is a way they have of making evil. A passion.
To fill their stomachs? Yes.

But the bird-hearts are not troubled.
Or quiet. They are filled with a kind of rapture. In the open
air there is room for the terrible.

Do not listen for cries in the night.
One can learn to hear too well, if even the birds love
claws. There is no one to blame.

Laurence Lieberman (1935– )

QUESTIONS

1. Can you think of any reason why this poem should have this shape?
2. Do you see any rhythmic similarity among the first lines of each of the stanzas? Is there any resemblance common to the long middle lines? Can you give any reason for patterns of rhythmic repetition that you find?

Many modern poems have lines with set numbers of syllables or words. Lines measured by syllables are called syllabics. A poet may assign the same number of words or syllables to all the lines (a normative count) or he may establish an arrangement in the first stanza and repeat the same arrangement in all succeeding stanzas (a quantitative count). Notice the 3–1, 3–1, 3–1 count in the following poem.

*The Red Wheelbarrow*

so much depends
upon

a red wheel
barrow

glazed with rain
water

beside the white
chickens.

William Carlos Williams (1883–1963)

QUESTIONS

1. Is there any reason to regard this as a possible "shape" poem?
2. Does the way your eyes move from line to line have any bearing on the way the poem affects you?
3. Do you notice anything distinctive about the way the poet uses compound words?

Parallelism in phrasing is a much used basis for rhythm. Any series of prepositional phrases or dependent clauses, for example, can set up a rhythmical pattern. If overused, this kind of rhythm gets monotonous, but poets can often build powerful effects, as does Whitman or his disciple, Allen Ginsberg.

*A Supermarket in California*

1 What thoughts I have of you tonight, Walt Whitman, for I walked down the sidestreets under the trees with a headache self-conscious looking at the full moon.

2 In my hungry fatigue, and shopping for images, I went into the neon fruit supermarket, dreaming of your enumerations!

3 What peaches and what penumbras! Whole families shopping at night! Aisles full of husbands! Wives in the avocados, babies in the tomatoes! —and you, Garcia Lorca, what were you doing down by the watermelons?

4 I saw you, Walt Whitman, childless, lonely old grubber, poking among the meats in the refrigerator and eyeing the grocery boys.

5 I heard you asking questions of each: Who killed the pork chops? What price bananas? Are you my Angel?

6 I wandered in and out of the brilliant stacks of cans following you, and followed in my imagination by the store detective.

7 We strode down the open corridors together in our solitary fancy tasting artichokes, possessing every frozen delicacy, and never passing the cashier.

8 Where are we going, Walt Whitman? The doors close in an hour. Which way does your beard point tonight?

9 (I touch your book and dream of our odyssey in the supermarket and feel absurd.)

10 Will we walk all night through solitary streets? The trees add shade to shade, lights out in the houses, we'll both be lonely.

11 Will we stroll dreaming of the lost America of love past blue automobiles in driveways, home to our silent cottage?

12 Ah, dear father, graybeard, lonely old courage-teacher, what America did you have when Charon quit poling his ferry and you got out on a smoking bank and stood watching the boat disappear on the black waters of Lethe?

Allen Ginsberg (1926– )

## *Poems for Analysis*

The poems that follow lend themselves to metrical analysis for a variety of reasons. Study them to discover what is remarkable about their rhythm. Try to notice particularly how rhythm affects your emotional response. If the poem is metered, scan it to notice what part the interplay of regularity and irregularity may play in the composition. If the poem is in free verse, try to judge whether or not the rhythm is organically effective. Remember that a reader does not fully understand a poem until he senses the tone, and that the rhythm and meter may bring about the most subtle variations in tone. The poems are given in chronological order, and, though they are not fully representative, they are intended to exemplify some trends in the use of rhythm through the years.

### *The Canonization*

For God's sake hold your tongue and let me love,
   Or chide my palsy or my gout,
   My five gray hairs or ruined fortune flout;
With wealth your state, your mind with arts improve;
   Take you a course, get you a place,
   Observe his honor, or his grace;
Or the king's real or his stamped face

Contemplate; what you will, approve—
So you will let me love.
Alas, alas, who's injured by my love?
What merchant's ships have my sighs drowned?
Who says my tears have overflowed his ground?
When did my colds a forward spring remove?
When did the heats which my veins fill
Add one more to the plaguey bill?
Soldiers find wars, and lawyers find out still
Litigious men which quarrels move,
Though she and I do love.

Call us what you will, we are made such by love;
Call her one, me another fly,
We're tapers too, and at our own cost die;
And we in us find the eagle and the dove,
The phoenix riddle hath more wit
By us: we two being one, are it.
So to one neutral thing both sexes fit,
We die and rise the same, and prove
Mysterious by this love.

We can die by it, if not live by love,
And if unfit for tomb or hearse
Our legend be, it will be fit for verse;
And if no piece of chronicle we prove,
We'll build in sonnets pretty rooms;
As well a well-wrought urn becomes
The greatest ashes, as half-acre tombs;
And by these hymns all shall approve
Us canonized for love,

And thus invoke us: "You, whom reverend love
Made one another's hermitage;
You, to whom love was peace, that now is rage;
Who did the whole world's soul contract, and drove
Into the glasses of your eyes
(So made such mirrors, and such spies,
That they did all to you epitomize)
Countries, towns, courts, beg from above
A pattern of your love."

John Donne (1572–1631)

## from *An Essay on Criticism*

True ease in writing comes from art, not chance,
As those move easiest who have learned to dance.
'Tis not enough no harshness gives offense,
The sound must seem an echo to the sense:
Soft is the strain when Zephyr gently blows,
And the smooth stream in smoother numbers flows;

But when loud surges lash the sounding shore,
The hoarse, rough verse should like the torrent roar;
When Ajax strives some rock's vast weight to throw,
The line too labors, and the words move slow;
Not so, when swift Camilla scours the plain,
Flies o'er the unbending corn, and skims along the main.
Hear how Timotheus' varied lays surprise,
And bid alternate passions fall and rise!

Alexander Pope (1688–1744)

## *Poem*

As the cat
climbed over
the top of

the jamcloset
first the right
forefoot

carefully
then the hind
stepped down

into the pit of
the empty
flowerpot

William Carlos Williams (1883–1963)

## *You, Andrew Marvell*

And here face down beneath the sun
And here upon earth's noonward height

To feel the always coming on
The always rising of the night:

To feel creep up the curving east
The earthy chill of dusk and slow
Upon those under lands the vast
And ever climbing shadow grow

And strange at Ecbatan the trees
Take leaf by leaf the evening strange
The flooding dark about their knees
The mountains over Persia change

And now at Kermanshah the gate
Dark empty and the withered grass
And through the twilight now the late
Few travelers in the westward pass

And Baghdad darken and the bridge
Across the silent river gone
And through Arabia the edge
Of evening widen and steal on

And deepen on Palmyra's street
The wheel rut in the ruined stone
And Lebanon fade out and Crete
High through the clouds and overblown

And over Sicily the air
Still flashing with the landward gulls
And loom and slowly disappear
The sails above the shadowy hulls

And Spain go under and the shore
Of Africa the gilded sand
And evening vanish and no more
The low pale light across that land

Nor now the long light on the sea:

And here face downward in the sun
To feel how swift how secretly
The shadow of the night comes on . . .

Archibald MacLeish (1892– )

*Chapter 12*

# Rhyme and Other Musical Effects

FOR the moment, let us presume that everyone knows what rhyme is and get straight to the questions of how and why poets work with it. Consider what the following poem would lose (a) if it did not have rhyme, and (b) if the rhyme were not used in the way it is used here.

### *Pitcher*

His art is eccentricity, his aim
How not to hit the mark he seems to aim at,

His passion how to avoid the obvious,
His technique how to vary the avoidance.

The others throw to be comprehended. He
Throws to be a moment misunderstood.

Yet not too much. Not errant, arrant, wild,
But every seeming aberration willed.

Not to, yet still, still to communicate
Making the batter understand too late.

Robert Francis (1901–    )

The poet is attempting to make the sounds of the poem reinforce not only the meaning, but also the mental image of a pitcher preparing his delivery. Just as a pitcher works up to a pitch, the poem works up to its rhyme, holding it in suspense until the last of several, mostly misleading, motions. Like the pitcher, the poet's passion is "how to avoid the obvious." Notice how in every couplet he repeats words—"his," "how," "aim," "avoid," "throw," "not," and "still." In the couplet which contains the least obvious repetition (lines 7 and 8) we get two sets of words which are nearly rhymes, "errant" and "arrant" and "willed" and "wild." Then in the last couplet, the rhymes "communicate" and "late" bring the poem to an emphatic close. The poet has given us many kinds of repetition to build our expectation for more of the same, but at the last moment he gives the resolute rhyme.

It becomes evident in discussing the musical effects of the poem above that repetitions of sound come in more than one variety. In order to describe accurately all that goes on in the poem, we need to backtrack momentarily and make some distinctions.

### *Rhyme*

*Rhyme* is the correspondence in the terminal syllables among two or more words. True rhyme always involves the last accented syllable and any subsequent unaccented syllables. If only one syllable corresponds, the rhyme is called *masculine,* as in "delight" and "night," "word" and "bird" (note that "sword" and "word" do not rhyme, despite the similar spellings). When two consecutive syllables correspond, the rhyme is called *feminine,* as in "master" and "faster." Occasionally, poets use rhymes with three or four syllables or rhyme a polysyllabic word with a phrase, as in "possibilities" and "a boss who's ill at ease." Rhymes of this sort are of small use in serious poems, but have been put to entertaining work in comic and satirical verse with great success, as in Byron's *Don Juan.*

*End rhyme* is the name given to the corresponding sounds when they occur at the ends of lines. This is by far the commonest type partly because rhymed words appearing at the ends of lines make good use of the emphatic, terminal position. Moreover, this kind of rhyme serves to organize verse into stanzas, giving poetry a kind of coherence of sound not available in other forms of composition. When rhyme is one of the distinguishing marks of a stanza, the stanza is said to have a *rhyme scheme.* The scheme not only sets the formal limits of the stanza, but, when used to parallel thought groups, assists in ordering the content of a poem. Though the rhyme scheme may be confining, most of what may be lost in freedom is gained in control over thought and word by the poet who finds rhyme congenial to his style. Perhaps the most concise way of illustrating how the end rhyme works to enhance a poem's unity, coherence, and emphasis is through the sonnet. The sonnet given below contains three quatrains (stanzas of four lines each) with alternately rhyming lines, and with a new set of rhymes for each quatrain. This sonnet ends with a rhyming couplet (a two-line stanza).

*Sonnet 17*

Who will believe my verse in time to come a
If it were fill'd with your most high deserts? b
Though yet, heaven knows, it is but as a tomb a
Which hides your life and shows not half your parts. b
If I could write the beauty of your eyes c
And in fresh numbers number all your graces, d
The age to come would say 'This poet lies; c
Such heavenly touches ne'er touch'd earthly faces.' d
So should my papers yellow'd with their age e
Be scorn'd like old men of less truth than tongue, f
And your true rights be term'd a poet's rage e
And stretched metre of an antique song: f
But were some child of yours alive that time, g
You should live twice; in it and in my rhyme. g

William Shakespeare (1564–1616)

Three of the rhymes in this poem do not ring true today because of a shift in the pronunciation of certain vowel sounds which has occurred since Shakespeare's time, but the pattern is clear. In three successive quatrains, the poet drives home the idea that in time to come no one will believe a person could be as beautiful as the poet claims. Though each quatrain advances the thought with some new image, we are strongly aware of the repetitions. Then, when the pattern is broken to accompany a shift of thought, the couplet lends the argument heightened emphasis.

Rhyming sounds occurring within the line are called *internal rhymes*. These are not so useful in giving a work its structure as are end rhymes. Their main advantage lies in the songful quality they give a poem. Internal rhyme is just one among many devices of sound repetition in the stanza below, taken from the opening chorus of Swinburne's *Atalanta in Calydon*.

For winter's rains and ruins are over,
  And all the season of snows and sins;
The days dividing lover and lover,
  The light that loses, the night that wins;
And time remembered is grief forgotten,
And frosts are slain and flowers begotten,
And in green underwood and cover
  Blossom by blossom the spring begins.

This excerpt may give the impression that Swinburne's use of the galloping rhythm and plentiful sound effects is excessive. But the poem, as a song in celebration of the coming of spring, is deliberately strong in its sensuous appeal to the sounds and rhythm.

True rhymes are built on the differences that we hear when the first consonant in a syllable is altered. The rhymes may easily be found by making substitutions for the initial consonant or consonant blend. Thus the rhymes for "ate" would be "bait," "Kate," "date," "gait," "gate," "great," "fate," "fete," "freight," "hate," "late," "mate," "Nate," "plait," "plate," "pate," "prate," "rate," "slate," "strait," "trait," "wait," and "weight." If the poet needs a sound repetition that is not so strong as the true rhyme, there are numerous possibilities available to him. For example, he may use *slant rhyme,* also called *half rhyme* or near rhyme. This sound effect is gained not by altering the initial consonant, but by substituting for the last consonant another sound which is similar to it. Thus a near rhyme for "which" is "wish," for "bags" is "backs," and for "fate," "faith." In near rhyme the first consonant may be altered too, as in "sings" and "brinks." One who is not aware of the similarities among the basic sounds of the language might have trouble thinking of near rhymes, but he will have no trouble in recognizing them. The most obvious similarities occur between the voiced and voiceless pairs of consonants. This is noticeable in the words "bus" and "buzz," the first of which ends without the vocal cord's vibration, and the second of which ends with the vibration. Other paired sounds are:

| | | | | | | |
|---|---|---|---|---|---|---|
| Voiceless | pot | bath | beck | match | heft | miser |
| Voiced | pod | bathe | beg | Madge | heaved | measure |

Unsophisticated readers make the mistake of thinking that poets settle for near rhymes when they cannot find the appropriate true rhymes. In fact, finding the near rhyme is no less difficult than finding the true; the test is in finding the word which fits best not only in sound, but in sense as well.

In the following poem, Robert Francis uses the slight incongruity of sound in slant rhymes to create a subtle imbalance suitable to the subject.

## *High Diver*

How deep is his duplicity who in a flash
Passes from resting bird to flying bird to fish,

Who momentarily is sculpture, then all motion,
Speed and splash, then climbs again to contemplation.

He is the archer who himself is bow and arrow.
He is the upper-under-world-commuting hero.

His downward going has the air of sacrifice
To some dark seaweed-bearded seagod face to face

Or goddess. Rippling and responsive lies the water
For him to contemplate, then powerfully to enter.

Robert Francis (1901–     )

### QUESTIONS

1. This poem seeks to evoke not only the image of a diver, but his emotions as well. Study the rhythm. Do you find the lines to be smooth, halting, or some combination? How does this bear upon the poem's effect? Comment on the effect of the last line.

2. The patterns of internal repetition in these lines may be a reflection of the ritual repetitions of athletes as they concentrate to develop the inner composure that perfection requires. What internal rhymes (true or slant) and what repeated words and syllables do you find? Are you aware of these repetitions before you search for them?

John Ciardi's poem captures the combination of grace and awkwardness of landing gulls, who fold their large wings with difficulty as they seem to take a few steps in air before finally touching down.

*Gulls Land and Cease to Be*

Spread back across the air, wings wide,
legs out, the wind delicately
dumped in balance, the gulls ride
down, down, hang, and exactly
touch, folding not quite at once
into their gangling weight, but
taking one step, two, wings still askance,
reluctantly, at last, shut,
twitch one look around
and are aground.

John Ciardi (1916–    )

QUESTIONS

1. What is the effect of the words ending lines 5 and 7? What is the term used to describe this repetition? Why does the poet alternate true rhyme with near rhyme in the first eight lines?

2. Notice that the last four lines grow increasingly shorter. Why?

3. What is the effect of placing the last two rhyming words so close together? What kind of rhyme is this?

4. Describe the rhythm accompanying the motion portrayed in this poem.

## *Other Musical Effects*

Aside from rhyme, the poet has an assortment of types of repetition that is so varied that there is no suitable catalog of terms to describe them. We will accept the limits of the following terms: alliteration, assonance, consonance, onomatopoeia, phonic echo, cacophony and euphony, and refrain.

### *Alliteration*

In its most limited sense, *alliteration* is the repetition of the initial consonant sound in a series of words that are not far apart, as in the opening line of Shakespeare's sonnet 146:

Poor soul, the centre of my sinful earth

Notice that since English spelling is not strictly phonetic, the reader who wishes to be fully aware of the sound in any poem must not presume that the repetition of letters parallels the repetition of sounds. In the familiar tongue twister,

> She sells sea shells by the sea shore,

one notices that the letter "s" has come to represent more than one sound. Not only does the "s" indicate more than one sound, but the three sounds given here are spelled in a variety of ways. For example, the "sh" sound in "gracious," "nation," and "fission" represent only three of the eleven possible spellings of the sound. The crux of the problem is that the English alphabet has only twenty-six characters to represent its approximately forty-five distinct sounds. It would seem at a glance that nineteen of the characters would have to do double duty, but in fact the matter is much more complex since the twenty-eight consonants alone are spelled in 116 different ways, some letters are not pronounced at all, and some words have sounds that are not represented by any letter. Poetry is first of all an auditory art, and the written words are merely approximate records of the sounds involved. The written word completely overlooks the rise and fall (that is, the pitch) of the spoken word or of the arrangement of stress. The reader who wishes to have a good understanding of the sound effects in poetry will miss much if he thinks that sound and spelling are synonymous.

Vowel alliteration occurs when a series of words begin with vowel sounds, as in Tennyson's "Morte d'Arthur":

> And slowly answered Arthur from the Barge:
>
> 'The older order changeth, yielding place to new.

This kind of concentration on the initial sounds may lead us to overlook the really important and more subtle repetitions that accumulate within words. Once again the possible difficulty arises when we depend on our eyes instead of our ears to analyze the sound effects. With the spoken word there are no actual spaces separating individual words; all the sounds run together with an occasional pause or drop in the voice. The sounds which need the closest attention are not the initial ones, but those which are emphasized or which work into a pattern of repetition. The tercets (three-line stanzas) below are from Shelley's "Ode to the West Wind."

Thou who didst waken from his summer dreams a
The blue Mediterranean, where he lay, b
Lulled by the coil of his crystálline streams, a

Beside a pumice isle in Baiae's bay, b
And saw in sleep old palaces and towers c
Quivering within the wave's intenser day, b

Shelley has laced these lines with forms of musical repetition so varied that the devices do not even have individual names. In the last line of each tercet the poet has used consonant sounds to make the subparts of the lines interlock. Here the "l" and "k" sounds merge in the third line, and the "w" and "v" sounds knit together the parts of the sixth. Elaborations in the sound patterns such as this help the poet sustain a sense of rhapsodic excitement. The use of the "p" sound in support of the "b's" in "Beside a pumice isle in Baiae's bay," shows how the musical effects may be gained through sounds that are similar though not identical.

### *Assonance*

So far, this discussion might seem to imply that the consonants are the sounds solely responsible for musical effects. The next two types of repetition, assonance and consonance, will illustrate that this is not the case. First let us consider *assonance,* the repetition of, or similarity between, vowel sounds. Once we realize that the vowels, which are all voiced sounds, are made by varying the size of the oral cavity and the arrangement of the lips and tongue, we can see how the poet can control the pitch of a line by his selection of vowels. In general, the larger the oral cavity, the more echoing the quality of the vowel; the smaller the cavity, the less the echoing effect. Vowels are said to be high or low according to whether the jaw is raised or lowered to utter them. By saying the words "hot," "hat," "hit," and "heat" in succession and in a normal tone of voice, we notice that we gradually raise the jaw and thus reduce the size of the oral cavity. We can also reduce the size of the cavity by moving the tongue from back to front in articulating vowel sounds. Here is a line by Keats using assonance:

As though a Rose Should shut and be a bud again

Variety of vowel sounds, of course, contribute as much to musicality as repetition. In analyzing vowel qualities, be sure not to equate spelling with sound.

*Consonance*

Consonance occurs when two syllables end with the same consonant, but do not have the same vowel, as in "hatch" and "etch." Notice the difference between this and the slant rhymes "hash" and "hatch." Sometimes consonance involves both the first and last consonants in a syllable or word, as in "hit," "hat," "hot," "height," "heat," "hoot," and "hate."

A basic way of building the word stock of the language is to form new words and syllables by varying the internal vowel or diphthong. Since there are fourteen easily recognized vowels and four chief diphthongs in English, the possibilities of building words through consonance are many. Unattentive readers may be unaware of this, but no poet who prizes sound repetitions overlooks consonance.

In just one combination of two consonants, "p" and "t," nine words may be formed by changing the internal vowel or diphthong as follows: "pat," "pate," "peat," "pot," "pit," "pet," "put," "putt," and "pout." A few syllables which are not independent words may be added to the list, including "despite," and "dispute." It would be difficult to find a syllable or monosyllabic word that cannot be meaningfully varied by this kind of rearrangement.

The general effect gained through either of these devices is similar, however; both tend to evoke a sense of uncertainty. Since they use sounds which are not quite rhymes, they may induce a feeling of uneasiness and apprehension in the reader.

Notice how W. H. Auden manipulates sounds to great advantage in the poem below.

*That Night When Joy Began*

That night when joy began
Our narrowest veins to flush,
We waited for the flash
Of morning's levelled gun.

But morning let us pass,
And day by day relief
Outgrows his nervous laugh,
Grown credulous of peace,

As mile by mile is seen
No trespasser's reproach,
And love's best glasses reach
No fields but are his own.

W. H. Auden (1907–1973)

QUESTIONS

1. Before examining the musical appeal of this poem, consider the meaning. Does the central metaphor relate love to the imagery of hunting or war? Why? What, specifically, is the difference between what the speaker expected and what he finds?

2. What might be the effect if the stanzas rhymed *a a b b* instead of *a b b a*?

3. In analyzing the sounds of this poem, do you find that Auden's scheme works consistently throughout? Comment on the use of sounds at the end of lines 9 and 12, and note that the sound repetitions need not be confined to whole words.

## *Onomatopoeia*

Words whose sounds suggest their meaning are called *onomatopoetic.* "Buzz," "click," "screech," "tinkle," and so forth, carry a phonetic hint of their meaning, though, of course, if one did not already know what the words mean, he would probably not understand them. Every language has its own words for the calls of animals, and though "bow-wow" or "moo" seem perfectly logical to speakers of English, a Russian, whose equivalent for "bow-wow" is "gaf-gaf," would have to learn these words in order to understand them in English, just as he would have to learn the words for "dog" and "cow."

Onomatopoeia is sometimes evident in poetry, though it is more talked about than used. Most of the sound-meaning relationships are far subtler and dependent on the interplay of rhythm and sound.

*Phonic Echoes*

When in reading a poem, one notices a recurrence of sounds which are, though not onomatopoetic, suggestive of generalized meanings, he may be feeling the effects of *phonic echoes.* "Inkle," or "ingle" in themselves, have no lexical meaning, yet, when they occur within some words, they call up a strongly consistent reaction—"tingle," "twinkle," "jingle," "sprinkle." Add to these any words with "ink" or "ing" or words beginning with "tw" or "spr," and the effect might be to intensify the reaction to the other words; for example, "twirl," "spring," "sprint," or "twitch."

Robert Burns applies this use of sound when, in "To a Mouse," he says,

That wee-bit heap o' leaves an' stibble° *stubble*
Has cost thee mony a weary nibble!
Now thou's turned out, for a' thy trouble,
    But house or hald,° *land*
To thole° the winter's sleety dribble, *endure*
    An' cranreuch° cauld! *hoarfrost*

The image of quick, small motions is reinforced by the repetition of "ibble."

So many words beginning with the blend, "gl," have to do with visual experience, that the impression of transient light may be heightened by repetition of the "gl" sound. In "Dover Beach," Matthew Arnold draws upon this response in the lines,

. . . on the French coast the light
Gleams and is gone; the cliffs of England stand,
Glimmering and vast, out in the tranquil bay.

In the poem which follows, W. S. Merwin reflects on a sound which, once heard, can never be forgotten, and which unfailingly calls up an eerie sense of lost and obscure loneliness.

## *Fog-Horn*

Surely that moan is not the thing
That men thought they were making, when they
Put it there, for their own necessities.
That throat does not call to anything human
But to something men had forgotten,
That stirs under fog. Who wounded that beast
Incurably, or from whose pasture
Was it lost, full grown, and time closed round it
With no way back? Who tethered its tongue
So that its voice could never come
To speak out in the light of clear day,
But only when the shifting blindness
Descends and is acknowledged among us,
As though from under a floor it is heard,
Or as though from behind a wall, always
Nearer than we had remembered? If it
Was we that gave tongue to this cry
What does it bespeak in us, repeating
And repeating, insisting on something
That we never meant? We only put it there
To give warning of something we dare not
Ignore, lest we should come upon it
Too suddenly, recognize it too late,
As our cries were swallowed up and all hands lost.

W. S. Merwin (1927– )

QUESTIONS

1. The key word in line 1, "moan," is onomatopoetic. Which words echo the sound of "moan"? What are the connotative effects of the words with echoing sounds? Consider not only close resemblances of sound, but all words having nasal or low back vowel qualities.

2. What does this poem say about the relationship of the creator and his creatures? Do the sound effects contribute to the seriousness of the tone?

*Cacophony and Euphony*

In our treatment of connotative words, the point was made that people react to words as well as understand them. A specific application of this notion should be made in the study of poetic sound effects. Harsh sounding (*cacophonic*) and sweet sounding (*euphonious*) words play an important role in the matching of sound and sense. Moreover, individual phonemes (the smallest meaningful units of sound) have harsh and pleasant effects on the ear depending partly on the relative ease or effort involved in producing the sound and on the possibility of giving the sound resonance. The plosive sounds (b, d, t, p), especially those made in the back of the mouth (g and k), for example, require an effort to make. They produce an unpleasant effect when they occur in quick succession, as in "gawk," "squawk," and "hawk." Low back vowels do more to minimize shrillness than high front vowels.

| *Low Back* | | *High Front* | |
|---|---|---|---|
| bought | not | neat | beet |
| boat | note | nit | bit |
| boot | nut | net | bet |

All the vowels can be "held," thus giving resonance to words. Many consonants can also be "held" because their sounds are made by forcing air through a narrow passage, as with "sh," "th," "f," "v," etc. The nasal sounds (m, n, and ng) lend resonance and the "r's" and "l's" blend well. No one needs to be told a pleasant sound from an unpleasant one, but in analyzing poetry's sound effects, one should try to be less passively affected and more aware of just what causes his reaction.

Analyze the sounds in the following poem, keeping in mind that in studying the effects of words the way in which they are said is inseparable from what they mean.

*Dulce et Decorum Est*

Bent double, like old beggars under sacks,
Knock-kneed, coughing like hags, we cursed through sludge,
Till on the haunting flares we turned our backs
And towards our distant rest began to trudge.

Men marched asleep. Many had lost their boots,
But limped on, blood-shod. All went lame; all blind;
Drunk with fatigue; deaf even to the hoots
Of tired, outstripped Five-Nines that dropped behind.

Gas! GAS! Quick, boys!—An ecstasy of fumbling,
Fitting the clumsy helmets just in time;
But someone still was yelling out and stumbling
And flound'ring like a man in fire or lime . . .
Dim through the misty panes and thick green light,
As under a green sea, I saw him drowning.

In all my dreams before my helpless sight,
He plunges at me, guttering, choking, drowning.

If in some smothering dreams, you too could pace
Behind the wagon that we flung him in,
And watch the white eyes writhing in his face,
His hanging face, like a devil's sick of sin;
If you could hear, at every jolt, the blood
Come gargling from the froth-corrupted lungs,
Obscene as cancer, bitter as the cud
Of vile, incurable sores on innocent tongues, —
My friend, you would not tell with such high zest
To children ardent for some desperate glory,
The old lie: *Dulce et decorum est*
*Pro patria mori.*

Wilfred Owen (1893–1918)

## QUESTIONS

1. The Latin quotation which ends the poem is from Horace and means, "It is sweet and fitting to die for one's country." How does this sound when read aloud, and how does the sound affect the meaning?

2. What cacophonic effects do you find in the first eight lines, and how do these affect the poem's rhythm?

3. In lines 9 through 14, what sounds within the lines intensify or echo the word "fumbling"?

4. What is the effect of using only one complete sentence in the poem's last twelve lines? Does this have any bearing on the poem's emphasis?

5. You may notice that the structure of this poem roughly resembles two interlocking sonnets, with the last two lines of the first fourteen lines rhyming

with the first two lines in the second fourteen. What is the strategy of organization here? Why does the poem's last line not fit the pentameter pattern of the rest of the poem?

## *Refrain*

So far this discussion has been limited to repeated units of sound and clusters of sound. A larger unit of speech (word, phrase, and line) when repeated is called a *refrain*. The refrain serves as a kind of musical partition, emphasizing the stages of a poem's story or thought. It may be a series of nonsense words, a strategically repeated idea, or a progression of slightly varied phrases which can create the fundamental pleasure of combined surprise and recognition.

### *Forget Not Yet*

Forget not yet the tried° intent — *proven*
Of such a truth as I have meant;
My great travail so gladly spent,
  Forget not yet.

Forget not yet when first began
The weary life ye know, since when
The suit, the service none tell can,
  Forget not yet.

Forget not yet the great assays,° — *attempts*
The cruel wrong, the scornful ways;
The painful patience in denays,° — *denials*
  Forget not yet.

Forget not yet, forget not this:
How long ago hath been, and is
The mind that never meant amiss.
  Forget not yet.

Forget not then thine own approved,° — *proven lover*
The which so long hath thee so loved,
Whose steadfast faith yet never moved;
  Forget not this.

Sir Thomas Wyatt (1503–1542)

QUESTIONS

1. This, like many of the lyrics of the English Renaissance, lends itself readily to instrumental accompaniment. What musical qualities do you find within the lines? What is the effect of the frequently repeated "t" sound in the first stanza? The "f" in the second? The "rg," "gr," and "cr" blends in the third?

2. What musical advantage may lie in making the refrain a half line, that is, in using four syllables instead of the expected eight? Does this influence the time you rest between stanzas?

3. What tempo of instrumental accompaniment would be most appropriate for this poem?

The next song uses a nonsense refrain for its rollicking effect.

*Mush Mush*

Oh! 'twas there I learned readin' and writin',
At Bill Bracket's where I went to school,
And 'twas there I learned howlin' and fightin'
From my schoolmaster, Mister O'Toole.
Him and me we had many a scrimmage,
And the divil a copy I wrote.
There was ne'er a garsun in the village,
Dared tread on the tail o' me . . .

*Refrain:*

Mush, mush, mush tu-ral-i-ady,
Singin' mush, mush, mush tu-ral-i-ay,
There was ne'er a garsun in the village
Dared tread on the tail o' me coat.

Oh 'twas there that I learn't all my courtin',
Many lessons I took in the art;
Till Cupid, the blackguard, in sportin'
An arrow drove straight thro' me heart.
Molly Connor, she lived right forninst me
And tender lines to her I wrote,
If you dare say one hard word agin her,
I'll tread on the tail of your . . .

*Refrain*

But a blackguard called Mickey Maloney
Came and stole her affections away,

He had money and I hadn't any,
So I sent him a challenge next day.
That evening we met be the woodbine,
The Shannon we crossed in a boat,
And I leathered him with my shillelah,
For he trod on the tail of my . . .

*Refrain*

Oh, my fame went abroad thro' the nation,
And folks came a-flocking to see,
And they cried out without hesitation
'You're a fightin' man, Billy McGee.'
I cleaned out the Finnegan faction
And I licked all the Murphy's afloat,
If you're in for a row or a ruction,
Just tread on the tail o' me . . .

*Refrain*

There are several good reasons for drinkin'
And another one enters me head
If a fella can't drink while he's living
How the hell can he drink when he's dead.

*Refrain*

Anonymous

QUESTIONS

1. If you think of this as a "drinking song," how would the refrain be sung?
2. Is the speaker supposed to be a sympathetic character? What keeps you from taking his unsuccessful courtship seriously?

## *Poems and Music*

No discussion of the music in poetry should end without some mention of song lyrics. Anyone who listens much to the radio or to records probably hears more verse sung than he reads. Most of the lyrics are simple enough for us to follow their meaning without being absorbed by it, because our attention belongs as much to the music as to words. If we read the lyrics to a song we know, it is impossible to keep the music from influencing whatever pleasure the words give. When we sing, the whole question of "holding" a sound is different than in reading. We have all sung these words of Robert Burns (1759–1796), and in reading them are affected by the memory of the tune:

Should auld acquaintance be forgot,
  And never brought to min'?
Should auld acquaintance be forgot
  And auld lang syne?

For auld lang syne, my dear,
  For auld lang syne,
We'll tak a cup o' kindness yet,
  For auld lang syne.

Our consciousness of the music influences the reading, and it is very likely that we enjoy the lyrics to songs we like. Many of the poems in this book, including the old ballads and Byron's "So We'll Go No More A-Roving," were meant to be sung to music that is now forgotten, but the words, having an intrinsic appeal of their own, have lasted on.

Since lyrics tend to use traditional symbols and images, and since most songs make a fairly direct appeal to the emotions, they may not have what it takes for a "rich" experience in reading. Popular songs are by nature short-lived, since they are geared for the present. The same of course might be said of anything that is written, because only a few favorites will last. Here is one by Thomas Moore (1779–1852) which is in its sentiment and imagery a typical old lyric. It was once a popular song.

Believe me if all those endearing young charms
  Which I gaze on so fondly today
Were to change by tomorrow and fleet in my arms
  Like a fairy gift fading away,

Thou would still be adored
  As this moment thou art
Let thy loveliness fade as it will
  And around the dear ruin each wish of my heart
Would entwine itself verdantly still.

Aside from a few songs, Moore's work is no longer read. But the rhythm, the sentiment, and the metaphor of this lyric still have a certain appeal when sung.

Lately there has been a definite swing towards giving popular music something to say about modern problems. The late Woody Guthrie's reputation rests as much on his moving portrayal of social injustice as it does on his music. Bob Dylan's work follows in this tradition with lyrics that may comment on anything from racial issues ("The Death of Emmet Till") to war ("John Brown"). His most enthusiastic admirers call him the country's best loved poet, notwithstanding Dylan's own statement that he is *not* a poet. But works like his are proof that song lyrics do not have to be bland or meaningless. At times, as in his half-sung, half-talked songs in the blues vein, the music seems even secondary. The vitality of these lyrics, like those of Paul Simon, Leonard Cohen, and Pete Seeger, is not debatable. But only when the music has passed from popularity will the poetry in the lyrics be put to the test.

One aspect, along with relevance, that makes some popular lyrics admirable is their avoidance of the stock, sentimental response, as in this one by the Beatles.

### *A Day in the Life*

I read the news today oh boy
about a lucky man who made the grade
and though the news was rather sad
well I just had to laugh
I saw the photograph
He blew his mind out in a car
he didn't notice that the lights had
changed
a crowd of people stood and stared
they'd seen his face before
nobody was really sure
if he was from the House of Lords.
I saw a film today oh boy
the English Army had just won the war
a crowd of people turned away
but I just had to look
having read the book.
I'd love to turn you on
Woke up, got out of bed,

dragged a comb across my head
found my way downstairs and drank a cup,
and looking up I noticed I was late.
Found my coat and grabbed my hat
made the bus in seconds flat
found my way upstairs and had a smoke,
and somebody spoke and I went into a dream
I heard the news today oh boy
four thousand holes in Blackburn,
Lancashire
and though the holes were rather small
they had to count them all
now they know how many holes it takes
to fill the Albert Hall.
I'd love to turn you on.

### QUESTIONS

1. What part does irony play in setting the tone of this poem? What is it about the words that makes them so unmistakably modern?
2. What does the poem "say" about the meaning of daily existence? What details lead you to this conclusion?
3. Does the speaker understand what he reads? Why?
4. What is the effect of the "refrain"? If you know the music to this, how does it affect your reading?

Another productive source of popular lyrics is the musical theater, which has proven capable of great variety in both music and subject matter. These lyrics usually aim at clarity since the words are used to advance the story and depict character. Like the words of a playscript, they are delivered just once. But, as Stephen Sondheim, one of our best librettists and composers has pointed out, there is no need to sacrifice either intelligence or entertainment. He describes the aim of musical theater as the "total integration of book, music, and movement into a seamless form."

The next lyric comes from the musical *Candide,* based on Voltaire's classic satire. First produced in 1957, the show is set for a revival in the 70's, with music by Leonard Bernstein, book by Lillian Hellman and lyrics by Richard Wilbur, Dorothy Parker and John Latouche. "Quiet," by Richard Wilbur, is well calculated to contribute to an exciting, musical-theatrical moment, not to stand alone. To contrast Wilbur's poetic style with this work, see his "Years-End" (p. 159), or "Mind" (p. 146). Notice how completely he adjusts the voice to fit the occasion. In this case the dramatic occasion involves an old woman who, after a life of danger and adventure, finds herself bored with the peacefulness of life in a governor's palace. The young woman, Cunegonde, wants to drop her role as the governor's mistress and become his wife. The hero, Candide, thinks meanwhile that she is the most virtuous of all possible girls. All the governor wants is "quiet."

### *Quiet*

OLD LADY

*(She sings)*

No doubt you'll think I'm giving in
To petulance and malice,
But in candor I am forced to say
That I'm sick of gracious living in
This stuffy little palace.
And I wish that I could leave today.
I have suffered a lot
And I'm certainly not
Unaware that this life has its black side.
I have starved in a ditch,
I've been burned for a witch,
And I'm missing the half of my backside.
I've been beaten and whipped
And repeatedly stripped,
I've been forced into all kinds of whoredom;
But I'm finding of late
That the very worst fate
Is to perish of comfort and BOREDOM.

GOVERNOR

*(Speaking)*

Quiet.

(CUNEGONDE *sings to* GOVERNOR)

It was three years ago
As you very well know
That you said we would soon have a wedding;

Every day you forget
What you promised, and yet
 You continue to rumple my bedding.
I'll no longer bring shame
On my family name.
 I had rather lie down and be buried;
No, I'll not lead the life
Of an unwedded wife.
 Tell me, when are we going to be MARRIED?

GOVERNOR

*(Speaking)*

Quiet.

(OLD LADY *sings*)

I was once, what is more,
Nearly sawed in four
 By a specially clumsy magician;
And you'd think I would feel
After such an ordeal
 That there's charm in my present position.
But I'd far rather be
In a tempest at sea,
 Or a bloody North African riot,
Than to sit in this dump
On what's left of my rump
 And put up with this terrible QUIET.

(CUNEGONDE, *joining in*)

When are we going to be MARRIED?

(OLD LADY *sings*)

Comfort and boredom and QUIET. . . .

(CUNEGONDE *sings, crescendo*)

When are we going to be—

*Simultaneously*

(GOVERNOR *sings*)

QUIET!

Richard Wilbur (1921– )

*Chapter 13*

# Characterization

A person's character is the sum of all his traits, and characterization is the portrayal of character resulting from an artist's synthesis of these traits in a consistent and intelligible pattern. People in daily life get to understand one another by observing each other's traits. If we know how to interpret them accurately, every choice, every reaction we perceive in another's behavior is a clue to his total character, for an individual's choices reflect to some extent the kind of person he wants to be and the kind of life he wants to have. The concrete, observable facts of one's behavior—his things, his speech, and his performance—provide the most objective source of material for both every man's day-to-day study of human nature and for the artist's portrayal of character.

People, of course, do not merely interpret each other; they interpret themselves to themselves (as in diaries) and to each other (as in self-revelation through writing and conversation). Through these sources, we get to know how a person wishes to appear and, perhaps, by comparing what he omits with what is known, what he has to hide.

A third source of detail about character comes in the form of hearsay—the condensed results of other people's observations which should be heard and judged as testimony, and which can be no more reliable than its source. Most of what we know about celebrities or politicians of national prominence is the sum of their public pose (often called their image) and the reportedly intimate looks into their private lives through interviews and journalistic reports.

The ultimate source—a direct look into a person's mind—remains beyond our grasp. Finally, no one can know anyone fully, not even himself, for his understanding of his own mind can hardly be objective. Yet artists have tried to show the working of the mind in motion by portraying the stream of consciousness. Though each of us may be isolated in his own consciousness, the principle of the human mind's operation is true for all. No poet could fully portray the exact movement of the mind at all levels any more than a physicist can stop light, but through the stream of words, symbols, and images, he can suggest the mixed awareness of sensory perceptions, reveries, thoughts, and reflections, all in free association and ungoverned by logic.

In poetic characterization, the distinction is usually made between described and enacted portrayal. The poet may tell us about a character, he may create a role through which the character reveals himself, or he may use his own commentary to support and explain a role. The distinction is determined by whether the poet uses third person or first person. In the third person, the poet may presume much or little about what goes on in his character's mind. At one end of the scale he uses only observable, objective detail; at the other he describes the stream of consciousness. A like scale applies to portrayal in first person, with the actual, heard speech of a character forming one limit, and the interior monologue, in which none of the speaker's most secret thought is screened, forming the other.

In longer narrative and dramatic poems all the means of portrayal are likely to be used, but in shorter works the poet is likely to limit both his means and his aim, focusing on the dominant trait of a single character. In recent times, prose fiction and drama have become the main instruments for characterization, but poetry has retained its claim on those sudden flashes of insight into human nature which do not require a fully detailed set of events as a setting.

Virtually every poem creates character in some degree because poetry as a whole is really a vast collection of people speaking, with voices that summon us to understand. The poems which follow represent a wide range of time and technique in character portrayal. Here is a contemporary work which accomplishes with unusual detachment the very difficult job of self-caricature.

### *Unwanted*

The poster with my picture on it
Is hanging on the bulletin board in the Post Office.

I stand by it hoping to be recognized
Posing first full face and then profile

But everybody passes by and I have to admit
The photograph was taken some years ago.

I was unwanted then and I'm unwanted now
Ah guess ah'll go up echo mountain and crah.

I wish someone would find my fingerprints somewhere
Maybe on a corpse and say, You're it.

Description: Male, or reasonably so
White, but not lily-white and usually deep-red

Thirty-fivish, and looks it lately
Five-feet-nine and one-hundred-thirty pounds: no physique

Black hair going gray, hairline receding fast
What used to be curly, now fuzzy

Brown eyes starey under beetling brow
Mole on chin, probably will become a wen

It is perfectly obvious that he was not popular at school
No good at baseball, and wet his bed.

His aliases tell his history: Dumbell, Good-for-nothing,
Jewboy, Fieldinsky, Skinny, Fierce Face, Greaseball, Sissy.

Warning: This man is not dangerous, answers to any name
Responds to love, don't call him or he will come.

Edward Field (1924– )

## QUESTIONS

1. What evidence is there in the poem that the author may be speaking of himself?

2. At what stage in the poem does the language shift to the idiom used in "Wanted" bulletins? Before this shift, how seriously does the speaker seem to be taking himself? Explain.

3. What effect does the mock-communique language have on the tone of the poem?

4. Ordinarily, a person cannot say that nobody wants him without seeming to indulge in self-pity. Explain why this is so or why not in "Unwanted."

## *Cora Punctuated with Strawberries*

Sandra and that boy that's going to get her in trouble
one of these days were out in the garden where anyone in
Mother's sickroom could see them out the upperleft corner of the
window sitting behind the garage feeding each other
blueberries and Cherry was helping with the dishes alone in the
kitchen and
um good strawberries if we did grow them just can't can without
popping one in every so often Henry was at it again in the
attic with that whatchamacallit of his when the Big
Bomb fell smack in the MacDonalds' yard you know over on
Elm and they got into Life and the papers and all all very
well but they might have been in when it hit and it would have
been a very different story for Lucy MacDonald then I'll tell
you well they say it was right in the Geographic Center of the
country the Geographic
woody Center you could hear it just as plain I thought the
elevator had blown up and I guess you read yourself the awful
things it would have
ak another one woody I tell you I don't know what's got
into these strawberries used to be so juicy they
say they only had the one and it's all it would have took well I
always knew we could beat the enemy they made such
shoddy tricks and spring-toys and puzzles and fuses and
things and besides, it wouldn't have been right.

George Starbuck (1931– )

### QUESTIONS

1. Explain the significance of the title. Where in her speech does Cora eat the strawberries?

2. Part of the comic tension in this poem results from the counterpoint between her gossip and her talk of canning. What kind of subjects are interesting to Cora, and what does her speech tell us about her mind?

3. Can you deduce from the poem where the speaker lives, what level of society she is in, and at what point in time she is speaking?

Good poetic characterization satisfies a reader's idea about human nature. That is, it produces an effect consistent with what is universally true about people. A good portrait need not be complete in all detail, for as in real experience, a character may be all the more remarkable because of its mystery. Sensitive readers often disagree about the characters in literature as if they were actual people with complex motives. Two readers who understand a character in literature equally well might disagree sharply over whether the character is likable, mistreated, or high-minded. The poem that follows depicts two characters in crisis and in conflict. In reading the poem, try to notice how Robinson uses the elements of imagery and symbolism to suggest more about the characters than is explicitly stated.

## *John Gorham*

"Tell me what you're doing over here, John Gorham,
Sighing hard and seeming to be sorry when you're not;
Make me laugh or let me go now, for long faces in the
   moonlight
Are a sign for me to say again a word that you forgot."—

"I'm over here to tell you what the moon already
May have said or maybe shouted ever since a year ago;
I'm over here to tell you what you are, Jane Wayland,
And to make you rather sorry, I should say, for being so."—

"Tell me what you're saying to me now, John Gorham,
Or you'll never see as much of me as ribbons any more;
I'll vanish in as many ways as I have toes and fingers,
And you'll not follow far for one where flocks have been
   before."—

"I'm sorry now you never saw the flocks, Jane Wayland,
But you're the one to make of them as many as you need.
And then about the vanishing. It's I who mean to vanish;
And when I'm here no longer you'll be done with me indeed."—

"That's a way to tell me what I am, John Gorham!
How am I to know myself until I make you smile?
Try to look as if the moon were making faces at you,
And a little more as if you meant to stay a little while."—

"You are what it is that over rose-blown gardens
Make a pretty flutter for a season in the sun;
You are what it is that with a mouse, Jane Wayland,
Catches him and lets him go and eats him up for fun."—

"Sure I never took you for a mouse, John Gorham;
All you say is easy, but so far from being true
That I wish you wouldn't ever be again the one to think so;
For it isn't cats and butterflies that I would be to you."—

"All your little animals are in one picture—
One I've had before me since a year ago to-night;
And the picture where they live will be of you, Jane Wayland,
Till you find a way to kill them or to keep them out of sight."—

"Won't you ever see me as I am, John Gorham,
Leaving out the foolishness and all I never meant?
Somewhere in me there's a woman, if you know the way to
find her.
Will you like me any better if I prove it and repent?"—

"I doubt if I shall ever have the time, Jane Wayland;
And I dare say all this moonlight lying round us might as well
Fall for nothing on the shards of broken urns that are forgotten,
As on two that have no longer much of anything to tell."

Edwin Arlington Robinson (1869–1935)

## QUESTIONS

1. What has gone on between the couple before this dialogue begins?
2. What is the difference between what Jane Wayland and John Gorham want out of their relationship?
3. How does the poet use irony and rhythm to distinguish the characters?
4. One of these characters makes clearer sense than the other. Which one tends to be obscure, and why?
5. One test of whether characters are credible specimens of human nature is whether the reader becomes interested in their affairs? Which character more fully engages your sympathies and why?

## from "The General Prologue" to *The Canterbury Tales*

Ther was also a nonne, a PRIORESSE,
That of hir smylyng was ful symple and coy° *unaffected and quiet*
Hir gretteste ooth was but by Seint Loy;
And she was cleped° Madame Eglentyne. *called*
Ful wel she soong the servyce dyvyne,
Entuned in hir nose ful semely,
And Frenssh she spak ful faire and fetisly,° *neatly*
After the scole of Stratford-atte-Bowe,
For Frenssh of Parys was to hire unknowe.
At mete° wel ytaught was she with alle: *meals*
She leet no morsel from hir lippes falle,
Ne wette hir fyngres in hir sauce depe.
Wel koude she carie a morsel and wel kepe
That no drope ne fille up-on hir brest.
In curteisie was set ful muchel hir lest.
Hir over lippe wyped she so clene
That in hir coppe ther was no ferthyng sene
Of grece, whan she dronken hadde hir draughte.
Ful semely after hir mete she raughte.° *reached*
And sikerly° she was of greet desport,° *certainly good cheer*
And ful plesaunt, and amyable of port,
And peyned hire to countrefete cheere
Of court, and to been estatlich° of manere, *stately*
And to been holden digne° of reverence. *worthy*
But, for to speken of hir conscience,° *feelings*
She was so charitable and so pitous° *piteous*
She wolde wepe, if that she sawe a mous
Caught in a trappe, if it were deed or bledde.
Of smale houndes hadde she, that she fedde
With rosted flessh, or mylk and wastel breed.° *fine white bread*
But soore wepte she if oon of hem were deed,
Or if men smoot it with a yerde° smerte;° *stick sharply*
And al was conscience and tendre herte.
Ful semely hir wympel° pynched was; *head covering*
Hir nose tretys,° hir eyen greye as glas, *well-shaped*
Hir mouth ful smal, and ther-to softe and reed;
But sikerly she hadde a fair forheed:
It was almoost a spanne brood, I trowe;
For, hardily, she was nat undergrowe.
Ful fetys° was hir cloke, as I was war. *well made*

Of smal coral aboute hir arm she bar
A peyre of bedes, gauded° al with grene, *with large beads*
And ther-on heng a brooch of gold ful shene, *(gauds)*
On which ther was first writen a crowned A,
And after Amor vincit omnia.° *love conquers all*

Geoffrey Chaucer (ca. 1343–1400)

QUESTIONS

1. Does Chaucer ever look directly into the nun's thoughts? Is he sympathetic in his portrayal, or does he disapprove of her? How can you tell?

2. What clues do you have about the nun's attitude toward herself? What can you say of her emotional makeup?

3. What does the inscription on her brooch (Love Conquers All) tell you about her character?

## *Felix Randal*

Felix Randal the farrier, O is he dead then? my duty all ended,
Who have watched his mould of man, big-boned and hardy-handsome
Pining, pining, till time when reason rambled in it and some
Fatal four disorders, fleshed there, all contended?

Sickness broke him. Impatient he cursed at first, but mended
Being anointed and all; though a heavenlier heart began some
Months earlier, since I had our sweet reprieve and ransom
Tendered to him. Ah well, God rest him all road ever he offended!

This seeing the sick endears them to us, us too it endears.
My tongue had taught thee comfort, touch had quenched thy tears,
Thy tears that touched my heart, child, Felix, poor Felix Randal;

How far from then forethought of, all thy more boisterous years,
When thou at the random grim forge, powerful amidst peers,
Didst fettle for the great grey drayhorse his bright and battering sandal!

Gerard Manley Hopkins (1844–1889)

QUESTIONS

1. How does the poet produce a sense of immediacy (here and now)? What is the occasion of the speech? What is the relationship between the speaker and the subject?

2. What contrasting mental pictures does the speaker have of Felix Randal? Trace the sequence of the priest's thoughts about Felix.

3. The speaker begins by addressing some living person and shifts, after line eight, to addressing Felix. Is there a shift of emotion here as well? Explain.

4. In the last stage of the poem, the tone is high-spirited rather than mournful. Does the ending seem suitable? What is the effect of comparing the horseshoes to sandals?

5. In the process of making a picture of Felix, does the speaker characterize himself? Is he a simple or complex character?

## *The Dramatic Monologue Defined*

The *dramatic monologue* is a lyric poem in which a speaker in a well-defined situation addresses another person who remains silent. The speaker is usually not the poet, but rather some fictional or historical personage, and his speech reveals facets of his character which he himself may not understand or wish to reveal. Implied in his speech are details about the time, the place, and the listener so that the reader may build a mental picture of the scene.

The *soliloquy* differs from the dramatic monologue in that the speaker has no silent listener and is, in effect, addressing himself. Most lyric poems have some or all of the aspects of the dramatic monologue.

### *Ulysses*

It little profits that an idle king,
By this still hearth, among these barren crags,
Matched with an agèd wife, I mete and dole
Unequal laws unto a savage race,
That hoard, and sleep, and feed, and know not me.
I cannot rest from travel; I will drink
Life to the lees. All times I have enjoyed
Greatly, have suffered greatly, both with those
That loved me, and alone; on shore, and when
Through scudding drifts the rainy Hyades
Vext the dim sea. I am become a name;
For always roaming with a hungry heart
Much have I seen and known—cities of men
And manners, climates, councils, governments,

Myself not least, but honored of them all—
And drunk delight of battle with my peers,
Far on the ringing plains of windy Troy.
I am a part of all that I have met;
Yet all experience is an arch wherethrough
Gleams that untraveled world, whose margin fades
For ever and for ever when I move.
How dull it is to pause, to make an end,
To rust unburnished, not to shine in use!
As though to breathe were life! Life piled on life
Were all too little, and of one to me
Little remains; but every hour is saved
From that eternal silence, something more,
A bringer of new things; and vile it were
For some three suns to store and hoard myself,
And this gray spirit yearning in desire
To follow knowledge, like a sinking star,
Beyond the utmost bound of human thought.

This is my son, mine own Telemachus,
To whom I leave the scepter and the isle—
Well-loved of me, discerning to fulfil
This labor, by slow prudence to make mild
A rugged people, and through soft degrees
Subdue them to the useful and the good.
Most blameless is he, centered in the sphere
Of common duties, decent not to fail
In offices of tenderness, and pay
Meet adoration to my household gods,
When I am gone. He works his work, I mine.

There lies the port; the vessel puffs her sail;
There gloom the dark, broad seas. My mariners,
Souls that have toiled, and wrought, and thought with me—
That ever with a frolic welcome took
The thunder and the sunshine, and opposed
Free hearts, free foreheads—you and I are old;
Old age hath yet his honor and his toil.
Death closes all; but something ere the end,
Some work of noble note, may yet be done,
Not unbecoming men that strove with gods.
The lights begin to twinkle from the rocks;
The long day wanes; the slow moon climbs; the deep
Moans round with many voices. Come, my friends,

'Tis not too late to seek a newer world.
Push off, and sitting well in order smite
The sounding furrows; for my purpose holds
To sail beyond the sunset, and the baths
Of all the western stars, until I die.
It may be that the gulfs will wash us down;
It may be we shall touch the Happy Isles,
And see the great Achilles, whom we knew.
Though much is taken, much abides; and though
We are not now that strength which in old days
Moved earth and heaven, that which we are, we are—
One equal temper of heroic hearts,
Made weak by time and fate, but strong in will
To strive, to seek, to find, and not to yield.

Alfred, Lord Tennyson (1809–1892)

## QUESTIONS

Poets of the Victorian age often adopted the persona of some well-known figure, real or fictional, from the past. Ulysses, the hero of Homer's *Odyssey,* has tempted many poets to recreate his image in the context of their own eras. In Dante's *Inferno,* Ulysses (damned because he was a pagan) tells of his final voyage. Shakespeare depicted him as a shrewd and practical strategist in *Troilus and Cressida.* Here, Tennyson pictures Ulysses at the moment when he is about to set off on the final journey as reported in the *Inferno.* Recall that Ulysses had spent ten years in fighting the Trojan war and another ten in returning to his kingdom and his family.

1. Is this poem an interior monologue, an explicit dramatic monologue, or some combination of these? Is there some point at which the poem goes from being a reflection to being a speech? Where? What is Ulysses' dominant trait?
2. Does Ulysses reveal any traits which would be considered flaws by today's standards of behavior? What are they?
3. If you had already formed an opinion about the character of Ulysses, does Tennyson's picture seem consistent with that opinion? Consider his stance toward his subjects, his wife, and his son.
4. In an old sense of the word, a hero is one who undergoes great tribulation for the welfare of his community. Is the Ulysses depicted here such a hero? How would he seem heroic in nineteenth or twentieth century terms?
5. Does Tennyson's diction and meter affect the way you imagine Ulysses? What is "heroic" about the speech?

*Browning and the Dramatic Monologue*

If we exclude the characters given to us by Shakespeare and the gallery of portraits in Chaucer's prologue to *The Canterbury Tales,* Robert Browning's characters are probably those best known to readers of English poetry. Browning found the dramatic monologue to be the form of expression best suited for his genius in analyzing unusual personalities.

In Browning's hands, the dramatic monologue became an instrument for revealing character in a dynamic context rather than in a static one. Dialogue had always been able to do this through the exchange of speech which can make constant transitions from one subject to another; but the monologue, before Browning's work, rarely kept up a sense of the excitement which a reader needs to follow a single speaker through a variety of attitudes. Lyric poetry, which may leave a reader with a definite impression about the character of the speaker, usually concentrates on a single attitude and a single moment of crisis. Love poems, for example, give us the lover in a number of poses—the rejected lover, the lover called to war, the coaxing lover, the jealous lover, and many others. But to show the lover's attitude to religion, politics, art, and family life, the poet is most likely to choose a narrative or dramatic structure. Browning manages to accomplish all this within the monologue.

"My Last Duchess" makes a fine example of his accomplishment in this form. Here we see Browning's fascination with the Italian Renaissance and with abnormal behavior. Though the poem is in rhymed couplets, the rhymes are barely audible because the poet has so carefully adapted his verse to the rhythms of speech, and because the strict formality of the couplets suits the speaker's personality so well.

The monologue itself implies all we need to know about the scene, the dramatic situation, and the people involved. Instead of telling the story in chronological order, Browning blends into the Duke's speech all the ingredients of a story so that plot, theme, and character become clear in our minds. The poem is based on an actual person, Alfonso, Duke of Ferrara, whose young duchess died mysteriously in 1561. Pandolf and Claus of Innsbruck are fictitious artists.

## *My Last Duchess*

Ferrara

That's my last Duchess painted on the wall,
Looking as if she were alive. I call
That piece a wonder, now: Frà Pandolf's hands
Worked busily a day, and there she stands.
Will't please you sit and look at her? I said
"Frà Pandolf" by design, for never read
Strangers like you that pictured countenance,
The depth and passion of its earnest glance,
But to myself they turned (since none puts by
The curtain I have drawn for you, but I)
And seemed as they would ask me, if they durst,
How such a glance came there; so, not the first
Are you to turn and ask thus. Sir 'twas not
Her husband's presence only, called that spot
Of joy into the Duchess' cheek: perhaps
Frà Pandolf chanced to say, "Her mantle laps
Over my lady's wrist too much," or "Paint
Must never hope to reproduce the faint
Half-flush that dies along her throat." Such stuff
Was courtesy, she thought, and cause enough
For calling up that spot of joy. She had
A heart—how shall I say?—too soon made glad,
Too easily impressed; she liked whate'er
She looked on, and her looks went everywhere.
Sir, 'twas all one! My favor at her breast,
The drooping of the daylight in the West,
The bough of cherries some officious fool
Broke in the orchard for her, the white mule
She rode with round the terrace—all and each
Would draw from her alike the approving speech,
Or blush, at least. She thanked men,—good! but thanked
Somehow—I know not how—as if she ranked
My gift of a nine-hundred-years-old name
With anybody's gift. Who'd stoop to blame
This sort of trifling? Even had you skill
In speech—which I have not—to make your will
Quite clear to such an one, and say, "Just this
Or that in you disgusts me; here you miss,
Or there exceed the mark"—and if she let

Herself be lessoned so, nor plainly set
Her wits to yours, forsooth, and made excuse—
E'en then would be some stooping; and I choose
Never to stoop. Oh, sir, she smiled, no doubt,
Whene'er I passed her; but who passed without
Much the same smile? This grew; I gave commands;
Then all smiles stopped together. There she stands
As if alive. Will't please you rise? We'll meet
The company below, then. I repeat,
The Count your master's known munificence
Is ample warrant that no just pretense
Of mine for dowry will be disallowed;
Though his fair daughter's self, as I avowed
At starting, is my object. Nay, we'll go
Together down, sir. Notice Neptune, though,
Taming a sea-horse, thought a rarity,
Which Claus of Innsbruck cast in bronze for me!

Robert Browning (1812–1889)

QUESTIONS

1. Summarize the story which is sketched into this poem. What were the Duchess' dominant traits? In what way is the Duke representative of his time and rank?

2. If the Duke's statement "I gave commands" (line 45) is all but an admission that he had his wife killed, why would he let the envoy know this?

3. Count the number of times the Duke uses a first personal pronoun. What is the effect?

4. The poem is full of dramatic irony. Explain it, and tell how far the Duke himself is aware of any irony.

5. Part of the difficulty in making a convincing monologue is in advancing the idea as it might happen in speech, rather than in an essay or in a dialogue. Can you see any subdivisions in the poem where the speech passes from stage to stage? Note the shift of tone in the concluding lines.

## *Other Monologues*

Many poems do not aim at creating a self-portrait of the speaker. In Ezra Pound's "Portrait d'une Femme," the focal point is the subject being addressed and not the speaker. This poem has all the elements of the dramatic monologue except the intention to emphasize the speaker's character. In order to follow the unifying comparison in this poem, one must know that the Sargasso Sea is a region in the Atlantic where mixing ocean currents nourish vast stretches of floating seaweeds. In legend it is a hazardous place where weed-entangled ships sink and litter the deep with their cargoes.

## *Portrait d'une Femme*

Your mind and you are our Sargasso Sea,
London has swept about you this score years
And bright ships left you this or that in fee:
Ideas, old gossip, oddments of all things,
Strange spars of knowledge and dimmed wares of price.
Great minds have sought you—lacking someone else.
You have been second always. Tragical?
No. You preferred it to the usual thing:
One dull man, dulling and uxorious,
One average mind—with one thought less, each year.
Oh, you are patient. I have seen you sit
Hours, where something might have floated up.
And now you pay one. Yes, you richly pay.
You are a person of some interest, one comes to you
And takes strange gain away:
Trophies fished up; some curious suggestion;
Fact that leads nowhere; and a tale for two,
Pregnant with mandrakes, or with something else
That might prove useful and yet never proves,
That never fits a corner or shows use,
Or finds its hour upon the loom of days:
The tarnished, gaudy, wonderful old work;
Idols, and ambergris and rare inlays.
These are your riches, your great store; and yet
For all this sea-hoard of deciduous things,
Strange woods half sodden, and new brighter stuff:
In the slow float of differing light and deep,
No! there is nothing! In the whole and all,
Nothing that's quite your own.
Yet this is you.

Ezra Pound (1885–1972)

## QUESTIONS

1. What about the woman is attractive? What does she want out of life, and what has she had to give up?

2. How would you describe the speaker's relationship with the woman? Is his involvement purely intellectual? If not, how would you describe the emotional element?

3. A unifying strain of vocabulary in the poem involves wealth and the exchange of merchandise. Find six examples of this. Does this detail effectively communicate to you an impression about the woman's values?

4. Why does the poet not say exactly what men give her and receive from her? Contrast the connotation of the names of things she accepts "in fee" and the names of things she pays. Does the poet think that the woman cheats herself?

The next selection comes from Earle Birney's "Damnation of Vancouver." The speaker, a Sechelt chief, recollects his tribe's way of life and its final extinction at the hands of the whites. In the original context the chief's speech is part of a dialogue. It is presented here as a monologue which builds a sense of the speaker's character as he tells his story. The tribes mentioned lived along the west coast of British Columbia and on Vancouver Island.

### from *Damnation of Vancouver*

There was something, I do not know,
a way of life that died for yours to live. . . .

Each summer the salmon came, the deer were plump in the
river groves. . . .

Sometimes a young man would be many months in the woods
thinking, alone as a heron,
and learning the powers of the creatures.
I lay and watched the little grey doctor, the lizard;
I studied the spirit of bear; I came by their songs.
When I was chief I carved Brother Bear on my houseposts,
took the red earths and the white and painted his strength. . . .

In those times we drank only our sounds and thoughts,
giving unhurt to those who gave.
When your fathers took our food and left us little coins,
when they took our songs and left us little hymns,
the music and the potlatch stopped. . . .

Before even the Captain's cloud-canoe, before I was chief,
the Sechelts held a great gift-giving on the tiderim.
Something, flung gleaming through the air, fell in the water.
I dived; my fingers clutched a gun, a flintlock.
Spaniards had made it;
the Nootkas gave its height in otter skins.
Now it was mine; I shot the deer my arrows fainted to reach.
With other years came other traders
and stronger fire unsealed from iron tube and bottle;
I gave my only son the flintlock.
He walked into the whiskey-house they built in our village;
he drank its madness;
he killed his cousin, my brother's heir.
The white men choked my son with a rope.
From that day my life was a walking backwards. . . .

What trails we would have stumbled on alone none now will
know.
In a moon of heat the tall priest came;
with his magic twig of fire he lit the dried grass
and spoke in the raven's voice of Hell,
unrolled a painting bright as the sundown,
showed us our dead in Hell's flame.
In fear we let the little wisps of our marvels
lose themselves in the black cloud of his god.
And ever the whites came crowding our shoreline
like summer smelts, and the deer fled.
My grandsons, my hunters, went to grease logs for the skidders;
one died under a felled tree,
the other black and gasping with smallpox. . . .

I had yet two daughters; their eyes were chaste.
To one a sailor gave rum, and a glass necklace,
and the secret rot of his thighs; she died barren and young.
The other went to be squaw to a trader;
when he had turned her away,
before she spat out her lungs with his plague,
she bore him my only grand-daughter.
In my old age the child grew tall, fair as a waterfall.
The factor married her; he made her give up our people.
There are white chiefs now in Vancouver who carry her blood,
but it is a long time now and they do not know,
or they are ashamed.
These are all my descendants. . . .

When the measles passed from my village, ten of us lived
to bury our ninety, and I, their Chief, was blind.
We left the longhouses for the burning,
the burial grove and the carvings to loggers.
They sent me over the Sound to sit
dark and alone by the smokehouse fire of my cousins.
One night I felt with shuffling feet the beach-path.
I walked into the saltwater,
I walked down to the home of the Seal Brother . . . .

Earle Birney (1904– )

*Chapter 14*

# The Full Analysis

THE premises on which this study has been built are, first, that the more one notices about the things that please him, the greater his appreciation will be; second, that the trained observer sees more than a casual reader; and third, that all systematic training requires time so that a focus may be methodically directed from one element to the next. The paradox of this approach is that in order to develop his powers of observation, one must go through a process of limiting the scope of his vision. Almost arbitrarily, we have limited topics for discussion about any poem to include only those elements which have been "covered." In the chapters which precede the treatment of symbolism, for example, it was often difficult to abstain from raising the tempting question of symbolic meanings. The result of all this is intended to be cumulative, even at the expense of temporarily overlooking important poetic elements.

By now, the need to train our sights on a secluded area of poetry should be passed. What remains is a review of the total process and an application of that process to three poems which, though they pose a certain resistance to the intelligence, are nevertheless accessible through analysis.

## *Suggestions for Analysis*

A. First read the poem through to sense the tone. When you have an idea about what kind of voice the poem requires, rehearse it, using the voice you feel is appropriate.

B. Summarize the content, trying to follow the internal structure, that is, the arrangement of thought.

1. For idea-oriented poems, outline the presentation of thought. Note whether the poem defines, compares, classifies, or explains causes or processes.
2. For poems which express feelings, trace the flow of emotion. Note how emotions succeed one another and how the poet introduces, advances, and concludes his statement.
3. For narrative poems, outline the plot's subdivisions, showing how the action advances from the opening situation, through the complication and climax to a conclusion. If the poem suggests a story without using a full plot, notice which elements of plot are present and show how the rest are implied.
4. For poems with a thesis to prove, outline the argument, noting the order of the proofs offered and the effectiveness of the presentation.
5. For poems which are primarily word pictures, explain the order in which details are observed and the way the poet's attitude toward the picture affects the choice and pattern of presentation.

C. Observe any visual signs of structuring in the poem (indentations, unusual spacing, division into stanzas, shifts in line length, etc.), and try to ascertain the rationale behind the arrangement which may be related to the progress of the thought content.

D. Word Choice. Be certain of the meaning of every word in the poem. If you think you know the meaning, but cannot understand the usage of a word, consult your dictionary to determine if the word is being used according to some unfamiliar definition.

1. Relate the dominant emotional impression with which the poem leaves you to the cumulative effect of the connotative words. Sort out the pleasant connotations from the unpleasant ones, and try to judge how the blending of emotionally charged words settles into a unified impression. Note all overlapping meanings.
2. Notice the poet's selection of abstract and concrete words to determine how these ingredients influence the dominant impression.

3. Review the word choice with an emphasis on imagery. Classify the image-making words according to the sense impressions involved, noticing all patterns of repetition which may contribute to the poem's substructure.
4. Evaluate the fitness of the diction as a whole, noting whether its relative formality or informality seems appropriate. Judge the word choice for its freshness and vitality.

E. Allusion. If the poem contains any direct or indirect reference to historical, literary, biblical, or legendary material, satisfy yourself that you understand the meaning and intention of the poet by consulting the appropriate reference source. Estimate the connotative value of the allusion and determine whether it is a part of some larger pattern of association.

F. Figurative Language. Reexamine the imagery to see if the images are free or are introduced through figurative comparisons. Notice if the images which are tied to figures of speech function as the concrete means by which the poet advances his thoughts.

1. Explain any poetic logic by which the figurative comparisons are related to one another. Notice if the figures of speech constitute one of the bases on which the poem is structured.
2. Classify the figures of speech according to the way in which they relate image to idea (metaphor, simile, etc.).

G. Irony. Be aware that any unobserved irony may spoil your interpretation of a poem. Try to measure any ironic distance between the poet and the speaker of the poem. Assess how aware the speaker of the poem is to those ironies which affect his voice or his situation.

1. Reconsider the tension by which opposite forces come together to create a unified effect. See how irony and paradox contribute to this.
2. Evaluate the effect which irony plays in satiric poems.

H. Symbols. Point out those details which have symbolic meaning, outlining any patterns of recurrence (e.g., religious, sexual, or animal symbols). Ascertain whether the symbols have allegorical meaning or whether their meanings are deliberately kept open for multiple interpretation.

I. Meter. If the poem is metered, scan it to find the metrical basis. Note and explain the significance of any departures from the base pattern. Show how the meter fits the poem's content and helps to set the emotional tone.

J. Musical Effects. Listen for musical effects resulting from such sound repetitions as alliteration, assonance, and rhyme. Cite any role sound plays in the external organization of the poem, and interpret any connections you find between the emotional tone and the musical quality.

* * *

At every stage of your analysis, treat the poem as you would treat a playscript to be rehearsed for a performance. Use marginal notes freely and mark the poem for its verbal dynamics. Let these markings be a visual reminder of the many submerged designs in poetry which may not be evident in the first few readings.

## *The Love Song of J. Alfred Prufrock*

*S'io credessi che mia risposta fosse*
*a persona che mai tornasse al mondo,*
*questa fiamma staria senza più scosse.*
*Ma per ciò che giammai di questo fondo*
*non tornò vivo alcun, s'i'odo il vero,*
*senza tema d'infamia ti rispondo.*

Let us go then, you and I,
When the evening is spread out against the sky
Like a patient etherised upon a table;
Let us go, through certain half-deserted streets,
The muttering retreats
Of restless nights in one-night cheap hotels
And sawdust restaurants with oyster-shells:

*The Italian epigraph* is from Dante's *Inferno,* XXVII, 61–66. The words are spoken by Guido da Montefeltro, who speaks without inhibition to Virgil, one with whom secrets are safe. He says, "If I believed I were speaking to one who might return to the world, this flame would be still, but since no living person has ever left this pit, if what I hear is the truth, I answer you without fear of Infamy." Guido, in Hell's eighth circle, has the shape of flame, and the wavering of the flame is his speech.

Streets that follow like a tedious argument
Of insidious intent
To lead you to an overwhelming question. . .
Oh, do not ask, 'What is it?'
Let us go and make our visit.

In the room the women come and go
Talking of Michelangelo.

The yellow fog that rubs its back upon the window-panes,
The yellow smoke that rubs its muzzle on the window-panes,
Licked its tongue into the corners of the evening,
Lingered upon the pools that stand in drains,
Let fall upon its back the soot that falls from chimneys,
Slipped by the terrace, made a sudden leap,
And seeing that it was a soft October night,
Curled once about the house, and fell asleep.

And indeed there will be time
For the yellow smoke that slides along the street
Rubbing its back upon the window-panes;
There will be time, there will be time
To prepare a face to meet the faces that you meet;
There will be time to murder and create,
And time for all the works and days of hands
That lift and drop a question on your plate;
Time for you and time for me,
And time yet for a hundred indecisions,
And for a hundred visions and revisions,
Before the taking of a toast and tea.

In the room the women come and go
Talking of Michelangelo.

And indeed there will be time
To wonder, 'Do I dare?' and, 'Do I dare?'
Time to turn back and descend the stair,
With a bald spot in the middle of my hair—
(They will say: 'How his hair is growing thin!')
My morning coat, my collar mounting firmly to the chin,
My necktie rich and modest, but asserted by a simple pin—
(They will say: 'But how his arms and legs are thin!')
Do I dare
Disturb the universe?

In a minute there is time
For decisions and revisions which a minute will reverse.

For I have known them all already, known them all—
Have known the evenings, mornings, afternoons,
I have measured out my life with coffee spoons;
I know the voices dying with a dying fall
Beneath the music from a farther room.
  So how should I presume?

And I have known the eyes already, known them all—
The eyes that fix you in a formulated phrase,
And when I am formulated, sprawling on a pin,
When I am pinned and wriggling on the wall,
Then how should I begin
To spit out all the butt-ends of my days and ways?
  And how should I presume?

And I have known the arms already, known them all—
Arms that are braceleted and white and bare
(But in the lamplight, downed with light brown hair!)
Is it perfume from a dress
That makes me so digress?
Arms that lie along a table, or wrap about a shawl.
  And should I then presume?
  And how should I begin?

. . . . . .

Shall I say, I have gone at dusk through narrow streets
And watched the smoke that rises from the pipes
Of lonely men in shirt-sleeves, leaning out of windows? . . .

I should have been a pair of ragged claws
Scuttling across the floors of silent seas.

. . . . . .

And the afternoon, the evening, sleeps so peacefully!
Smoothed by long fingers,
Asleep . . . tired . . . or it malingers,
Stretched on the floor, here beside you and me.
Should I, after tea and cakes and ices,
Have the strength to force the moment to its crisis?
But though I have wept and fasted, wept and prayed,

Though I have seen my head (grown slightly bald) brought in
upon a platter,
I am no prophet—and here's no great matter;
I have seen the moment of my greatness flicker,
And I have seen the eternal Footman hold my coat, and snicker,
And in short, I was afraid.

And would it have been worth it, after all,
After the cups, the marmalade, the tea,
Among the porcelain, among some talk of you and me,
Would it have been worth while,
To have bitten off the matter with a smile,
To have squeezed the universe into a ball
To roll it towards some overwhelming question,
To say: 'I am Lazarus, come from the dead,
Come back to tell you all, I shall tell you all'—
If one, settling a pillow by her head,
Should say: 'That is not what I meant at all.
That is not it, at all.'

And would it have been worth it, after all,
Would it have been worth while,
After the sunsets and the dooryards and the sprinkled streets,
After the novels, after the teacups, after the skirts that trail
along the floor—
And this, and so much more?—
It is impossible to say just what I mean!
But as if a magic lantern threw the nerves in patterns on a
screen:
Would it have been worth while
If one, settling a pillow or throwing off a shawl,
And turning toward the window, should say:
'That is not it at all,
That is not what I meant, at all.'

. . . . .

*Lines 82–83: See Matthew 14: 1–11 for the story of Salome and John the Baptist.*
*Lines 92–93: See lines 41–42 of Andrew Marvell's "To His Coy Mistress."*
*Line 94: See John 11: 1–44 for the account of Christ's raising Lazarus from the dead; and Luke 16: 19–25 for the story of Lazarus and Dives.*

No! I am not Prince Hamlet, nor was meant to be;
Am an attendant lord, one that will do
To swell a progress, start a scene or two,
Advise the prince; no doubt, an easy tool,
Deferential, glad to be of use,
Politic, cautious, and meticulous;
Full of high sentence, but a bit obtuse;
At times, indeed, almost ridiculous—
Almost, at times, the Fool.

I grow old . . . I grow old . . .
I shall wear the bottoms of my trousers rolled.

Shall I part my hair behind? Do I dare to eat a peach?
I shall wear white flannel trousers, and walk upon the beach.
I have heard the mermaids singing, each to each.

I do not think that they will sing to me.

I have seen them riding seaward on the waves
Combing the white hair of the waves blown back
When the wind blows the water white and black.

We have lingered in the chambers of the sea
By sea-girls wreathed with seaweed red and brown
Till human voices wake us, and we drown.

T. S. Eliot (1888–1965)

## *Sunday Morning*

I

Complacencies of the peignoir, and late
Coffee and oranges in a sunny chair,
And the green freedom of a cockatoo
Upon a rug mingle to dissipate
The holy hush of ancient sacrifice.
She dreams a little, and she feels the dark
Encroachment of that old catastrophe,
As a calm darkens among water-lights.

Lines *111–119: These lines may allude to Hamlet himself, to Osric, Polonius, or Rosencrantz and Gildenstern, all from Shakespeare's* Hamlet.
*Lines 124–125: See John Donne's "Song" (Go and catch a falling star).*

The pungent oranges and bright, green wings
Seem things in some procession of the dead,
Winding across wide water, without sound.
The day is like wide water, without sound,
Stilled for the passing of her dreaming feet
Over the seas, to silent Palestine,
Dominion of the blood and sepulchre.

II

Why should she give her bounty to the dead?
What is divinity if it can come
Only in silent shadows and in dreams?
Shall she not find in comforts of the sun,
In pungent fruit and bright, green wings, or else
In any balm or beauty of the earth,
Things to be cherished like the thought of heaven?
Divinity must live within herself:
Passions of rain, or moods in falling snow;
Grievings in loneliness, or unsubdued
Elations when the forest blooms; gusty
Emotions on wet roads on autumn nights;
All pleasures and all pains, remembering
The bough of summer and the winter branch.
These are the measures destined for her soul.

III

Jove in the clouds had his inhuman birth.
No mother suckled him, no sweet land gave
Large-mannered motions to his mythy mind.
He moved among us, as a muttering king,
Magnificent, would move among his hinds,
Until our blood, commingling, virginal,
With heaven, brought such requital to desire
The very hinds discerned it, in a star.
Shall our blood fail? Or shall it come to be
The blood of paradise? And shall the earth
Seem all of paradise that we shall know?
The sky will be much friendlier then than now,
A part of labor and a part of pain,
And next in glory to enduring love,
Not this dividing and indifferent blue.

IV

She says "I am content when wakened birds,
Before they fly, test the reality
Of misty fields, by their sweet questionings;
But when the birds are gone, and their warm fields
Return no more, where, then, is paradise?"
There is not any haunt of prophecy,
Nor any old chimera of the grave,
Neither the golden underground, nor isle
Melodious, where spirits gat them home,
Nor visionary south, nor cloudy palm
Remote on heaven's hill, that has endured
As April's green endures; or will endure
Like her remembrance of awakened birds,
Or her desire for June and evening, tipped
By the consummation of the swallow's wings.

V

She says, "But in contentment I still feel
The need of some imperishable bliss."
Death is the mother of beauty; hence from her,
Alone, shall come fulfilment to our dreams
And our desires. Although she strews the leaves
Of sure obliteration on our paths,
The path sick sorrow took, the many paths
Where triumph rang its brassy phrase, or love
Whispered a little out of tenderness,
She makes the willow shiver in the sun
For maidens who were wont to sit and gaze
Upon the grass, relinquished to their feet.
She causes boys to pile new plums and pears
On disregarded plate. The maidens taste
And stray impassioned in the littering leaves.

VI

Is there no change of death in paradise?
Does ripe fruit never fall? Or do the boughs
Hang always heavy in that perfect sky,
Unchanging, yet so like our perishing earth,
With rivers like our own that seek for seas
They never find, the same receding shores

That never touch with inarticulate pang?
Why set the pear upon those river-banks
Or spice the shores with odors of the plum?
Alas, that they should wear our colors there,
The silken weavings of our afternoons,
And pick the strings of our insipid lutes!
Death is the mother of beauty, mystical,
Within whose burning bosom we devise
Our earthly mothers waiting, sleeplessly.

VII

Supple and turbulent, a ring of men
Shall chant in orgy on a summer morn
Their boisterous devotion to the sun,
Not as a god, but as a god might be,
Naked among them, like a savage source.
Their chant shall be a chant of paradise,
Out of their blood, returning to the sky;
And in their chant shall enter, voice by voice,
The windy lake wherein their lord delights,
The trees, like serafin, and echoing hills,
That choir among themselves long afterward.
They shall know well the heavenly fellowship
Of men that perish and of summer morn.
And whence they came and whither they shall go
The dew upon their feet shall manifest.

VIII

She hears, upon that water without sound,
A voice that cries, "The tomb in Palestine
Is not the porch of spirits lingering.
It is the grave of Jesus, where he lay."
We live in an old chaos of the sun,
Or old dependency of day and night,
Or island solitude, unsponsored, free,
Of that wide water, inescapable.
Deer walk upon our mountains, and the quail
Whistle about us in their spontaneous cries;
Sweet berries ripen in the wilderness;

And, in the isolation of the sky,
At evening, casual flocks of pigeons make
Ambiguous undulations as they sink,
Downward to darkness, on extended wings.

Wallace Stevens (1879–1955)

## *Middle Passage*

### I.

*Jesús, Estrella, Esperanza, Mercy:*

Sails flashing to the wind like weapons,
sharks following the moans the fever and the dying;
horror the corposant and compass rose.

Middle Passage:
voyage through death
to life upon these shores.

"10 April 1800—
Blacks rebellious. Crew uneasy. Our linguist says
their moaning is a prayer for death,
ours and their own. Some try to starve themselves.
Lost three this morning leaped with crazy laughter
to the waiting sharks, sang as they went under."

*Desire, Adventure, Tartar, Ann:*

Standing to America, bringing home
black gold, black ivory, black seed.

*Deep in the festering hold thy father lies,*
*of his bones New England pews are made,*
*those are altar lights that were his eyes.*

Title. *The Middle Passage is the transatlantic crossing, or middle phase of the slave's journey from his village to the American plantation.* 1. *names of ships active in slave trade, also lines 14, 48, and 122.* 4. corposant, *St. Elmo's fire, the flamelike discharge of static electricity from prominent parts of a ship in stormy weather. St. Elmo is the patron saint of sailors.* 8. *Lines in quotation marks represent the records and testimony of whites.*

Jesus Saviour Pilot Me
Over Life's Tempestuous Sea

We pray that Thou wilt grant, O Lord,
safe passage to our vessels bringing
heathen souls unto Thy chastening.

Jesus Saviour

"8 bells. I cannot sleep, for I am sick
with fear, but writing eases fear a little
since still my eyes can see these words take shape
upon the page & so I write, as one
would turn to exorcism. 4 days scudding,
but now the sea is calm again. Misfortune
follows in our wake like sharks (our grinning
tutelary gods). Which one of us
has killed an albatross? A plague among
our blacks—Ophthalmia: blindness—& we
have jettisoned the blind to no avail.
It spreads, the terrifying sickness spreads.
Its claws have scratched sight from the Capt.'s eyes
& there is blindness in the fo'c'sle
& we must sail 3 weeks before we come
to port."

*What port awaits us, Davy Jones'*
*or home? I've heard of slavers drifting, drifting,*
*playthings of wind and storm and chance, their crews*
*gone blind, the jungle hatred*
*crawling up on deck.*

Thou Who Walked On Galilee

"Deponent further sayeth *The Bella J*
left the Guinea Coast
with cargo of five hundred blacks and odd
for the barracoons of Florida:

"That there was hardly room 'tween-decks for half
the sweltering cattle stowed spoon-fashion there;
that some went mad of thirst and tore their flesh
and sucked the blood:

20, 21, *lines from a hymn, along with lines 25, 47, and 69 make an ironic refrain: the sailor's prayer for safety.* 51. barracoons, *barracks where slaves were kept temporarily.*

"That Crew and Captain lusted with the comeliest
of the savage girls kept naked in the cabins;
that there was one they called The Guinea Rose
and they cast lots and fought to lie with her:

"That when the Bo's'n piped all hands, the flames
spreading from starboard already were beyond
control, the negroes howling and their chains
entangled with the flames:

"That the burning blacks could not be reached,
that the Crew abandoned ship,
leaving their shrieking negresses behind,
that the Captain perished drunken with the wenches:

"Further Deponent sayeth not."

Pilot Oh Pilot Me

II.

Aye, lad, and I have seen those factories,
Gambia, Rio Pongo, Calabar;
have watched the artful mongos baiting traps
of war wherein the victor and the vanquished

Were caught as prizes for our barracoons.
Have seen the nigger kings whose vanity
and greed turned wild black hides of Fellatah,
Mandingo, Ibo, Kru to gold for us.

And there was one—King Anthracite we named him—
fetish face beneath French parasols
of brass and orange velvet, impudent mouth
whose cups were carven skulls of enemies:

He'd honor us with drum and feast and conjo
and palm-oil glistening wenches deft in love,
and for tin crowns that shone with paste,
red calico and German-silver trinkets

70. *Section II is a dramatic monologue spoken by an old slave trader.* 72. [M]ongos, *members of a Bantu group of tribes in the Southern Congo.* 76. Fellatah, *Negroes from Egypt and the Sudan.* 77. Mandingo, *Sudanese tribesmen;* Ibo, *Negro tribesmen from the Lower Niger River area;* Kru, *members of a Negro tribe in the region of Liberia.* 82. conjo, *charms and fetish objects used in rituals.*

Would have the drums talk war and send
his warriors to burn the sleeping villages
and kill the sick and old and lead the young
in coffles to our factories.

Twenty years a trader, twenty years,
for there was wealth aplenty to be harvested
from those black fields, and I'd be trading still
but for the fevers melting down my bones.

III.

Shuttles in the rocking loom of history,
the dark ships move, the dark ships move,
their bright ironical names
like jests of kindness on a murderer's mouth;
plough through thrashing glister toward
fata morgana's lucent melting shore,
weave toward New World littorals that are
mirage and myth and actual shore.
Voyage through death,
voyage whose chartings are unlove.
A charnel stench, effluvium of living death
spreads outward from the hold,
where the living and the dead, the horribly dying,
lie interlocked, lie foul with blood and excrement.

*Deep in the festering hold thy father lies,*
*the corpse of mercy rots with him,*
*rats eat love's rotten gelid eyes.*

*But, oh, the living look at you*
*with human eyes whose suffering accuses you,*
*whose hatred reaches through the swill of dark*
*to strike you like a leper's claw.*

*You cannot stare that hatred down*
*or chain the fear that stalks the watches*
*and breathes on you its fetid scorching breath;*
*cannot kill the deep immortal human wish,*
*the timeless will.*

"But for the storm that flung up barriers
of wind and wave, *The Amistad,* señores,
would have reached the port of Príncipe in two,
three days at most; but for the storm we should
have been prepared for what befell.
Swift as the puma's leap it came. There was
that interval of moonless calm filled only
with the water's and the rigging's usual sounds,
then sudden movement, blows and snarling cries
and they had fallen on us with machete
and marlinspike. It was as though the very
air, the night itself were striking us.
Exhausted by the rigors of the storm,
we were no match for them. Our men went down
before the murderous Africans. Our loyal
Celestino ran from below with gun
and lantern and I saw, before the cane-
knife's wounding flash, Cinquez,
that surly brute who calls himself a prince,
directing, urging on the ghastly work.
He hacked the poor mulatto down, and then
he turned on me. The decks were slippery
when daylight finally came. It sickens me
to think of what I saw, of how these apes
threw overboard the butchered bodies of
our men, true Christians all, like so much jetsam.
Enough, enough. The rest is quickly told:
Cinquez was forced to spare the two of us
you see to steer the ship to Africa,
and we like phantoms doomed to rove the sea
voyaged east by day and west by night,
deceiving them, hoping for rescue,
prisoners on our own vessel, till
at length we drifted to the shores of this
your land, America, where we were freed

121. *From this point on in the poem, details refer to the* Amistad *mutiny of 1839 in which 53 slaves led by Joseph Cinque successfully overcame their Spanish crew. A Spanish prisoner, pretending to navigate towards Africa, steered the ship into U.S. waters where it was captured and taken to New London, Conn. Placed on trial, the men were defended by John Quincy Adams. In 1841, after a famous Supreme Court decision, the men were freed and allowed to return to Africa.*

from our unspeakable misery. Now we
demand, good sirs, the extradition of
Cinquez and his accomplices to La
Havana. And it distresses us to know
there are so many here who seem inclined
to justify the mutiny of these blacks.
We find it paradoxical indeed
that you whose wealth, whose tree of liberty
are rooted in the labor of your slaves
should suffer the august John Quincy Adams
to speak with so much passion of the right
of chattel slaves to kill their lawful masters
and with his Roman rhetoric weave a hero's
garland for Cinquez. I tell you that
we are determined to return to Cuba
with our slaves and there see justice done. Cinquez—
or let us say 'the Prince'—Cinquez shall die."

The deep immortal human wish,
the timeless will:

Cinquez its deathless primaveral image,
life that transfigures many lives.

Voyage through death
to life upon these shores.

Robert Hayden (1913– )

# Part II

# ANTHOLOGY

# Anthology

*Edward*

"Why dois your brand° sae° drop wi' bluid, *sword so*
Edward, Edward?
Why dois your brand sae drop wi' bluid,
And why sae sad gang° yee O?" *go*
"O I hae killed my hauke sae guid,
Mither, mither:
O I hae killed my hauke sae guid,
And I had nae mair bot hee O."

"Your haukis bluid was nevir sae reid,° *red*
Edward, Edward:
Your haukis bluid was nevir sae reid,
My deir son I tell thee O."
"O I hae killed my reid-roan steid,
Mither, mither:
O I hae killed my reid-roan steid,
That erst was sae fair and free O."

"Your steid was auld, and ye hae gat mair,
Edward, Edward:
Your steid was auld, and ye hae gat mair,
Sum other dule° ye drie° O." *grief suffer*
"O, I hae killed my fadir deir,
Mither, mither,
O, I hae killed my fadir deir,
Alas, and wae° is mee, O!" *woe*

"And whatten° penance wul ye drie for that, *what kind of*
Edward, Edward?
And whatten penance will ye drie for that?
My deir son, now tell me, O."
"Ile set my feit in yonder boat,

Mither, mither,
Ile set my feit in yonder boat,
And Ile fare ovir the sea, O."

"And what wul ye doe wi' your towirs and your ha',
Edward, Edward,
And what wul ye doe wi' your towirs and your ha',
That were sae fair to see, O?"
"Ile let thame stand tul they doun fa',
Mither, mither,
Ile let thame stand tul they doun fa',
For here nevir mair maun° I bee, O." *must*

"And what wul ye leive to your bairns° and your wife, *children*
Edward, Edward?
And what wul ye leive to your bairns and your wife,
When ye gang ovir the sea, O?"
"The warldis° room, late° them beg thrae° life, *world's let through*
Mither, mither,
The warldis room, late them beg thrae life,
For thame nevir mair wul I see, O."

"And what wul ye leive to your ain° mither deir, *own*
Edward, Edward?
And what wul ye leive to your ain mither deir?
My deir son, now tell me, O."
"The curse of hell frae me sall ye beir,
Mither, mither,
The curse of hell frae me sall ye beir,
Sic° counseils° ye gave to me, O." *such counsels*

Anonymous

## *The Twa Corbies*

As I was walking all alane,
I heard two corbies° making a mane;° *carrion crows, moan*
The tane° unto the t'other say, *one*
"Where sall we gang° and dine today?" *shall we go*

"In behint yon auld fail dyke,° *turf wall*
I wot° there lies a new-slain knight; *know*
And naebody kens° that he lies there, *knows*
But his hawk, his hound, and lady fair.

"His hound is to the hunting gane,
His hawk to fetch the wild-fowl hame,
His lady's ta'en another mate,
So we may mak our dinner sweet.

"Ye'll sit on his white hause-bane,° *neck-bone*
And I'll pick out his bonny blue een;° *eyes*
Wi ae lock o' his gowden hair
We'll theek° our nest when it grows bare. *thatch*

"Mony a one for him makes mane,
But nane sall ken where he is gane;
O'er his white banes when they are bare,
The wind sall blaw for evermair."

Anonymous

## *My Galley*

My galley chargèd with forgetfulness
Thorough sharp seas, in winter nights, doth pass
'Tween rock and rock; and eke° mine enemy, alas, *also*
That is my lord, steereth with cruelness—
And every oar a thought in readiness,
As though that death were light in such a case.
An endless wind doth tear the sail apace,
Of forcèd sighs and trusty fearfulness;
A rain of tears, a cloud of dark disdain,
Hath done the wearied cords great hinderance,
Wreathèd with error and eke with ignorance.
The stars be hid that led me to this pain;
Drownèd is reason, that should me consort,
And I remain despairing of the port.

Sir Thomas Wyatt (1503–1542)

## *Whoso List to Hunt*

Whoso list to hunt, I know where is an hind,
But as for me, alas, I may no more.
The vain travail hath wearied me so sore,
I am of them that farthest come behind.
Yet may I by no means my wearied mind
Draw from the deer; but as she fleeth afore
Fainting I follow. I leave off therefore,
Since in a net I seek to hold the wind.

Who list her hunt, I put him out of doubt,
As well as I may spend his time in vain.
And graven with diamonds in letters plain
There is written, her fair neck round about:
*Noli me tangere*°, for Caesar's I am, *do not touch*
And wild for to hold, though I seem tame.

Sir Thomas Wyatt (1503–1542)

## from *Astrophel and Stella*

### 31

With how sad steps, O Moon, thou climb'st the skies!
How silently, and with how wan a face!
What! may it be that even in heavenly place
That busy archer his sharp arrows tries?
Sure, if that long-with-love-acquainted eyes
Can judge of love, thou feel'st a lover's case;
I read it in thy looks: thy languished grace,
To me that feel the like, thy state descries.
Then, even of fellowship, O Moon, tell me,
Is constant love deemed there but want of wit?
Are beauties there as proud as here they be?
Do they above love to be loved, and yet
Those lovers scorn whom that love doth possess?
Do they call virtue there ungratefulness?

### 39

Come sleep! O sleep, the certain knot of peace,
The baiting° place of wit, the balm of woe, *resting*
The poor man's wealth, the prisoner's release,
Th' indifferent° judge between the high and low; *objective*
With shield of proof° shield me from out the prease° *tested* *crowd*
Of those fierce darts despair at me doth throw;
O make in me those civil wars to cease;
I will good tribute pay, if thou do so.
Take thou of me smooth pillows, sweetest bed,
A chamber deaf to noise and blind to light,
A rosy garland and a weary head;
And if these things, as being thine by right,
Move not thy heavy grace, thou shalt in me,
Livelier than elsewhere, Stella's image see.

Sir Philip Sidney (1554–1547)

## from *Delia*

### 45

Care-charmer sleep, son of the sable night,
Brother to death, in silent darkness born,
Relieve my languish and restore the light;
With dark forgetting of my care, return.
And let the day be time enough to mourn
The shipwreck of my ill-adventured youth;
Let waking eyes suffice to wail their scorn
Without the torment of the night's untruth.
Cease, dreams, th' images of day-desires,
To model forth the passions of the morrow;
Never let rising sun approve you liars,
To add more grief to aggravate my sorrow.
Still let me sleep, embracing clouds in vain,
And never wake to feel the day's disdain.

Samuel Daniel (1562–1619)

## *Sleep*

Care-charming Sleep, thou easer of all woes,
Brother to Death, sweetly thyself dispose
On this afflicted prince; fall like a cloud
In gentle showers; give nothing that is loud
Or painful to his slumbers; easy, sweet,
And as a purling stream, thou son of Night,
Pass by his troubled senses; sing his pain,
Like hollow murmuring wind or silver rain;
Into this prince gently, oh, gently slide,
And kiss him into slumbers like a bride.

John Fletcher (1579–1625)

## *The Silver Swan*

The silver swan, who living had no note,
When death approached, unlocked her silent throat;
Leaning her breast against the reedy shore,
Thus sung her first and last, and sung no more.
Farewell, all joys; O death, come close mine eyes;
More geese than swans now live, more fools than wise.

Orlando Gibbons (1583–1625)

## from *Amoretti*

### 75

One day I wrote her name upon the strand,
But came the waves and washed it away;
Again I wrote it with a second hand,
But came the tide, and made my pains his prey.
"Vain man," said she, "that dost in vain essay
A mortal thing so to immortalize,
For I myself shall like to this decay,
And eke my name be wipèd out likewise."
"Not so (quoth I) let baser things devise
To die in dust, but you shall live by fame;
My verse your virtues rare shall eternize,
And in the heavens write your glorious name,
Where whenas death shall all the world subdue,
Our love shall live, and later life renew."

### 79

Men call you fair, and you do credit it,
For that yourself you daily such do see:
But the true fair, that is the gentle wit
And virtuous mind, is much more praised of me.
For all the rest, how ever fair it be,
Shall turn to nought and loose that glorious hue:
But only that is permanent and free
From frail corruption, that doth flesh ensue.
That is true beauty: that doth argue you
To be divine and born of heavenly seed:
Derived from that fair Spirit, from whom all true
And perfect beauty did at first proceed.
He only fair, and what he fair hath made,
All other fair like flowers untimely fade.

Edmund Spenser (1552–1599)

## from *Idea's Mirrour*

### 6

How many paltry, foolish, painted things,
That now in coaches trouble ev'ry street,
Shall be forgotten, whom no poet sings,
Ere they be well wrapped in their winding sheet!

Where I to thee eternity shall give,
When nothing else remaineth of these days,
And queens hereafter shall be glad to live
Upon the alms of thy superfluous praise;
Virgins and matrons reading these my rhymes
Shall be so much delighted with thy story
That they shall grieve they lived not in these times,
To have seen thee, their sex's only glory.
So shalt thou fly above the vulgar throng,
Still to survive in my immortal song.

Michael Drayton (1563–1613)

## from *Sonnets*

### 29

When in disgrace with fortune and men's eyes,
I all alone beweep my outcast state,
And trouble deaf heaven with my bootless cries,
And look upon myself, and curse my fate,
Wishing me like to one more rich in hope,
Featured like him, like him with friends possessed,
Desiring this man's art and that man's scope,
With what I most enjoy contented least;
Yet in these thoughts myself almost despising,
Haply I think on thee; and then my state,
Like to the lark at break of day arising
From sullen earth, sings hymns at heaven's gate;
For thy sweet love remembered such wealth brings
That then I scorn to change my state with kings.

### 30

When to the sessions of sweet silent thought
I summon up remembrance of things past,
I sigh the lack of many a thing I sought,
And with old woes new wail my dear times' waste:
Then can I drown an eye, unused to flow,
For precious friends hid in death's dateless night,
And weep afresh love's long since cancelled woe,
And moan the expense of many a vanished sight:
Then can I grieve at grievances foregone,
And heavily from woe to woe tell o'er
The sad account of fore-bemoanèd moan,

Which I new pay as if not paid before.
  But if the while I think on thee, dear friend,
  All losses are restored and sorrows end.

116

Let me not to the marriage of true minds
Admit impediments. Love is not love
Which alters when it alteration finds,
Or bends with the remover to remove.
O, no! it is an ever-fixèd mark,
That looks on tempests and is never shaken;
It is the star to every wandering bark,
Whose worth's unknown, although his height be taken.° *measured by sextant*
Love's not Time's fool, though rosy lips and cheeks
Within his bending sickle's compass come;
Love alters not with his brief hours and weeks,
But bears it out even to the edge of doom.
  If this be error and upon me proved,
  I never writ, nor no man ever loved.

129

The expense of spirit in a waste of shame
Is lust in action; and till action, lust
Is perjured, murderous, bloody, full of blame,
Savage, extreme, rude, cruel, not to trust;
Enjoyed no sooner but despisèd straight;
Past reason hunted; and no sooner had,
Past reason hated, as a swallowed bait,
On purpose laid to make the taker mad:
Mad in pursuit, and in possession so;
Had, having, and in quest to have, extreme;
A bliss in proof,°—and proved, a very woe; *in the act*
Before, a joy proposed; behind, a dream.
  All this the world well knows; yet none knows well
  To shun the heaven that leads men to this hell.

William Shakespeare (1564–1616)

## from *Cymbeline*

Fear no more the heat o' the sun,
  Nor the furious winter's rages;

Thou thy worldly task hast done,
  Home art gone, and ta'en thy wages.
Golden lads and girls all must,
As chimney-sweepers, come to dust.

Fear no more the frown o' the great;
  Thou art past the tyrant's stroke;
Care no more to clothe and eat;
  To thee the reed is as the oak.
The sceptre, learning, physic, must
All follow this, and come to dust.

Fear no more the lightning-flash,
  Nor the all-dreaded thunder-stone;
Fear not slander, censure rash;
  Thou hast finished joy and moan.
All lovers young, all lovers must
Consign to thee, and come to dust.

No exorciser harm thee!
  Nor no witchcraft charm thee!
Ghost unlaid forbear thee!
  Nothing ill come near thee!
Quiet consummation have;
And renownèd be thy grave!

William Shakespeare (1564–1616)

## *Song: To Celia*

Drink to me only with thine eyes,
  And I will pledge with mine;
Or leave a kiss but in the cup
  And I'll not look for wine.
The thirst that from the soul doth rise
  Doth ask a drink divine;
But might I of Jove's nectar sup,
  I would not change for thine.

I sent thee late a rosy wreath,
  Not so much honoring thee
As giving it a hope that there
  It could not withered be.

But thou thereon didst only breathe,
  And sent'st it back to me;
Since when it grows, and smells, I swear,
  Not of itself, but thee!

Ben Jonson (1572–1637)

## *Queen and Huntress*

Queen and huntress, chaste and fair,
Now the sun is laid to sleep,
Seated in thy silver chair.
State in wonted manner keep;
    Hesperus entreats thy light,
    Goddess, excellently bright.

Earth, let not thy envious shade
Dare itself to interpose;
Cynthia's shining orb was made
Heaven to clear, when day did close;
    Bless us then with wishèd sight,
    Goddess, excellently bright.

Lay thy bow of pearl apart,
And thy crystal-shining quiver;
Give unto the flying hart
Space to breathe, how short soever;
    Thou that mak'st a day of night,
    Goddess, excellently bright.

Ben Jonson (1572–1637)

## *On My First Son*

Farewell, thou child of my right hand, and joy;
My sin was too much hope of thee, loved boy:
Seven years thou wert lent to me, and I thee pay,
Exacted by thy fate, on the just day.
O could I lose all father now! for why
Will man lament the state he should envy,
To have so soon 'scaped world's and flesh's rage,
And, if no other misery, yet age?

Title. *Cynthia, or Diana, goddess of the moon and of the hunt.*

Rest in soft peace, and asked, say, "Here doth lie
Ben Jonson his best piece of poetry."
For whose sake henceforth all his vows be such
As what he loves may never like too much.

Ben Jonson (1572–1637)

## *Come, My Celia*

Come, my Celia, let us prove,
While we can, the sports of love;
Time will not be ours for ever,
He, at length, our goods will sever.
Spend not then his gifts in vain:
Suns that set may rise again;
But if once we lose this light,
'Tis with us perpetual night.
Why should we defer our joys?
Fame and rumour are but toys.
Cannot we delude the eyes
Of a few poor household spies?
Or his easier ears beguile,
Thus removèd by our wile?
'Tis no sin love's fruits to steal,
But the sweet thefts to reveal;
To be taken, to be seen,
These have crimes accounted been.

Ben Jonson (1572–1637)

## *The Flea*

Mark but this flea, and mark in this,
How little that which thou deniest me is;
It sucked me first, and now sucks thee,
And in this flea our two bloods mingled be;
Thou know'st that this cannot be said
A sin, nor shame, nor loss of maidenhead;
  Yet this enjoys before it woo,
  And, pampered, swells with one blood made of two;
  And this, alas, is more than we would do.

Oh stay, three lives in one flea spare,
Where we almost, yea, more than married are.

This flea is you and I, and this
Our marriage bed and marriage temple is;
Though parents grudge, and you, we're met,
And cloistered in these living walls of jet.
  Though use make you apt to kill me,
  Let not to that, self-murder added be,
  And sacrilege, three sins in killing three.

Cruel and sudden, hast thou since
Purpled thy nail in blood of innocence?
Wherein could this flea guilty be,
Except in that drop which it sucked from thee?
Yet thou triumph'st and say'st that thou
Find'st not thyself, nor me, the weaker now.
  'Tis true, then learn how false fears be:
  Just so much honor, when thou yield'st to me,
  Will waste, as this flea's death took life from thee.

John Donne (1572–1631)

## from *The Holy Sonnets*

### 10

Death, be not proud, though some have callèd thee
Mighty and dreadful, for thou art not so;
For those whom thou think'st thou dost overthrow
Die not, poor death, nor yet canst thou kill me.
From rest and sleep, which but thy pictures be,
Much pleasure—then, from thee much more must flow;
And soonest our best men with thee do go,
Rest of their bones and soul's delivery.
Thou art slave to fate, chance, kings, and desperate men,
And dost with poison, war, and sickness dwell;
And poppy or charms can make us sleep as well,
And better than thy stroke. Why swell'st thou then?
One short sleep passed, we wake eternally,
And death shall be no more; death, thou shalt die.

John Donne (1572–1631)

## *Song*

Go and catch a falling star,
  Get with child a mandrake root,

Tell me where all past years are,
   Or who cleft the devil's foot;
Teach me to hear mermaids singing,
Or to keep off envy's stinging,
      And find
      What wind
Serves to advance an honest mind.

If thou be'st born to strange sights,
   Things invisible to see,
Ride ten thousand days and nights
   Till Age snow white hairs on thee;
Thou, when thou return'st, wilt tell me
All strange wonders that befell thee,
      And swear
      No where
Lives a woman true and fair.

If thou find'st one, let me know;
   Such a pilgrimage were sweet.
Yet do not; I would not go,
   Though at next door we might meet.
Though she were true when you met her,
And last till you write your letter,
      Yet she
      Will be
False, ere I come, to two or three.

John Donne (1572–1631)

## *The Pulley*

   When God at first made man,
Having a glass of blessings standing by,
"Let us," said He, "pour on him all we can.
Let the world's riches, which dispersèd lie,
   Contract into a span."

   So strength first made a way;
Then beauty flowed, then wisdom, honor, pleasure.
When almost all was out, God made a stay,
Perceiving that, alone of all his treasure,
   Rest in the bottom lay.

"For if I should," said He,
"Bestow this jewel also on my creature,
He would adore My gifts instead of Me,
And rest in nature, not the God of nature;
So both should losers be.

"Yet let him keep the rest,
But keep them with repining restlessness.
Let him be rich and weary, that at least
If goodness lead him not, yet weariness
May toss him to My breast."

George Herbert (1593–1633)

## *On a Girdle*

That which her slender waist confined
Shall now my joyful temples bind;
No monarch but would give his crown
His arms might do what this has done.

It was my heaven's extremest sphere,
The pale which held that lovely deer.
My joy, my grief, my hope, my love,
Did all within this circle move!

A narrow compass, and yet there
Dwelt all that's good and all that's fair;
Give me but what this riband bound,
Take all the rest the sun goes round.

Edmund Waller (1606–1687)

## *Methought I Saw My Late Espousèd Saint*

Methought I saw my late espousèd saint
Brought to me like Alcestis from the grave,
Whom Jove's great son to her glad husband gave,
Rescued from death by force, though pale and faint.
Mine, as whom washed from spot of child-bed taint
Purification in the old Law did save,

2. Alcestis, *from Euripides'* Alcestis, *wife of Admetus who was brought back from the dead by Hercules, son of Zeus.* 6. Law, *Hebrew law prescribing sacrifices to cleanse a woman after giving birth.*

And such as yet once more I trust to have
Full sight of her in heaven without restraint,
Came vested all in white, pure as her mind.
Her face was veiled; yet to my fancied sight,
Love, sweetness, goodness in her person shined
So clear as in no face with more delight.
But O as to embrace me she inclined,
I waked, she fled, and day brought back my night.

John Milton (1608–1674)

## *When I Consider How My Light Is Spent*

When I consider how my light is spent
Ere half my days, in this dark world and wide,
And that one talent which is death to hide,
Lodged with me useless, though my soul more bent
To serve therewith my Maker, and present
My true account, lest he returning chide;
"Doth God exact day-labor, light denied?"
I fondly ask; but Patience to prevent
That murmur, soon replies, "God doth not need
Either man's work or his own gifts; who best
Bear his mild yoke, they serve him best. His state
Is kingly. Thousands at his bidding speed
And post o'er land and ocean without rest:
They also serve who only stand and wait."

John Milton (1608–1674)

## *The Garden*

How vainly men themselves amaze
To win the palm, the oak, or bays,
And their incessant labours see
Crowned from some single herb, or tree,
Whose short and narrow-vergèd shade
Does prudently their toils upbraid;
While all flowers and all trees do close
To weave the garlands of repose!

1. amaze, *bewilder themselves.* 2. *symbols of achievement in war, athletics, and art.*

Fair Quiet, have I found thee here,
And Innocence, thy sister dear?
Mistaken long, I sought you then
In busy companies of men.
Your sacred plants, if here below,
Only among the plants will grow;
Society is all but rude
To this delicious solitude.

No white nor red was ever seen
So amorous as this lovely green.
Fond lovers, cruel as their flame,
Cut in these trees their mistress' name:
Little, alas, they know or heed
How far these beauties hers exceed!
Fair trees, wheresoe'er your barks I wound,
No name shall but your own be found.

When we have run our passion's heat,
Love hither makes his best retreat.
The gods, that mortal beauty chase,
Still in a tree did end their race:
Apollo hunted Daphne so,
Only that she might laurel grow;
And Pan did after Syrinx speed,
Not as a nymph, but for a reed.

What wondrous life is this I lead!
Ripe apples drop about my head;
The luscious clusters of the vine
Upon my mouth do crush their wine;
The nectarine and curious peach
Into my hands themselves do reach;
Stumbling on melons, as I pass,
Insnared with flowers, I fall on grass.

Meanwhile the mind, from pleasure less
Withdraws into its happiness;
The mind, that ocean where each kind
Does straight its own resemblance find;
Yet it creates, transcending these,

27–32. *When pursued by Pan, Daphne escaped by becoming a laurel, Syrinx by becoming a reed (Ovid's* Metamorphoses, *Book I).* 41. from pleasure less, *pleasure of a lower order.* 43. *The idea was that all terrestrial things have a counterpart in the ocean, and in the human mind.*

Far other worlds and other seas,
Annihilating all that's made
To a green thought in a green shade.

Here at the fountain's sliding foot,
Or at some fruit-tree's mossy root,
Casting the body's vest aside,
My soul into the boughs does glide:
There, like a bird, it sits and sings,
Then whets and combs its silver wings,
And, till prepared for longer flight,
Waves in its plumes the various light.

Such was that happy garden-state,
While man there walked without a mate:
After a place so pure and sweet,
What other help could yet be meet!
But 'twas beyond a mortal's share
To wander solitary there:
Two paradises 'twere in one
To live in paradise alone.

How well the skilful gardener drew,
Of flowers and herbs, this dial new;
Where, from above, the milder sun
Does through a fragrant zodiac run;
And, as it works, the industrious bee
Computes its time as well as we!
How could such sweet and wholesome hours
Be reckoned but with herbs and flowers?

Andrew Marvell (1621–1678)

## *A Description of the Morning*

Now hardly here and there a Hackney-Coach
Appearing, showed the Ruddy Morns Approach.
Now Betty from her Masters Bed had flown,
And softly stole to discompose her own.
The Slipshod Prentice from his Masters Door,
Had pared the Dirt, and sprinkled round the Floor.
Now Moll had whirled her Mop with dex'trous Airs,

60. *There is a pun between "help . . . meet" and "helpmate," which were homonyms in Marvell's English.* 68. *In the formal garden, flowers were planted in the design of the zodiac, hence, "fragrant zodiac."*

Prepared to scrub the Entry and the Stairs.
The Youth with Broomy Stumps began to trace
The Kennel-Edge, where Wheels had worn the Place.
The Smallcoal-Man was heard with Cadence deep,
'Till drowned in Shriller Notes of Chimney-Sweep,
Duns at his Lordships Gate began to meet,
And Brickdust Moll had screamed through half the Street.
The Turnkey now his Flock returning sees,
Duly let out a Nights to steal for Fees.
The watchful Bailiffs take their silent Stands,
And School-Boys lag with Satchels in their Hands.

Jonathan Swift (1667–1745)

## *Epistle to Miss Blount*

As some fond virgin, whom her mother's care
Drags from the town to wholesome country air,
Just when she learns to roll a melting eye,
And hear a spark, yet think no danger nigh—
From the dear man unwilling she must sever,
Yet takes one kiss before she parts forever—
Thus from the world fair Zephalinda flew,
Saw others happy, and with sighs withdrew;
Not that their pleasures caused her discontent:
She sighed not that they stayed, but that she went.

She went—to plain-work and to purling brooks,
Old-fashioned halls, dull aunts, and croaking rooks;
She went from opera, park, assembly, play,
To morning walks, and prayers three hours a day;
To part her time 'twixt reading and bohea,
To muse, and spill her solitary tea;
Or o'er cold coffee trifle with the spoon,
Count the slow clock, and dine exact at noon;
Divert her eyes with pictures in the fire,
Hum half a tune, tell stories to the squire;
Up to her godly garret after seven,
There starve and pray, for that's the way to heaven.

10. Kennel-edge, *gutter.* 15. The Turnkey, *or jailer, apparently lets his prisoners free during the night, but locks them up during the day.*

7. Zephalinda, *pet name for Miss Blount.* 15. bohea, *a variety of tea.*

Some squire, perhaps, you take delight to rack,
Whose game is "whisk," whose treat a toast in sack;
Who visits with a gun, presents you birds,
Then gives a smacking buss, and cries, "No words!"
Or with his hound comes hollowing from the stable,
Makes love with nods, and knees beneath a table;
Whose laughs are hearty, though his jests are coarse,
And loves you best of all things—but his horse.

In some fair evening, on your elbow laid,
You dream of triumphs in the rural shade;
In pensive thought recall the fancied scene,
See coronations rise on every green:
Before you pass the imaginary sights
Of Lords and Earls and Dukes and gartered Knights,
While the spread fan o'ershades your closing eyes,
Then gives one flirt, and all the vision flies.
Thus vanish sceptres, coronets, and balls,
And leave you in lone woods, or empty walls.

So when your slave, at some dear idle time
(Not plagued with headaches or the want of rhyme)
Stands in the streets, abstracted from the crew,
And while he seems to study, thinks of you;
Just when his fancy paints your sprightly eyes,
Or sees the blush of Parthenissa rise—
Gay pats my shoulder, and you vanish quite,
Streets, chairs, and coxcombs rush upon my sight.
Vexed to be still in town, I knit my brow,
Look sour, and hum a tune—as you may now.

Alexander Pope (1688–1744)

## from *An Essay on Man*

I. Know then thyself, presume not God to scan;
The proper study of Mankind is Man.
Plac'd on this isthmus of a middle state,
A being darkly wise, and rudely great:
With too much knowledge for the Sceptic side,
With too much weakness for the Stoic's pride,
He hangs between; in doubt to act, or rest,
In doubt to deem himself a God, or Beast;

46. Parthenissa, *sister of Miss Blount.*

In doubt his Mind or Body to prefer,
Born but to die, and reas'ning but to err;
Alike in ignorance, his reason such,
Whether he thinks too little, or too much:
Chaos of Thought and Passion, all confus'd;
Still by himself abus'd, or disabus'd;
Created half to rise, and half to fall;
Great lord of all things, yet a prey to all;
Sole judge of Truth, in endless Error hurl'd:
The glory, jest, and riddle of the world!

Alexander Pope (1688–1744)

## *Elegy Written in a Country Churchyard*

The Curfew tolls the knell of parting day,
  The lowing herd winds slowly o'er the lea,
The plowman homeward plods his weary way,
  And leaves the world to darkness and to me.

Now fades the glimmering landscape on the sight,
  And all the air a solemn stillness holds,
Save where the beetle wheels his droning flight,
  And drowsy tinklings lull the distant folds;

Save that from younder ivy-mantled tower
  The moping owl does to the moon complain
Of such, as wand'ring near her secret bower,
  Molest her ancient solitary reign.

Beneath those rugged elms, that yew-tree's shade,
  Where heaves the turf in many a mold'ring heap,
Each in his narrow cell for ever laid,
  The rude Forefathers of the hamlet sleep.

The breezy call of incense-breathing Morn,
  The swallow twitt'ring from the straw-built shed,
The cock's shrill clarion, or the echoing horn,
  No more shall rouse them from their lowly bed.

For them no more the blazing hearth shall burn,
  Or busy housewife ply her evening care:
No children run to lisp their sire's return,
  Or climb his knees the envied kiss to share.

Oft did the harvest to their sickle yield,
  Their furrow oft the stubborn glebe has broke;
How jocund did they drive their team afield!
  How bowed the woods beneath their sturdy stroke!

Let not Ambition mock their useful toil,
  Their homely joys, and destiny obscure;
Nor Grandeur hear with a disdainful smile,
  The short and simple annals of the poor.

The boast of heraldry, the pomp of power,
  And all that beauty, all that wealth e'er gave,
Await alike th' inevitable hour.
  The paths of glory lead but to the grave.

Nor you, ye proud, impute to these the fault,
  If Memory o'er their tomb no trophies raise,
Where through the long-drawn aisle and fretted vault
  The pealing anthem swells the note of praise.

Can storied urn or animated bust
  Back to its mansion call the fleeting breath?
Can Honor's voice provoke the silent dust,
  Or Flattery soothe the dull cold ear of Death?

Perhaps in this neglected spot is laid
  Some heart once pregnant with celestial fire;
Hands that the rod of empire might have swayed,
  Or waked to ecstasy the living lyre.

But Knowledge to their eyes her ample page
  Rich with the spoils of time did ne'er unroll;
Chill Penury repressed their noble rage,
  And froze the genial current of the soul.

Full many a gem of purest ray serene,
  The dark unfathomed caves of ocean bear:
Full many a flower is born to blush unseen,
  And waste its sweetness on the desert air.

Some village Hampden, that, with dauntless breast
  The little tyrant of his fields withstood;

26. glebe, *lump of earth.* 39. fretted vault, *intricately carved arches.* 41. storied urn, *inscribed burial urn;* animated, *true to life.* 43. provoke, *call forth.*

Some mute inglorious Milton here may rest,
  Some Cromwell guiltless of his country's blood.

Th' applause of listening senates to command,
  The threats of pain and ruin to despise,
To scatter plenty o'er a smiling land,
  And read their history in a nation's eyes,

Their lot forbade: nor circumscribed alone
  Their growing virtues, but their crimes confined;
Forbade to wade through slaughter to a throne,
  And shut the gates of mercy on mankind.

The struggling pangs of conscious truth to hide,
  To quench the blushes of ingenuous shame,
Or heap the shrine of Luxury and Pride
  With incense kindled at the Muse's flame.

Far from the madding crowd's ignoble strife,
  Their sober wishes never learned to stray;
Along the cool sequestered vale of life
  They kept the noiseless tenor of their way.

Yet ev'n these bones from insult to protect
  Some frail memorial still erected nigh,
With uncouth rhymes and shapeless sculpture decked,
  Implores the passing tribute of a sigh.

Their names, their years, spelt by th' unlettered Muse,
  The place of fame and elegy supply:
And many a holy text around she strews,
  That teach the rustic moralist to die.

For who to dumb Forgetfulness a prey,
  This pleasing anxious being e'er resigned,
Left the warm precincts of the cheerful day,
  Nor cast one longing ling'ring look behind?

On some fond breast the parting soul relies,
  Some pious drops the closing eye requires;
Ev'n from the tomb the voice of Nature cries,
  Ev'n in our ashes live their wonted fires.

For thee, who mindful of th' unhonored dead
  Dost in these lines their artless tale relate;

57–60. Hampden, Milton, and Cromwell *all fought the tyranny of Charles I.*

If chance, by lonely contemplation led,
Some kindred spirit shall inquire thy fate,

Haply some hoary-headed swain may say,
"Oft have we seen him at the peep of dawn
Brushing with hasty steps the dews away
To meet the sun upon the upland lawn.

"There at the foot of yonder nodding beech
That wreathes its old fantastic roots so high,
His listless length at noontide would he stretch,
And pore upon the brook that babbles by.

"Hard by yon wood, now smiling as in scorn,
Mutt'ring his wayward fancies he would rove,
Now drooping, woeful wan, like one forlorn,
Or crazed with care, or crossed in hopeless love.

"One morn I missed him on the customed hill,
Along the heath and near his fav'rite tree;
Another came; nor yet beside the rill,
Nor up the lawn, nor at the wood was he;

"The next with dirges due in sad array
Slow through the churchway path we saw him borne.
Approach and read (for thou canst read) the lay,
Graved on the stone beneath yon aged thorn."

### *The Epitaph*

*Here rests his head upon the lap of earth,*
*A youth to Fortune and to Fame unknown.*
*Fair Science frowned not on his humble birth,*
*And Melancholy marked him for her own.*

*Large was his bounty, and his soul sincere;*
*Heaven did a recompense as largely send:*
*He gave to Misery all he had, a tear,*
*He gained from Heaven ('twas all he wished) a friend.*

*No farther seek his merits to disclose,*
*Or draw his frailties from their dread abode,*
*(There they alike in trembling hope repose)*
*The bosom of his Father and his God.*

Thomas Gray (1716–1771)

97. Haply, *by chance;* swain, *shepherd.*

## *A Red Red Rose*

O, my luve is like a red red rose
  That's newly sprung in June:
O, my luve is like the melodie
  That's sweetly played in tune.

As fair art thou, my bonie lass,
  So deep in luve am I;
And I will luve thee still, my dear,
  Till a' the seas gang dry.

Till a' the seas gang dry, my dear,
  And the rocks melt wi' the sun;
And I will luve thee still, my dear,
  While the sands o' life shall run.

And fare thee weel, my only luve!
  And fare thee weel a while!
And I will come again, my luve,
  Tho' it were ten thousand mile.

Robert Burns (1759–1796)

## *The Lamb*

  Little Lamb, who made thee?
  Dost thou know who made thee?
Gave thee life, and bid thee feed
By the stream and o'er the mead;
Gave thee clothing of delight,
Softest clothing, woolly, bright;
Gave thee such a tender voice,
Making all the vales rejoice?
  Little Lamb, who made thee?
  Dost thou know who made thee?

  Little Lamb, I'll tell thee,
  Little Lamb, I'll tell thee:
He is callèd by thy name,
For He calls Himself a Lamb.
He is meek, and He is mild;
He became a little child.

I a child, and thou a lamb,
We are callèd by his name.
Little Lamb, God bless thee!
Little Lamb, God bless thee!

William Blake (1757–1827)

## *Ah, Sun-flower*

Ah, Sun-flower! weary of time,
Who countest the steps of the sun,
Seeking after that sweet golden clime,
Where the traveler's journey is done;

Where the Youth pined away with desire,
And the pale Virgin shrouded in snow,
Arise from their graves, and aspire
Where my Sun-flower wishes to go.

William Blake (1757–1827)

## *The Little Black Boy*

My mother bore me in the southern wild,
And I am black, but O! my soul is white;
White as an angel is the English child,
But I am black, as if bereaved of light.

My mother taught me underneath a tree,
And, sitting down before the heat of day,
She took me on her lap and kissèd me,
And, pointing to the east, began to say:

"Look on the rising sun—there God does live,
And gives His light, and gives His heat away;
And flowers and trees and beasts and men receive
Comfort in morning, joy in the noonday.

"And we are put on earth a little space,
That we may learn to bear the beams of love;
And these black bodies and this sunburnt face
Is but a cloud, and like a shady grove.

"For when our souls have learned the heat to bear,
The cloud will vanish; we shall hear His voice,
Saying, 'Come out from the grove, My love and care,
And round my golden tent like lambs rejoice.' "

Thus did my mother say, and kissèd me,
And thus I say to little English boy:
When I from black and he from white cloud free,
And round the tent of God like lambs we joy,

I'll shade him from the heat, till he can bear
To lean in joy upon our Father's knee;
And then I'll stand and stroke his silver hair,
And be like him, and he will then love me.

William Blake (1757–1827)

## *Ode: Intimations of Immortality from Recollections of Early Childhood*

*The Child is father of the Man;*
*And I could wish my days to be*
*Bound each to each by natural piety.*

I

There was a time when meadow, grove, and stream,
The earth, and every common sight,
To me did seem
Appareled in celestial light,
The glory and the freshness of a dream.
It is not now as it hath been of yore—
Turn whereso'er I may,
By night or day,
The things which I have seen I now can see no more.

II

The Rainbow comes and goes,
And lovely is the Rose,
The Moon doth with delight
Look round her when the heavens are bare,
Waters on a starry night
Are beautiful and fair;
The sunshine is a glorious birth;
But yet I know, where'er I go,
That there hath passed away a glory from the earth.

Epigraph. *The last lines of "My Heart Leaps Up" by Wordsworth himself.*

III

Now, while the birds thus sing a joyous song,
And while the young lambs bound
As to the tabor's sound,
To me alone there came a thought of grief:
A timely utterance gave that thought relief,
And I again am strong:
The cataracts blow their trumpets from the steep;
No more shall grief of mine the season wrong;
I hear the echoes through the mountains throng,
The winds come to me from the fields of sleep,
And all the earth is gay;
Land and sea
Give themselves up to jollity,
And with the heart of May
Doth every beast keep holiday;—
Thou Child of Joy,
Shout round me, let me hear thy shouts, thou happy
Shepherd-boy!

IV

Ye blessèd Creatures, I have heard the call
Ye to each other make; I see
The heavens laugh with you in your jubilee;
My heart is at your festival,
My head hath its coronal,
The fulness of your bliss, I feel—I feel it all.
Oh evil day! if I were sullen
While earth herself is adorning,
This sweet May-morning,
And the children are culling
On every side,
In a thousand valleys far and wide,
Fresh flowers; while the sun shines warm,
And the Babe leaps up on his Mother's arm:—
I hear, I hear, with joy I hear!
—But there's a tree, of many, one,
A single field which I have looked upon,
Both of them speak of something that is gone;
The pansy at my feet
Doth the same tale repeat:
Whither is fled the visionary gleam?
Where is it now, the glory and the dream?

21. tabor, *drum.*

V

Our birth is but a sleep and a forgetting;
The Soul that rises with us, our life's Star,
Hath had elsewhere its setting,
And cometh from afar;
Not in entire forgetfulness,
And not in utter nakedness,
But trailing clouds of glory do we come
From God, who is our home;
Heaven lies about us in our infancy!
Shades of the prison-house begin to close
Upon the growing Boy,
But he beholds the light, and whence it flows,
He sees it in his joy;
The Youth, who daily farther from the east
Must travel, still is Nature's Priest,
And by the vision splendid
Is on his way attended;
At length the Man perceives it die away,
And fade into the light of common day.

VI

Earth fills her lap with pleasures of her own;
Yearnings she hath in her own natural kind,
And, even with something of a Mother's mind,
And no unworthy aim,
The homely Nurse doth all she can
To make her Foster-child, her Inmate Man,
Forget the glories he hath known,
And that imperial palace whence he came.

VII

Behold the Child among his newborn blisses,
A six-years' Darling of a pygmy size!
See, where 'mid work of his own hand he lies,
Fretted by sallies of his mother's kisses,
With light upon him from his father's eyes!
See, at his feet, some little plan or chart,
Some fragment from his dream of human life,
Shaped by himself with newly-learned art;
A wedding or a festival,

A mourning or a funeral;
And this hath now his heart,
And unto this he frames his song;
Then will he fit his tongue
To dialogues of business, love, or strife;
But it will not be long
Ere this be thrown aside,
And with new joy and pride
The little Actor cons another part;
Filling from time to time his "humorous stage"
With all the Persons, down to palsied Age,
That Life brings with her in her equipage;
As if his whole vocation
Were endless imitation.

VIII

Thou, whose exterior semblance doth belie
Thy Soul's immensity;
Thou best Philosopher, who yet dost keep
Thy heritage, thou Eye among the blind,
That, deaf and silent, read'st the eternal deep,
Haunted for ever by the eternal mind,—
Mighty Prophet! Seer blest!
On whom those truths do rest,
Which we are toiling all our lives to find,
In darkness lost, the darkness of the grave,
Thou, over whom thy Immortality
Broods like the Day, a Master o'er a Slave,
A Presence which is not to be put by;
Thou little Child, yet glorious in the might
Of heaven-born freedom on thy being's height,
Why with such earnest pains dost thou provoke
The years to bring the inevitable yoke,
Thus blindly with thy blessedness at strife?
Full soon thy Soul shall have her earthly freight,
And custom lie upon thee with a weight,
Heavy as frost, and deep almost as life!

IX

O joy! that in our embers
Is something that doth live,

104. humorous stage, *the "pretending" stage.*

That nature yet remembers
What was so fugitive!
The thought of our past years in me doth breed
Perpetual benediction: not indeed
For that which is most worthy to be blest;
Delight and liberty, the simple creed
Of childhood, whether busy or at rest,
With new-fledged hope still fluttering in his breast:—
Not for these I raise
The song of thanks and praise;
But for those obstinate questionings
Of sense and outward things,
Fallings from us, vanishings;
Blank misgivings of a Creature
Moving about in worlds not realised,
High instincts before which our mortal Nature
Did tremble like a guilty Thing surprised;
But for those first affections,
Those shadowy recollections,
Which, be they what they may,
Are yet the fountain light of all our day,
Are yet a master light of all our seeing;
Uphold us, cherish, and have power to make
Our noisy years seem moments in the being
Of the eternal Silence: truths that wake,
To perish never;
Which neither listlessness, nor mad endeavor,
Nor Man nor Boy,
Nor all that is at enmity with joy,
Can utterly abolish or destroy!
Hence in a season of calm weather
Though inland far we be,
Our Souls have sight of that immortal sea
Which brought us hither,
Can in a moment travel thither,
And see the Children sport upon the shore,
And hear the mighty waters rolling evermore.

X

Then sing, ye Birds, sing, sing a joyous song!
And let the young Lambs bound
As to the tabor's sound!
We in thought will join your throng,

Ye that pipe and ye that play,
Ye that through your hearts today
Feel the gladness of the May!
What though the radiance which was once so bright
Be now forever taken from my sight,
Though nothing can bring back the hour
Of splendor in the grass, of glory in the flower;
We will grieve not, rather find
Strength in what remains behind;
In the primal sympathy
Which having been must ever be;
In the soothing thoughts that spring
Out of human suffering;
In the faith that looks through death,
In years that bring the philosophic mind.

XI

And O, ye fountains, meadows, hills, and groves,
Forebode not any severing of our loves!
Yet in my heart of hearts I feel your might;
I only have relinquished one delight
To live beneath your more habitual sway.
I love the brooks which down their channels fret,
Even more than when I tripped lightly as they;
The innocent brightness of a new-born day
Is lovely yet;
The clouds that gather round the setting sun
Do take a sober coloring from an eye
That hath kept watch o'er man's mortality;
Another race hath been, and other palms are won.
Thanks to the human heart by which we live,
Thanks to its tenderness, its joys, and fears,
To me the meanest flower that blows can give
Thoughts that do often lie too deep for tears.

William Wordsworth (1770–1850)

## *Dejection: An Ode*

*Late, late yestreen I saw the new Moon,*
*With the old Moon in her arms;*
*And I fear, I fear, my Master dear!*
*We shall have a deadly storm.*

Ballad of Sir Patrick Spence

I

Well, if the Bard was weather-wise, who made
The grand old ballad of Sir Patrick Spence,
This night, so tranquil now, will not go hence
Unroused by winds, that ply a busier trade
Than those which mould yon cloud in lazy flakes,
Or the dull sobbing draft, that moans and rakes
Upon the strings of this Aeolian lute,
Which better far were mute.
For lo! the New-moon winter-bright!
And overspread with phantom light,
(With swimming phantom light o'erspread
But rimmed and circled by a silver thread)
I see the old Moon in her lap, foretelling
The coming-on of rain and squally blast.
And oh! that even now the gust were swelling,
And the slant night-shower driving loud and fast!
Those sounds which oft have raised me, whilst they awed,
And sent my soul abroad,
Might now perhaps their wonted impulse give,
Might startle this dull pain, and make it move and live!

II

A grief without a pang, void, dark, and drear,
A stifled, drowsy, unimpassioned grief,
Which finds no natural outlet, no relief,
In word, or sigh, or tear—
O Lady! in this wan and heartless mood,
To other thoughts by yonder throstle wooed,
All this long eve, so balmy and serene,
Have I been gazing on the western sky,
And its peculiar tint of yellow green:
And still I gaze—and with how blank an eye!
And those thin clouds above, in flakes and bars,
That give away their motion to the stars;
Those stars, that glide behind them or between,
Now sparkling, now bedimmed, but always seen:
Yon crescent Moon, as fixed as if it grew
In its own cloudless, starless lake of blue;
I see them all so excellently fair,
I see, not feel, how beautiful they are!

7. Aeolian lute *(named after Aeolus, god of the wind), a musical device with strings that vibrate in the wind.*

III

My genial spirits fail;
And what can these avail
To lift the smothering weight from off my breast?
It were a vain endeavour,
Though I should gaze forever
On that green light that lingers in the west:
I may not hope from outward forms to win
The passion and the life, whose fountains are within.

IV

O Lady! we receive but what we give,
And in our life alone does Nature live;
Ours is her wedding garment, ours her shroud!
And would we aught behold, of higher worth,
Than that inanimate cold world allowed
To the poor loveless ever-anxious crowd,
Ah! from the soul itself must issue forth
A light, a glory, a fair luminous cloud
Enveloping the earth—
And from the soul itself must there be sent
A sweet and potent voice, of its own birth,
Of all sweet sounds the life and element!

V

O pure of heart! thou need'st not ask of me
What this strong music in the soul may be!
What, and wherein it doth exist,
This light, this glory, this fair luminous mist,
This beautiful and beauty-making power.
Joy, virtuous Lady! Joy that ne'er was given,
Save to the pure, and in their purest hour,
Life, and life's effluence, cloud at once and shower,
Joy, Lady! is the spirit and the power,
Which wedding Nature to us gives in dower,
A new earth and new heaven,
Undreamt of by the sensual and the proud—
Joy is the sweet voice, joy the luminous cloud—
We in ourselves rejoice!
And thence flows all that charms or ear or sight,
All melodies the echoes of that voice,
All colors a suffusion from that light.

VI

There was a time when, though my path was rough,
  This joy within me dallied with distress,
And all misfortunes were but as the stuff
  Whence Fancy made me dreams of happiness;
For hope grew round me, like the twining vine,
And fruits, and foliage, not my own, seemed mine.
But now afflictions bow me down to earth,
Nor care I that they rob me of my mirth;
    But oh! each visitation
Suspends what nature gave me at my birth,
  My shaping spirit of Imagination.
For not to think of what I needs must feel,
  But to be still and patient, all I can;
And haply by abstruse research to steal
  From my own nature all the natural man—
  This was my sole resource, my only plan:
Till that which suits a part infects the whole,
And now is almost grown the habit of my soul.

VII

Hence, viper thoughts, that coil around my mind,
    Reality's dark dream!
I turn from you, and listen to the wind,
  Which long has raved unnoticed. What a scream
Of agony by torture lengthened out
That lute sent forth! Thou Wind, that rav'st without,
  Bare crag, or mountain-tairn, or blasted tree,
Or pine-grove whither woodman never clomb,
Or lonely house, long held the witches' home,
  Methinks were fitter instruments for thee,
Mad Lutanist! who in this month of showers,
Of dark-brown gardens, and of peeping flowers,
Mak'st Devils' yule, with worse than wintry song,
The blossoms, buds, and timorous leaves among.
  Thou Actor, perfect in all tragic sounds!
Thou mighty Poet, e'en to frenzy bold!
    What tell'st thou now about?
    'Tis of the rushing of an host in rout,
  With groans of trampled men, with smarting wounds—

100. devil's yule, *a wintery storm in springtime.*

At once they groan with pain, and shudder with the cold!
But hush! there is a pause of deepest silence!
And all that noise, as of a rushing crowd,
With groans, and tremulous shudderings—all is over—
It tells another tale, with sounds less deep and loud!
A tale of less affright,
And tempered with delight,
As Otway's self had framed the tender lay,—
'Tis of a little child
Upon a lonesome wild,
Not far from home, but she hath lost her way:
And now moans low in bitter grief and fear,
And now screams loud, and hopes to make her mother hear.

VIII

'Tis midnight, but small thoughts have I of sleep:
Full seldom may my friend such vigils keep!
Visit her, gentle Sleep! with wings of healing,
And may this storm be but a mountain-birth,
May all the stars hang bright above her dwelling,
Silent as though they watched the sleeping Earth!
With light heart may she rise,
Gay fancy, cheerful eyes,
Joy lift her spirit, joy attune her voice;
To her may all things live, from pole to pole,
Their life the eddying of her living soul!
O simple spirit, guided from above,
Dear Lady! friend devoutest of my choice,
Thus mayest thou ever, evermore rejoice.

Samuel Taylor Coleridge (1772–1834)

## *She Walks in Beauty*

She walks in beauty, like the night
Of cloudless climes and starry skies;
And all that's best of dark and bright
Meet in her aspect and her eyes:
Thus mellowed to that tender light
Which heaven to gaudy day denies.

120. Otway, *Jacobean playwright famous for his ability to stir the emotions.*

One shade the more, one ray the less,
  Had half impaired the nameless grace
Which waves in every raven tress,
  Or softly lightens o'er her face;
Where thoughts serenely sweet express,
  How pure, how dear their dwelling-place.

And on that cheek, and o'er that brow,
  So soft, so calm, yet eloquent,
The smiles that win, the tints that glow,
  But tell of days in goodness spent,
A mind at peace with all below,
  A heart whose love is innocent!

George Gordon, Lord Byron (1788–1824)

## *The Destruction of Sennacherib*

The Assyrian came down like the wolf on the fold,
And his cohorts were gleaming in purple and gold;
And the sheen of their spears was like stars on the sea,
When the blue wave rolls nightly on deep Galilee.

Like the leaves of the forest when Summer is green,
That host with their banners at sunset were seen:
Like the leaves of the forest when Autumn hath blown,
That host on the morrow lay withered and strown.

For the Angel of Death spread his wings on the blast,
And breathed in the face of the foe as he passed;
And the eyes of the sleepers waxed deadly and chill,
And their hearts but once heaved, and forever grew still!

And there lay the steed with his nostrils all wide,
But through it there rolled not the breath of his pride;
And the foam of his gasping lay white on the turf,
And cold as the spray of the rock-beating surf.

And there lay the rider distorted and pale,
With the dew on his brow, and the rust on his mail:
And the tents were all silent—the banners alone—
The lances unlifted—the trumpet unblown.

Title. Sennacherib, *Assyrian king whose army was destroyed by a plague while besieging Jerusalem.*

And the widows of Ashur are loud in their wail,
And the idols are broke in the temple of Baal;
And the might of the Gentile, unsmote by the sword,
Hath melted like snow in the glance of the Lord!

George Gordon, Lord Byron (1788–1824)

## *To Night*

I

Swiftly walk o'er the western wave,
   Spirit of Night!
Out of the misty eastern cave,
Where all the long and lone daylight,
Thou wovest dreams of joy and fear,
Which make thee terrible and dear,—
   Swift be thy flight!

II

Wrap thy form in a mantle grey,
   Star-inwrought!
Blind with thine hair the eyes of Day;
Kiss her until she be wearied out,
Then wander o'er city, and sea, and land,
Touching all with thine opiate wand—
   Come, long-sought!

III

When I arose and saw the dawn,
   I sighed for thee;
When light rode high, and the dew was gone,
And noon lay heavy on flower and tree,
And the weary Day turned to his rest,
Lingering like an unloved guest,
   I sighed for thee.

IV

Thy brother Death came, and cried,
   Wouldst thou me?
Thy sweet child Sleep, the filmy-eyed,

21. Ashur, *Assyrian*. 22. Baal, *Assyrian god.*

Murmured like a noon-tide bee,
Shall I nestle near thy side?
Wouldst thou me?—and I replied,
No, not thee!

V

Death will come when thou art dead,
Soon, too soon—
Sleep will come when thou art fled;
Of neither would I ask the boon
I ask of thee, belovèd Night—
Swift be thine approaching flight,
Come soon, soon!

Percy Bysshe Shelley (1792–1822)

## *Ode on a Grecian Urn*

Thou still unravished bride of quietness,
Thou foster-child of silence and slow time,
Sylvan historian, who canst thus express
A flowery tale more sweetly than our rhyme:
What leaf-fringed legend haunts about thy shape
Of deities or mortals, or of both,
In Tempe or the dales of Arcady?
What men or gods are these? What maidens loth?
What mad pursuit? What struggle to escape?
What pipes and timbrels? What wild ecstasy?

Heard melodies are sweet, but those unheard
Are sweeter; therefore, ye soft pipes, play on;
Not to the sensual ear, but, more endeared,
Pipe to the spirit ditties of no tone:
Fair youth, beneath the trees, thou canst not leave
Thy song, nor ever can those trees be bare;
Bold Lover, never, never canst thou kiss,
Though winning near the goal—yet, do not grieve;
She cannot fade, though thou hast not thy bliss,
For ever wilt thou love, and she be fair!

Ah, happy, happy boughs! that cannot shed
Your leaves, nor ever bid the Spring adieu;

7. Tempe, *A beautiful Grecian valley, especially favored by Apollo.* Arcady, *Arcadia, idyllic scene of many mythological stories.* 10. timbrels, *tambourines.*

And, happy melodist, unwearied,
For ever piping songs for ever new;
More happy love! more happy, happy love!
For ever warm and still to be enjoyed,
For ever panting and for ever young;
All breathing human passion far above,
That leaves a heart high-sorrowful and cloyed,
A burning forehead, and a parching tongue.

Who are these coming to the sacrifice?
To what green altar, O mysterious priest,
Lead'st thou that heifer lowing at the skies,
And all her silken flanks with garlands drest?
What little town by river or sea shore,
Or mountain-built with peaceful citadel,
Is emptied of its folk, this pious morn?
And, little town, thy streets for evermore
Will silent be; and not a soul to tell
Why thou art desolate, can e'er return.

O Attic shape! Fair attitude! with brede
Of marble men and maidens overwrought,
With forest branches and the trodden weed;
Thou, silent form, dost tease us out of thought
As doth eternity: Cold Pastoral!
When old age shall this generation waste,
Thou shalt remain, in midst of other woe
Than ours, a friend to man, to whom thou say'st,
Beauty is truth, truth beauty,—that is all
Ye know on earth, and all ye need to know.

John Keats (1795–1821)

## from *In Memoriam*

### I

I held it truth, with him who sings
To one clear harp in divers tones,
That men may rise on stepping-stones
Of their dead selves to higher things.

But who shall so forecast the years
And find in loss a gain to match?

41. brede, *design.*
1–2. *A reference to Goethe.*

Or reach a hand through time to catch
The far-off interest of tears?

Let Love clasp Grief lest both be drowned,
Let darkness keep her raven gloss.
Ah, sweeter to be drunk with loss,
To dance with Death, to beat the ground,

Than that the victor Hours should scorn
The long result of love, and boast,
"Behold the man that loved and lost,
But all he was is overworn."

## LIV

O yet we trust that somehow good
Will be the final goal of ill,
To pangs of nature, sins of will,
Defects of doubt, and taints of blood;

That nothing walks with aimless feet;
That not one life shall be destroyed,
Or cast as rubbish to the void,
When God hath made the pile complete;

That not a worm is cloven in vain;
That not a moth with vain desire
Is shriveled in a fruitless fire,
Or but subserves another's gain.

Behold, we know not anything;
I can but trust that good shall fall
At last—far off—at last, to all,
And every winter change to spring.

So runs my dream; but what am I?
An infant crying in the night;
An infant crying for the light,
And with no language but a cry.

Alfred, Lord Tennyson (1809–1892)

## *Soliloquy of the Spanish Cloister*

1

G-r-r—there go, my heart's abhorrence!
Water your damned flower-pots, do!
If hate killed men, Brother Lawrence,
God's blood, would not mine kill you!
What? your myrtle-bush wants trimming?
Oh, that rose has prior claims—
Needs its leaden vase filled brimming?
Hell dry you up with its flames!

2

At the meal we sit together:
*Salve tibi!*° I must hear — *Hail to thee*
Wise talk of the kind of weather,
Sort of season, time of year:
*Not a plenteous cork-crop: scarcely*
*Dare we hope oak-galls, I doubt:*
*What's the Latin name for "parsley"?*
What's the Greek name for Swine's Snout?

3

Whew! We'll have our platter burnished,
Laid with care on our own shelf!
With a fire-new spoon we're furnished,
And a goblet for ourself,
Rinsed like something sacrificial
Ere 'tis fit to touch our chaps—
Marked with L for our initial!
(He-he! There his lily snaps!)

4

*Saint,* forsooth! While brown Dolores
Squats outside the Convent bank
With Sanchicha, telling stories,
Steeping tresses in the tank,
Blue-black, lustrous, thick like horsehairs,
—Can't I see his dead eye glow,
Bright as 'twere a Barbary corsair's?° — *African pirates*
(That is, if he'd let it show!)

5

When he finishes refection,
   Knife and fork he never lays
Cross-wise, to my recollection,
   As do I, in Jesu's praise.
I the Trinity illustrate,
   Drinking watered orange-pulp—
In three sips the Arian° frustrate; *disbeliever in the Trinity*
   While he drains his at one gulp.

6

Oh, those melons! If he's able
   We're to have a feast! so nice!
One goes to the Abbot's table,
   All of us get each a slice.
How go on your flowers? None double?
   Not one fruit-sort can you spy?
Strange!—And I, too, at such trouble,
   Keep them close-nipped on the sly!

7

There's a great text in Galatians,
   Once you trip on it, entails
Twenty-nine distinct damnations,
   One sure, if another fails:
If I trip him just a-dying,
   Sure of heaven as sure can be,
Spin him round and send him flying
   Off to hell, a Manichee?° *one who believes God and Satan equal*

8

Or, my scrofulous French novel
   On grey paper with blunt type!
Simply glance at it, you grovel
   Hand and foot in Belial's° gripe: *spirit of lust*
If I double down its pages
   At the woeful sixteenth print,
When he gathers his greengages,
   Ope a sieve and slip it in't?

9

Or, there's Satan!—one might venture
   Pledge one's soul to him, yet leave

Such a flaw in the indenture
  As he'd miss till, past retrieve,
Blasted lay that rose-acacia
  We're so proud of! *Hy, Zy, Hine*° . . . *occult incantation?*
'St, there's Vespers! *Plena gratiâ,*° *full of grace*
  *Ave, Virgo!*° G-r-r—you swine! *hail virgin*

Robert Browning (1812–1889)

## *Recorders Ages Hence*

Recorders ages hence,
Come, I will take you down underneath this impassive exterior, I will tell you what to say of me,
Publish my name and hang up my picture as that of the tenderest lover,
The friend the lover's portrait, of whom his friend his lover was fondest,
Who was not proud of his songs, but of the measureless ocean of love within him, and freely pour'd it forth,
Who often walk'd lonesome walks thinking of his dear friends, his lovers,
Who pensive away from one he lov'd often lay sleepless and dissatisfied at night,
Who knew too well the sick, sick dread lest the one he lov'd might secretly be indifferent to him,
Whose happiest days were far away through fields, in woods, on hills, he and another wandering hand in hand, they twain apart from other men,
Who oft as he saunter'd the streets curv'd with his arm the shoulder of his friend, while the arm of his friend rested upon him also.

Walt Whitman (1819–1892)

## *To a Common Prostitute*

Be composed—be at ease with me—I am Walt Whitman, liberal and lusty as Nature,
Not till the sun excludes you do I exclude you,
Not till the waters refuse to glisten for you and the leaves to rustle for you, do my words refuse to glisten and rustle for you.

My girl I appoint with you an appointment, and I charge you that you make preparation to be worthy to meet me,
And I charge you that you be patient and perfect till I come.

Till then I salute you with a significant look that you do not forget me.

Walt Whitman (1819–1892)

## *The Maldive Shark*

About the Shark, phlegmatical one,
Pale sot of the Maldive sea,
The sleek little pilot-fish, azure and slim,
How alert in attendance be.
From his saw-pit of mouth, from his charnel of maw,
They have nothing of harm to dread,
But liquidly glide on his ghastly flank
Or before his Gorgonian head;
Or lurk in the port of serrated teeth
In white triple tiers of glittering gates,
And there find a haven when peril's abroad,
An asylum in jaws of the Fates!
They are friends; and friendly they guide him to prey,
Yet never partake of the treat—
Eyes and brains to the dotard lethargic and dull,
Pale ravener of horrible meat.

Herman Melville (1819–1891)

## *Lucifer in Starlight*

On a starred night Prince Lucifer uprose.
  Tired of his dark dominion, swung the fiend
  Above the rolling ball in cloud part screened,
Where sinners hugged their specter of repose.
Poor prey to his hot fit of pride were those.
  And now upon his western wing he leaned,
  Now his huge bulk o'er Afric's sands careened,
Now the black planet shadowed Arctic snows.

2. Maldive sea, *an area southwest of India.* 8. Gorgonian, *fiercely repulsive, like the Gorgon, a snake-haired female in Greek mythology, so ugly that to see her would turn a man to stone.*

Soaring through wider zones that pricked his scars
   With memory of the old revolt from Awe,
He reached a middle height, and at the stars,
Which are the brain of heaven, he looked, and sank.
Around the ancient track marched, rank on rank,
   The army of unalterable law.

George Meredith (1828–1909)

## *In the Restaurant*

"But hear. If you stay, and the child be born,
It will pass as your husband's with the rest,
While, if we fly, the teeth of scorn
Will be gleaming at us from east to west;
And the child will come as a life despised;
I feel an elopement is ill-advised!"

"O you realize not what it is, my dear,
To a woman! Daily and hourly alarms
Lest the truth should out. How can I stay here,
And nightly take him into my arms!
Come to the child no name or fame,
Let us go, and face it, and bear the shame."

Thomas Hardy (1840–1928)

## *The Man He Killed*

   "Had he and I but met
   By some old ancient inn,
We should have sat us down to wet
   Right many a nipperkin!

   "But ranged as infantry,
   And staring face to face,
I shot at him as he at me,
   And killed him in his place.

   "I shot him dead because—
   Because he was my foe,

4. nipperkin, *small cup.*

Just so: my foe of course he was;
That's clear enough; although

"He thought he'd 'list, perhaps,
Off-hand-like—just as I—
Was out of work—had sold his traps—
No other reason why.

"Yes; quaint and curious war is!
You shoot a fellow down
You'd treat, if met where any bar is,
Or help to half-a-crown."

Thomas Hardy (1840–1928)

## *The Darkling Thrush*

I leant upon a coppice gate
When Frost was specter-gray,
And Winter's dregs made desolate
The weakening eye of day.
The tangled bine-stems scored the sky
Like strings of broken lyres,
And all mankind that haunted nigh
Had sought their household fires.

The land's sharp features seemed to be
The Century's corpse outleant,
His crypt the cloudy canopy,
The wind his death-lament.
The ancient pulse of germ and birth
Was shrunken hard and dry,
And every spirit upon earth
Seemed fervorless as I.

At once a voice arose among
The bleak twigs overhead
In a fullhearted evensong
Of joy illimited;
An aged thrush, frail, gaunt, and small,
In blast-beruffled plume,

15. traps, *personal belongings.*

1. coppice, *a thicket of small trees.* 5. bine-stems, *stems of vines.*

Had chosen thus to fling his soul
 Upon the growing gloom.

So little cause for carolings
 Of such ecstatic sound
Was written on terrestrial things
 Afar or nigh around,
That I could think there trembled through
 His happy good-night air
Some blessed Hope, whereof he knew
 And I was unaware.

Thomas Hardy (1840–1928)

## *Byzantium*

The unpurged images of day recede;
The Emperor's drunken soldiery are abed;
Night resonance recedes, night-walkers' song
After great cathedral gong;
A starlit or a moonlit dome disdains
All that man is,
All mere complexities,
The fury and the mire of human veins.

Before me floats an image, man or shade,
Shade more than man, more image than a shade;
For Hades' bobbin bound in mummy-cloth
May unwind the winding path;
A mouth that has no moisture and no breath
Breathless mouths may summon;
I hail the superhuman;
I call it death-in-life and life-in-death.

Miracle, bird or golden handiwork,
More miracle than bird or handiwork,
Planted on the star-lit golden bough,
Can like the cocks of Hades crow,

Title. *Sixth century Byzantium (Istanbul) was to Yeats the ideal civilization where religion, art, and practical life went on in perfect harmony. Here he describes Byzantium as it might have been at the end of the first Christian millenium.* 20. Hades crow, *a bird of resurrection to waken the dead.*

Or, by the moon embittered, scorn aloud
In glory of changeless metal
Common bird or petal
And all complexities of mire or blood.

At midnight on the Emperor's pavement flit
Flames that no faggot feeds, nor steel has lit,
Nor storm disturbs, flames begotten of flame,
Where blood-begotten spirits come
And all complexities of fury leave,
Dying into a dance,
An agony of trance,
An agony of flame that cannot singe a sleeve.

Astraddle on the dolphin's mire and blood,
Spirit after spirit! The smithies break the flood,
The golden smithies of the Emperor!
Marbles of the dancing floor
Break bitter furies of complexity,
Those images that yet
Fresh images beget,
That dolphin-torn, that gong-tormented sea.

William Butler Yeats (1865–1939)

## *Among School Children*

I

I walk through the long schoolroom questioning;
A kind old nun in a white hood replies;
The children learn to cipher and to sing,
To study reading-books and history,
To cut and sew, be neat in everything
In the best modern way—the children's eyes
In momentary wonder stare upon
A sixty-year-old smiling public man.

II

I dream of a Ledaean body, bent
Above a sinking fire, a tale that she

8. sixty-year-old . . . man, *Yeats, an Irish senator, visited the schools.* 9. Ledaean, *child of Leda, Helen of Troy; see line 20.*

Told of a harsh reproof, or trivial event
That changed some childish day to tragedy—
Told, and it seemed that our two natures blent
Into a sphere from youthful sympathy,
Or else, to alter Plato's parable,
Into the yolk and white of the one shell.

III

And thinking of that fit of grief or rage
I look upon one child or t'other there
And wonder if she stood so at that age—
For even daughters of the swan can share
Something of every paddler's heritage—
And had that color upon cheek or hair,
And thereupon my heart is driven wild:
She stands before me as a living child.

IV

Her present image floats into the mind—
Did Quattrocento finger fashion it
Hollow of cheek as though it drank the wind
And took a mess of shadows for its meat?
And I though never of Ledaean kind
Had pretty plumage once—enough of that,
Better to smile on all that smile, and show
There is a comfortable kind of old scarecrow.

V

What youthful mother, a shape upon her lap
Honey of generation had betrayed,
And that must sleep, shriek, struggle to escape
As recollection or the drug decide,
Would think her son, did she but see that shape
With sixty or more winters on its head,
A compensation for the pang of his birth,
Or the uncertainty of his setting forth?

15. Plato's parable, *a parable explaining how lovers come to search for their counterparts.* 26. Quattrocento finger, *metonymy for fifteenth century artist.*

VI

Plato thought nature but a spume that plays
Upon a ghostly paradigm of things;
Soldier Aristotle played the taws
Upon the bottom of a king of kings;
World-famous golden-thighed Pythagoras
Fingered upon a fiddle-stick or strings
What a star sang and careless Muses heard:
Old clothes upon old sticks to scare a bird.

VII

Both nuns and mothers worship images,
But those the candles light are not as those
That animate a mother's reveries,
But keep a marble or a bronze repose.
And yet they too break hearts—O Presences
That passion, piety or affection knows,
And that all heavenly glory symbolize—
O self-born mockers of man's enterprise;

VIII

Labor is blossoming or dancing where
The body is not bruised to pleasure soul,
Nor beauty born out of its own despair,
Nor blear-eyed wisdom out of midnight oil.
O chestnut-tree, great-rooted blossomer,
Are you the leaf, the blossom or the bole?
O body swayed to music, O brightening glance,
How can we know the dancer from the dance?

William Butler Yeats (1865–1939)

## *Stopping by Woods on a Snowy Evening*

Whose woods these are I think I know.
His house is in the village though;
He will not see me stopping here
To watch his woods fill up with snow.

44. king of kings, *Alexander the Great, pupil of Aristotle.* 45. Pythagoras, *Greek philosopher who taught the transmigration of souls.*

My little horse must think it queer
To stop without a farmhouse near
Between the woods and frozen lake
The darkest evening of the year.

He gives his harness bells a shake
To ask if there is some mistake.
The only other sound's the sweep
Of easy wind and downy flake.

The woods are lovely, dark and deep,
But I have promises to keep,
And miles to go before I sleep,
And miles to go before I sleep.

Robert Frost (1874–1963)

## *Peter Quince at the Clavier*

I

Just as my fingers on these keys
Make music, so the selfsame sounds
On my spirit make a music, too.

Music is feeling, then, not sound;
And thus it is that what I feel,
Here in this room, desiring you,

Thinking of your blue-shadowed silk,
Is music. It is like the strain
Waked in the elders by Susanna.

Of a green evening, clear and warm,
She bathed in her still garden, while
The red-eyed elders watching, felt

Title. *Peter Quince, in Shakespeare's* A Midsummer-Night's Dream, *directs the interlude of "Pyramus and Thisbe." The clavier is a keyboard instrument, forerunner of the piano. In the play, as at the keyboard, Quince envisions strong passions and romantic melodrama.* 9. Susanna, *in Daniel 13 falsely accused by the lustful elders, is saved by Daniel's wise judgment.*

The bases of their beings throb
In witching chords, and their thin blood
Pulse pizzicati of Hosanna.

II

In the green water, clear and warm,
Susanna lay.
She searched
The touch of springs,
And found
Concealed imaginings.
She sighed,
For so much melody.

Upon the bank, she stood
In the cool
Of spent emotions.
She felt, among the leaves,
The dew
Of old devotions.

She walked upon the grass,
Still quavering.
The winds were like her maids,
On timid feet,
Fetching her woven scarves,
Yet wavering.

A breath upon her hand
Muted the night.
She turned—
A cymbal crashed,
And roaring horns.

III

Soon, with a noise like tambourines,
Came her attendant Byzantines.

15. pizzicati, *notes made by plucking rather than bowing a stringed instrument.*
42. Byzantines. *Susanna's servants.*

They wondered why Susanna cried
Against the elders by her side;

And as they whispered, the refrain
Was like a willow swept by rain.

Anon, their lamps' uplifted flame
Revealed Susanna and her shame.

And then, the simpering Byzantines
Fled, with a noise like tambourines.

IV

Beauty is momentary in the mind—
The fitful tracing of a portal;
But in the flesh it is immortal.
The body dies; the body's beauty lives.
So evenings die, in their green going,
A wave, interminably flowing.
So gardens die, their meek breath scenting
The cowl of winter, done repenting.
So maidens die, to the auroral
Celebration of a maiden's choral.
Susanna's music touched the bawdy strings
Of those white elders; but, escaping,
Left only Death's ironic scraping.
Now, in its immortality, it plays
On the clear viol of her memory,
And makes a constant sacrament of praise.

Wallace Stevens (1879–1955)

## *Base Details*

If I were fierce, and bald, and short of breath,
  I'd live with scarlet Majors at the Base,
And speed glum heroes up the line to death.
  You'd see me with my puffy petulant face,
Guzzling and gulping in the best hotel,
  Reading the Roll of Honour. "Poor young chap,"

I'd say—"I used to know his father well;
   Yes, we've lost heavily in this last scrap."
And when the war is done and youth stone dead,
I'd toddle safely home and die—in bed.

Siegfried Sassoon (1886–1967)

## *Spenser's Ireland*

has not altered;—
   a place as kind as it is green,
   the greenest place I've never seen.
Every name is a tune.
Denunciations do not affect
      the culprit; nor blows, but it
is torture to him to not be spoken to.
They're natural,—
         the coat, like Venus'
mantle lined with stars,
buttoned close at the neck,—the sleeves new from disuse.

If in Ireland
   they play the harp backward at need,
   and gather at midday the seed
of the fern, eluding
their 'giants all covered with iron', might
      there be fern seed for unlearn-
ing obduracy and for reinstating
the enchantment?
         Hindered characters
seldom have mothers
in Irish stories, but they all have grandmothers.

It was Irish;
   a match not a marriage was made
   when my great grandmother'd said
with native genius for

Title. *Edmund Spenser, the Elizabethan poet, spent many years in Ireland as an English official. He supported England's stringently oppressive policies against the Irish. In 1598, after his home in Cork was burned by the Irish, he returned to England.*

disunion, 'although your suitor be
perfection, one objection
is enough; he is not
Irish.' Outwitting
the fairies, befriending the furies,
whoever again
and again says, 'I'll never give in,' never sees

that you're not free
until you've been made captive by
supreme belief,—credulity
you say? When large dainty
fingers tremblingly divide the wings
of the fly for mid-July
with a needle and wrap it with peacock-tail,
or tie wool and
buzzard's wing, their pride,
like the enchanter's
is in care, not madness. Concurring hands divide

flax for damask
that when bleached by Irish weather
has the silvered chamois-leather
water-tightness of a
skin. Twisted torcs and gold new-moon-shaped
lunulae aren't jewelry
like the purple-coral fuchsia-tree's. Eire—
the guillemot
so neat and the hen
of the heath and the
linnet spinet-sweet—bespeak relentlessness? Then

they are to me
like enchanted Earl Gerald who
changed himself into a stag, to
a great green-eyed cat of
the mountain. Discommodity makes
them invisible; they've dis-
appeared. The Irish say your trouble is their
trouble and your

49. torcs, *necklace of twisted metal.* 50. lunulae, *crescent-shaped things.* 51. Eire, *Ireland.* 52. guillemot, *a narrow-billed diving bird.*

joy their joy? I wish
I could believe it;
I am troubled, I'm dissatisfied, I'm Irish.

Marianne Moore (1887–1972)

## *Morning at the Window*

They are rattling breakfast plates in basement kitchens,
And along the trampled edges of the street
I am aware of the damp souls of housemaids
Sprouting despondently at area gates.

The brown waves of fog toss up to me
Twisted faces from the bottom of the street,
And tear from a passer-by with muddy skirts
An aimless smile that hovers in the air
And vanishes along the level of the roofs.

T. S. Eliot (1888–1965)

## *Janet Waking*

Beautifully Janet slept
Till it was deeply morning. She woke then
And thought about her dainty-feathered hen,
To see how it had kept.

One kiss she gave her mother.
Only a small one gave she to her daddy
Who would have kissed each curl of his shining baby;
No kiss at all for her brother.

"Old Chucky, Old Chucky!" she cried,
Running across the world upon the grass
To Chucky's house, and listening. But alas,
Her Chucky had died.

It was a transmogrifying bee
Came droning down on Chucky's old bald head

And sat and put the poison. It scarcely bled,
But how exceedingly

And purply did the knot
Swell with the venom and communicate
Its rigor! Now the poor comb stood up straight
But Chucky did not.

So there was Janet
Kneeling on the wet grass, crying her brown hen
(Translated far beyond the daughters of men)
To rise and walk upon it.

And weeping fast as she had breath
Janet implored us, "Wake her from her sleep!"
And would not be instructed in how deep
Was the forgetful kingdom of death.

John Crowe Ransom (1888– )

## *Chaplinesque*

We make our meek adjustments,
Contented with such random consolations
As the wind deposits
In slithered and too ample pockets.

For we can still love the world, who find
A famished kitten on the step, and know
Recesses for it from the fury of the street,
Or warm torn elbow coverts.

We will sidestep, and to the final smirk
Dally the doom of that inevitable thumb
That slowly chafes its puckered index toward us,
Facing the dull squint with what innocence
And what surprise!

And yet these fine collapses are not lies
More than the pirouettes of any pliant cane;
Our obsequies are, in a way, no enterprise.

Title. *Like Charles Chaplin, the silent film actor.*

We can evade you, and all else but the heart:
What blame to us if the heart live on.

The game enforces smirks; but we have seen
The moon in lonely alleys make
A grail of laughter of an empty ash can,
And through all sound of gaiety and quest
Have heard a kitten in the wilderness.

Hart Crane (1899–1932)

## *Incident*

Once riding in old Baltimore
   Heart-filled, head-filled with glee,
I saw a Baltimorean
   Keep looking straight at me.

Now I was eight and very small,
   And he was no whit bigger,
And so I smiled, but he poked out
   His tongue, and called me, "Nigger."

I saw the whole of Baltimore
   From May until December;
Of all the things that happened there
   That's all that I remember.

Countee Cullen (1903–1946)

## *The Fury of Aerial Bombardment*

You would think the fury of aerial bombardment
Would rouse God to relent; the infinite spaces
Are still silent. He looks on shock-pried faces.
History, even, does not know what is meant.

You would feel that after so many centuries
God would give man to repent; yet he can kill

As Cain could, but with multitudinous will,
No farther advanced than in his ancient furies.

Was man made stupid to see his own stupidity?
Is God by definition indifferent, beyond us all?
Is the eternal truth man's fighting soul
Wherein the Beast ravens in its own avidity?

Of Van Wettering I speak, and Averill,
Names on a list, whose faces I do not recall
But they are gone to early death, who late in school
Distinguished the belt feed lever from the belt holding pawl.

Richard Eberhart (1904– )

## *Algonkian Burial*

Comes the time
I was suddenly aware of the difference.
And by and by the flesh fell away from the bones
and the joints clinked as the wind passed.
There was little left me of the quality of water.

I looked not out of place propped among the birch trees
with my pipe and tobacco and my cold supper beside me.
I could not help feeling
proud of the regularity of my ribs
and my soldierly erectness as I lay at attention
while the morning sun flickered in the hollow sockets of my eyes.

Alfred Goldsworthy Bailey (1905– )

## *Late-Flowering Lust*

My head is bald, my breath is bad,
Unshaven is my chin,
I have not now the joys I had
When I was young in sin.

I run my fingers down your dress
With brandy-certain aim
And you respond to my caress
And maybe feel the same.

But I've a picture of my own
  On this reunion night,
Wherein two skeletons are shewn
  To hold each other tight;

Dark sockets look on emptiness
  Which once was loving-eyed,
The mouth that opens for a kiss
  Has got no tongue inside.

I cling to you inflamed with fear
  As now you cling to me,
I feel how frail you are my dear
  And wonder what will be—

A week? or twenty years remain?
  And then—what kind of death?
A losing fight with frightful pain
  Or a gasping fight for breath?

Too long we let our bodies cling,
  We cannot hide disgust
At all the thoughts that in us spring
  From this late-flowering lust.

John Betjeman (1906–    )

## *In Westminster Abbey*

Let me take this other glove off
  As the *vox humana* swells,
And the beauteous fields of Eden,
  Bask beneath the Abbey bells.
Here, where England's statesmen lie,
Listen to a lady's cry.

Gracious Lord, oh bomb the Germans.
  Spare their women for Thy Sake,
And if that is not too easy
  We will pardon Thy Mistake.
But, gracious Lord, whate'er shall be,
Don't let anyone bomb me.

Keep our Empire undismembered
Guide our Forces by Thy Hand,
Gallant blacks from far Jamaica,
Honduras and Togoland;
Protect them Lord in all their fights,
And, even more, protect the whites.

Think of what our Nation stands for,
Books from Boots' and country lanes,
Free speech, free passes, class distinction,
Democracy and proper drains.
Lord, put beneath Thy special care
One-eighty-nine Cadogan Square.

Although dear Lord I am a sinner,
I have done no major crime;
Now I'll come to Evening Service
Whensoever I have the time.
So Lord, reserve for me a crown,
And do not let my shares go down.

I will labour for Thy Kingdom,
Help our lads to win the war,
Send white feathers to the cowards
Join the Women's Army Corps,
Then wash the Steps around Thy Throne
In the Eternal Safety Zone.

Now I feel a little better,
What a treat to hear Thy Word,
Where the bones of leading statesmen,
Have so often been interr'd.
And now, dear Lord, I cannot wait
Because I have a luncheon date.

John Betjeman (1906– )

## *Weed Puller*

Under the concrete benches,
Hacking at black hairy roots,—
Those lewd monkey-tails hanging from drainholes,—

Digging into the soft rubble underneath,
Webs and weeds,
Grubs and snails and sharp sticks,
Or yanking tough fern-shapes,
Coiled green and thick, like dripping smilax,
Tugging all day at perverse life:
The indignity of it!—
With everything blooming above me,
Lilies, pale-pink cyclamen, roses,
Whole fields lovely and inviolate,—
Me down in that fetor of weeds,
Crawling on all fours,
Alive, in a slippery grave.

Theodore Roethke (1908–1963)

## *Auto Wreck*

Its quick soft silver bell beating, beating,
And down the dark one ruby flare
Pulsing out red light like an artery,
The ambulance at top speed floating down
Past beacons and illuminated clocks
Wings in a heavy curve, dips down,
And brakes speed, entering the crowd.
The doors leap open, emptying light;
Stretchers are laid out, the mangled lifted
And stowed into the little hospital.
Then the bell, breaking the hush, tolls once,
And the ambulance with its terrible cargo
Rocking, slightly rocking, moves away,
As the doors, an afterthought, are closed.

We are deranged, walking among the cops
Who sweep glass and are large and composed.
One is still making notes under the light.
One with a bucket douches ponds of blood
Into the street and gutter.
One hangs lanterns on the wrecks that cling,
Empty husks of locusts, to iron poles.

8. smilax, *a vine with bright green leaves.* 14. fetor, *bad smell.*

Our throats were tight as tourniquets,
Our feet were bound with splints, but now,
Like convalescents intimate and gauche,
We speak through sickly smiles and warn
With the stubborn saw of common sense,
The grim joke and the banal resolution.
The traffic moves around with care,
But we remain, touching a wound
That opens to our richest horror.
Already old, the question Who shall die?
Becomes unspoken Who is innocent?
For death in war is done by hands;
Suicide has cause and stillbirth, logic;
And cancer, simple as a flower, blooms.
But this invites the occult mind,
Cancels our physics with a sneer,
And spatters all we knew of denouement
Across the expedient and wicked stones.

Karl Shapiro (1913– )

## *A Camp in the Prussian Forest*

I walk beside the prisoners to the road.
Load on puffed load,
Their corpses, stacked like sodden wood,
Lie barred or galled with blood

By the charred warehouse. No one comes today
In the old way
To knock the fillings from their teeth;
The dark, coned, common wreath

Is plaited for their grave—a kind of grief.
The living leaf
Clings to the planted profitable
Pine if it is able;

The boughs sigh, mile on green, calm, breathing mile,
From this dead file
The planners ruled for them. . . . One year
They sent a million here:

Here men were drunk like water, burnt like wood.
The fat of good
And evil, the breast's star of hope
Were rendered into soap.

I paint the star I sawed from yellow pine—
And plant the sign
In soil that does not yet refuse
Its usual Jews

Their first asylum. But the white, dwarfed star—
This dead white star—
Hides nothing, pays for nothing; smoke
Fouls it, a yellow joke,

The needles of the wreath are chalked with ash,
A filmy trash
Litters the black woods with the death
Of men; and one last breath

Curls from the monstrous chimney. . . . I laugh aloud
Again and again;
The star laughs from its rotting shroud
Of flesh. O star of men!

Randall Jarrell (1914–1965)

## *Dream Song 15*

What was Ashore, then? . . Cargoed with Forget,
My ship runs down a midnight winter storm
Between whirlpool and rock, and my white love's form
Gleams at the wheel, her hair streams. When we met
Seaward, Thought frank & guilty to each oar set
Hands careless of port as of the waters' harm.
Endless a wet wind wears my sail, dark swarm
Endless of sighs and veering hopes, love's fret.

Rain of tears, real, mist of imagined scorn,
No rest accords the fraying shrouds, all thwart
Already with mistakes, foresight so short.
Muffled in capes of waves my clear sighs, torn,

Hitherto most clear,—Loyalty and Art.
And I begin now to despair of port.

(AFTER PETRARCH & WYATT)

John Berryman (1914–1972)

## *Guitarreros*

Black against twisted black
The old mesquite
Rears up against the stars
Branch bridle hanging,
While the bull comes down from the mountain
Driven along by your fingers,
Twenty nimble stallions prancing up and down the *redil* of the guitars.
One leaning on the trunk, one facing—
Now the song:
Not cleanly flanked, not pacing,
But in a stubborn yielding that unshapes
And shapes itself again,
Hard-mouthed, zigzagged, thrusting,
Thrown not sung
One to the other.
The old man listens in his cloud
Of white tobacco smoke.
"It was so," he says,
"In the old days it was so."

Américo Paredes (1915– )

## *We Real Cool*

The Pool Players.
Seven at the Golden Shovel.

We real cool. We
Left school. We

Lurk late. We
Strike straight. We

Sing sin. We

Thin gin. We

Jazz June. We
Die soon.

Gwendolyn Brooks (1917–      )

## *Ezra Pound*

Horizontal in a deckchair on the bleak ward,
some feeble-minded felon in pajamas, clawing
a Social Credit broadside from your table, you saying,
". . . here with a black suit and black briefcase; in the briefcase,
an abomination, Possum's *hommage* to Milton."
Then sprung; Rapallo, and then the decade gone;
then three years, then Eliot dead, you saying,
"And who is left to understand my jokes?
My old Brother in the arts . . . and besides, he was a smash of a poet."
He showed us his blotched, bent hands, saying, "Worms.
When I talked that nonsense about Jews on the Rome
wireless, she knew it was shit, and still loved me."
And I, "Who else has been in Purgatory?"
And he, "To begin with a swelled head and end with swelled feet."

Robert Lowell (1917–      )

## *War*

When my young brother was killed
By a mute and dusty shell in the thorny brush
Crowning the boulders of the Villa Verde Trail
On the island of Luzon,

I laid my whole dry body down,
Dropping my face like a stone in a green park
On the east banks of the Rhine;

3. Social Credit, *a utopian economic theory, Pound's answer to capitalism.* 6. Rapallo, *the city in Italy where Pound lived before and during World War II.* 11–12. When . . . wireless, *Pound made pro-Fascist broadcasts during the war.*

On an airstrip skirting the Seine
His sergeant brother sat like a stick in his barracks
While cracks of fading sunlight
Caged the dusty air;

In the rocky rolling hills west of the Mississippi
His father and mother sat in a simple Norwegian parlor
With a photograph smiling between them on the table
And their hands fallen into their laps
Like sticks and dust;

And still other brothers and sisters,
Linking their arms together,
Walked down the dusty road where once he ran
And into the deep green valley
To sit on the stony banks of the stream he loved
And let the murmuring waters
Wash over their blood-hot feet with a springing crown of tears.

Joseph Langland (1917– )

## *Dirge*

The learned masseur McLuhan says books are dead. Why not?
It's a trend. Theologians tell us God is dead. And any day now
ornithologists announce to the next of kin the demise of birds.
Imperialism is dead. Colonialism is dead. Isolationism is
dead and the frontier is dead and the white man's burden and
peace in our time and the open door all dead, along with
domestic tranquillity and nonviolence and blushing brides.
Gandhi is long dead and Einstein and Schweitzer and Ford and
free enterprise and clear streams and pure air are dead
and of course Puritanism is dead and good taste is dead and
Lake Erie dead as denial and Lake Michigan being administered
final rites. Oh yes the Establishment is dead and so is the
antiestablishment dead. Hemingway is dead and Frost and Faulkner
and romanticism is dead and naturalism is dead and goodness knows
how many liberals agrarians one-worlders free traders
and oh my god Jack is dead and we all died with him a little.
MacArthur is dead Hirohito is dead and Hitler and Mussolini.

Bertrand the Russell and Charles the Grand and Norman the Mailer
and Ayn the Rand and Allen the Ginsberg and uncounted others all
dead from the neck up and more than I care to recall deeply dead
from the neck down. Why be half safe? Cigarettes kill you and
alcohol kills you and drugs kill you and automobiles and planes
and taxis and trains. Running to war will kill you and running
away from war will kill you just as dead and overeating will kill
you and not eating will kill you and if the high voltage doesn't
do it and the carbon monoxide misses and VD and a stroll through
the park at night both fail, there's always the ever-dependable
cancer and heart failure. Sarcophagus McAbre worked to death. Who's
for one hell of a wake? Buddy, you still there? Buddy??!!!

Ray Mizer (1918– )

## *Cognate Object*

True, love, you have a way with words.
Away with words! I would have you,
Both subject and object; or else
With linking verb (Subjective complement!)
In happy case and all sweet syntax be,
In perfect agreement,
That pure infinitive,
The subject understood.

You I would have,
Demonstrative if possible,
And possessive; intensive you,
So substantive, so causative,
O fair conjunction this!

The gender right past doubt.
O most emphatic conjugation!
Unmodified, absolute,
Beyond comparison.

Ray Mizer (1918– )

### *In Goya's greatest scenes*

In Goya's greatest scenes we seem to see
the people of the world
exactly at the moment when
they first attained the title of
'suffering humanity'
They writhe upon the page
in a veritable rage
of adversity
Heaped up
groaning with babies and bayonets
under cement skies
in an abstract landscape of blasted trees
bent statues bats wings and beaks
slippery gibbets
cadavers and carnivorous cocks
and all the final hollering monsters
of the
'imagination of disaster'
they are so bloody real
it is as if they really still existed

And they do

Only the landscape is changed

They still are ranged along the roads
plagued by legionaires

false windmills and demented roosters
They are the same people
only further from home
on freeways fifty lanes wide
on a concrete continent
spaced with bland billboards
illustrating imbecile illusions of happiness

The scene shows fewer tumbrils

Title. *Francisco José de Goya, 1746–1828, Spanish painter.*

but more maimed citizens
in painted cars
and they have strange license plates
and engines
that devour America

Lawrence Ferlinghetti (1919– )

## *The Goose Fish*

On the long shore, lit by the moon
To show them properly alone,
Two lovers suddenly embraced
So that their shadows were as one.
The ordinary night was graced
For them by the swift tide of blood
That silently they took at flood,
And for a little time they prized
Themselves emparadised.

Then, as if shaken by stage-fright
Beneath the hard moon's bony light,
They stood together on the sand
Embarrassed in each other's sight
But still conspiring hand in hand,
Until they saw, there underfoot,
As though the world had found them out,
The goose fish turning up, though dead,
His hugely grinning head.

There in the china light he lay,
Most ancient and corrupt and grey
They hesitated at his smile,
Wondering what it seemed to say
To lovers who a little while
Before had thought to understand,
By violence upon the sand,
The only way that could be known
To make a world their own.

It was a wide and moony grin
Together peaceful and obscene;
They knew not what he would express,
So finished a comedian
He might mean failure or success,
But took it for an emblem of
Their sudden, new and guilty love
To be observed by, when they kissed,
  That rigid optimist.

So he became their patriarch,
Dreadfully mild in the half-dark.
His throat that the sand seemed to choke,
His picket teeth, these left their mark
But never did explain the joke
That so amused him, lying there
While the moon went down to disappear
Along the still and tilted track
  That bears the zodiac.

Howard Nemerov (1920–    )

## *A Day Begins*

A headless squirrel, some blood
oozing from the unevenly
chewed-off neck

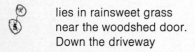

lies in rainsweet grass
near the woodshed door.
Down the driveway

the first irises
have opened since dawn,
ethereal, their mauve

almost a transparent gray,
their dark veins
bruise-blue.

Denise Levertov (1923–    )

## *You Were Wearing*

You were wearing your Edgar Allan Poe printed cotton blouse.
In each divided up square of the blouse was a picture of Edgar Allan Poe.
Your hair was blonde and you were cute. You asked me, "Do most boys think that most girls are bad?"
I smelled the mould of your seaside resort hotel bedroom on your hair held in place by a John Greenleaf Whittier clip.
"No," I said, "it's girls who think that boys are bad." Then we read *Snowbound* together
And ran around in an attic, so that a little of the blue enamel was scraped off my George Washington, Father of His Country, shoes.

Mother was walking in the living room, her Strauss Waltzes comb in her hair.
We waited for a time and then joined her, only to be served tea in cups painted with pictures of Herman Melville
As well as with illustrations from his book *Moby Dick* and from his novella, *Benito Cereno.*
Father came in wearing his Dick Tracy necktie: "How about a drink, everyone?"
I said, "Let's go outside a while." Then we went onto the porch and sat on the Abraham Lincoln swing.
You sat on the eyes, mouth, and beard part, and I sat on the knees.
In the yard across the street we saw a snowman holding a garbage can lid smashed into a likeness of the mad English king, George the Third.

Kenneth Koch (1925– )

## *The Mill*

It stands dark and isolated in a kind of dream,
unreal; the water falls like maidenhair,
and the miller's flesh has soured like cream
to sounds of thunder, and turned to air.

The rock abutment is worn like an old tooth
to a wet, darker color; some beams lie washing,
thick with fronds of grass. Submerged in truth,
they blink behind a rain of minnows flashing.

The solid floor where the miller walked
and felt his body jar, hard weight against another,
has turned to jelly in the shallows, pocked
by grasses greener than the wood, and tougher.

Most of all I know is like this: gone or old.
The splinter in the flesh can melt like snow
before the heat inside the finger can turn cold.
All hard things strain to be the first to go.

The dream lasts; I've dreamed it over and over:
a picture polished dark as glass in stone.
Sometimes at night I hear the water roar,
or hear the miller pacing on the boards, alone.

Jack Matthews (1925– )

## *Corner*

The cop slumps alertly on his motorcycle,
supported by one leg like a leather stork.
His glance accuses me of loitering.
I can see his eyes moving like fish
in the green depths of his green goggles.

His ease is fake. I can tell.
My ease is fake. And he can tell.
The fingers armored by his gloves
splay and clench, itching to change something.

As if he were my enemy or my death,
I just stand there watching.

I spit out my gum which has gone stale.
I knock out a new cigarette—
which is my bravery.

It is all imperceptible:
the way I shift my weight,
the way he creaks in his saddle.

The traffic is specific though constant.
The sun surrounds me, divides the street between us.
His crash helmet is whiter in the shade.
It is like a bull ring as they say it is just before the fighting.
I cannot back down. I am there.

Everything holds me back.
I am in danger of disappearing into the sunny dust.
My levis bake and my T shirt sweats.

My cigarette makes my eyes burn.
But I don't dare drop it.

Who made him my enemy?
Prince of coolness. King of fear.
Why do I lean here waiting?
Why does he lounge there watching?

I am becoming sunlight.
My hair is on fire. My boots run like tar.
I am hung-up by the bright air.

Something breaks through all of a sudden,
and he blasts off, quick as a craver,
one with his power; watching me watch.

Ralph Pomeroy (1926–     )

## *The Wife*

I know two women
  and the one
is tangible substance,
  flesh and bone.

The other in my mind
  occurs.
She keeps her strict
  proportion there.

But how should I
  propose to live
with two such creatures
  in my bed—

or how shall he
    who has a wife
yield two to one
    and watch the other die.

Robert Creeley (1926–    )

## *I Know a Man*

As I sd to my
friend, because I am
always talking,—John, I

sd, which was not his
name, the darkness sur-
rounds us, what

can we do against
it, or else, shall we &
why not, buy a goddamn big car,

drive, he sd, for
christ's sake, look
out where yr going.

Robert Creeley (1926–    )

## *Wait for Me*

*. . . give a man his*
I said to her,

*manliness: provide*
what you want I

*creature comfort*
want only

*for him and herself:*
more so. You

*preserve essential*
think marriage is

*hypocrisies—*
everything?

*in short, make a*
Oh well,

*home for herself.*
I said.

Robert Creeley (1926– )

## *Marvell's Garden*

Marvell's garden, that place of solitude,
is not where I'd choose to live
yet is the fixed sundial
that turns me round
unwillingly,
in a hot glade
as closer, closer I come to contradiction,
to the shade green within the green shade.

The garden where Marvell scorned love's solicitude—
that dream—and played instead an arcane solitaire,
shuffling his thoughts like shadowy chance
across the shrubs of ecstasy,
and cast the myths away to flowering hours
as, yes, his mind, that sea, caught at green
thoughts shadowing a green infinity.

And yet Marvell's garden was not Plato's
garden—and yet—he did care more for the form
of things than for the thing itself—
ideas and visions,
resemblances and echoes,
things seeming and being
not quite what they were.

That was his garden, a kind of attitude
struck out of an earth too carefully attended,
wanting to be left alone.
And I don't blame him for that.
God knows, too many fences fence us out
and his garden closed in on Paradise.

On Paradise! When I think of his hymning
Puritans in the Bermudas, the bright oranges

lighting up that night! When I recall
his rustling tinsel hopes
beneath the cold decree of steel,
Oh, I have wept for some new convulsion
to tear together this world and his.

But then I saw his luminous plumèd wings
prepared for flight,
and then I heard him singing glory
in a green tree,
and then I caught the vest he'd laid aside
all blest with fire.

And I have gone walking slowly in
his garden of necessity
leaving brothers, lovers, Christ
outside my walls
where they have wept without
and I within.

Phyllis Webb (1927– )

## *The Starry Night*

"That does not keep me from having a terrible need of—shall I say the word—religion. Then I go out at night to paint the stars."

—VINCENT VAN GOGH in a letter to his brother

The town does not exist
except where one black-haired tree slips
up like a drowned woman into the hot sky.
The town is silent. The night boils with eleven stars.
Oh starry starry night! This is how
I want to die.

It moves. They are all alive.
Even the moon bulges in its orange irons
to push children, like a god, from its eye.
The old unseen serpent swallows up the stars.
Oh starry starry night! This is how
I want to die:

into that rushing beast of the night,

Title. *A painting by Van Gogh.*

sucked up by that great dragon, to split
from my life with no flag,
no belly,
no cry.

Anne Sexton (1928–     )

## *Why Try?*

And she was brown
And she always dressed and wore brown
And she had a fine brown body
And she had two beautiful brown eyes
And she would sit in the Beat Cafe
on her brown behind on a hard brown bench
and listen to brown sounds entertain her brown thoughts
And she would often double cross her brown legs
And reveal her beautiful brown pleasing knees
And as she sat in the Beat Cafe on her brown behind on the
    hard brown bench
And listening to brown sounds coming from entertainers of
    brown bohemia
I saw a young white girl throw her brand
    new jar of
        suntan lotion and sigh: WHY TRY?

Ted Joans (1928–     )

## *Black Jackets*

In the silence that prolongs the span
Rawly of music when the record ends,
The red-haired boy who drove a van
In weekday overalls but, like his friends,

Wore cycle boots and jacket here
To suit the Sunday hangout he was in,
Heard, as he stretched back from his beer,
Leather creak softly round his neck and chin.

Before him, on a coal-black sleeve
Remote exertion had lined, scratched, and burned

Insignia that could not revive
The heroic fall or climb where they were earned.

On the other drinkers bent together,
Concocting selves for their impervious kit,
He saw it as no more than leather
Which, taut across the shoulders grown to it,

Sent through the dimness of a bar
As sudden and anonymous hints of light
As those that shipping give, that are
Now flickers in the Bay, now lost in night.

He stretched out like a cat, and rolled
The bitterish taste of beer upon his tongue,
And listened to a joke being told:
The present was the things he stayed among.

Thom Gunn (1929–    )

## *The Hag*

The old story went that the cajoling hag
Fattened the pretty princess within a fence
Of barbs the spiders poked their eight eyes out in
Even, the points were so close, fattened her
With pastry pies and would not let her incline
One inch toward the threshold from the table
Lest she slip off the hag's dish and exchange
The hag's narrow intestine for the wide world.
And this hag had to lie in a certain way
At night lest the horrible angular black hatred
Poke through her side and surprise the pretty princess
Who was well-deceived by this posture of love.

Now here is an old hag, as I see,
Has got this story direly drastically wrong,
Who has dragged her pretty daughter home from college,
Who has locked up her pretty eyes in a brick house
And has sworn her pretty mouth shall rot like fruit
Before the world shall make a jam of it

To spread on every palate. And so saying,
She must lie perforce at night in a certain way
Lest the heart break through her side and burst the walls
And surprise her daughter with an extravagance
Of tearful love, who finds it easier
To resign her hope of a world wide with love,
And even to rot in the dark, but easier under
Nine bolts of spite than on one leash of love.

Ted Hughes (1930– )

## *Crow's Last Stand*

Burning
burning
burning
there was finally something
The sun could not burn, that it had rendered
Everything down to—a final obstacle
Against which it raged and charred

And rages and chars

Limpid among the glaring furnace clinkers
The pulsing blue tongues and the red and the yellow
The green lickings of the conflagration

Limpid and black—

Crow's eye-pupil, in the tower of its scorched fort.

Ted Hughes (1930– )

## *Pike*

Pike, three inches long, perfect
Pike in all parts, green tigering the gold.
Killers from the egg: the malevolent aged grin.
They dance on the surface among the flies.

Or move, stunned by their own grandeur,
Over a bed of emerald, silhouette
Of submarine delicacy and horror.
A hundred feet long in their world.

In ponds, under the heat-struck lily pads—
Gloom of their stillness:
Logged on last year's black leaves, watching upwards.
Or hung in an amber cavern of weeds

The jaws' hooked clamp and fangs
Not to be changed at this date;
A life subdued to its instrument;
The gills kneading quietly, and the pectorals.

Three we kept behind glass,
Jungled in weed: three inches, four,
And four and a half: fed fry to them—
Suddenly there were two. Finally one

With a sag belly and the grin it was born with.
And indeed they spare nobody.
Two, six pounds each, over two feet long,
High and dry and dead in the willow-herb—

One jammed past its gills down the other's gullet:
The outside eye stared: as a vice locks—
The same iron in this eye
Though its film shrank in death.

A pond I fished, fifty yards across,
Whose lilies and muscular tench
Had outlasted every visible stone
Of the monastery that planted them—

Stilled legendary depth:
It was as deep as England. It held
Pike too immense to stir, so immense and old
That past nightfall I dared not cast

But silently cast and fished
With the hair frozen on my head
For what might move, for what eye might move.
The still splashes on the dark pond,

Owls hushing the floating woods
Frail on my ear against the dream
Darkness beneath night's darkness had freed,
That rose slowly towards me, watching.

Ted Hughes (1930–     )

## *Fields*

The wind sprays pale dirt into my mouth.
The small, almost invisible scars on my hands.

The pores on my throat and elbows
Have taken in a seed of dirt of their own

After a day in the grapefields near Rolinda
A fine silt, washed by sweat,
Has settled into the lines on my wrists and palms

Already I am becoming the valley,
A soil that sprouts nothing
For the worker

Gary Soto (1952–        )

## *Marriage*

Should I get married? Should I be good?
Astound the girl next door with my velvet suit and faustus hood?
Don't take her to movies but to cemeteries
tell all about werewolf bathtubs and forked clarinets
then desire her and kiss her and all the preliminaries
and she going just so far and I understanding why
not getting angry saying You must feel! It's beautiful to feel!
Instead take her in my arms lean against an old crooked tombstone
and woo her the entire night the constellations in the sky—

When she introduces me to her parents
back straightened, hair finally combed, strangled by a tie,
should I sit knees together on their 3rd degree sofa
and not ask Where's the bathroom?
How else to feel other than I am,
often thinking Flash Gordon soap—
O how terrible it must be for a young man
seated before a family and the family thinking
We never saw him before! He wants our Mary Lou!
After tea and homemade cookies they ask What do you do for a living?

Should I tell them? Would they like me then?
Say All right get married, we're losing a daughter
but we're gaining a son—
And should I then ask Where's the bathroom?
O God, and the wedding! All her family and her friends
and only a handful of mine all scroungy and bearded
just wait to get at the drinks and food—
And the priest! he looking at me as if I masturbated
asking me Do you take this woman for your lawful wedded wife?
And I trembling what to say say Pie Glue!
I kiss the bride all those corny men slapping me on the back
She's all yours, boy, Ha-ha-ha!
And in their eyes you could see some obscene honeymoon going on—

Then all that absurd rice and clanky cans and shoes
Niagara Falls! Hordes of us! Husbands! Wives! Flowers! Chocolates!
All streaming into cozy hotels
All going to do the same thing tonight
The indifferent clerk he knowing what was going to happen
The lobby zombies they knowing what
The whistling elevator man he knowing
The winking bellboy knowing
Everybody knowing! I'd be almost inclined not to do anything!
Stay up all night! Stare that hotel clerk in the eye!
Screaming: I deny honeymoon! I deny honeymoon!
running rampant into those almost climactic suites
yelling Radio belly! Cat shovel!
O I'd live in Niagara forever! in a dark cave beneath the Falls
I'd sit there the Mad Honeymooner
devising ways to break marriages, a scourge of bigamy
a saint of divorce—

But I should get married I should be good
How nice it'd be to come home to her
and sit by the fireplace and she in the kitchen
aproned young and lovely wanting my baby
and so happy about me she burns the roast beef
and comes crying to me and I get up from my big papa chair
saying Christmas teeth! Radiant brains! Apple deaf!

God what a husband I'd make! Yes, I should get married!
So much to do! like sneaking into Mr Jone's house late at night
and cover his golf clubs with 1920 Norwegian books
Like hanging a picture of Rimbaud on the lawnmower
like pasting Tannu Tuva postage stamps all over the picket fence
like when Mrs Kindhead comes to collect for the Community Chest
grab her and tell her There are unfavorable omens in the sky!
And when the mayor comes to get my vote tell him
When are you going to stop people killing whales!
And when the milkman comes leave him a note in the bottle
Penguin dust, bring me penguin dust, I want penguin dust—

Yet if I should get married and it's Connecticut and snow
and she gives birth to a child and I am sleepless, worn,
up for nights, head bowed against a quiet window, the past behind me,
finding myself in the most common of situations a trembling man
knowledged with responsibility not twig-smear nor Roman coin soup—
O what would that be like!
Surely I'd give it for a nipple a rubber Tacitus
For a rattle a bag of broken Bach records
Tack Della Francesca all over its crib
Sew the Greek alphabet on its bib
And build for its playpen a roofless Parthenon

No, I doubt I'd be that kind of father
not rural not snow no quiet window
but hot smelly tight New York City
seven flights up, roaches and rats in the walls
a fat Reichian wife screeching over potatoes Get a job!
And five nose running brats in love with Batman
And the neighbors all toothless and dry haired
like those hag masses of the 18th century
all wanting to come in and watch TV
The landlord wants his rent
Grocery store Blue Cross Gas & Electric Knights of Columbus
Impossible to lie back and dream Telephone snow, ghost parking—

No! I should not get married I should never get married!
But—imagine If I were married to a beautiful sophisticated woman
tall and pale wearing an elegant black dress and long black gloves
holding a cigarette holder in one hand and a highball in the other
and we lived high up in a penthouse with a huge window
from which we could see all of New York and ever farther on clearer days
No, can't imagine myself married to that pleasant prison dream—

O but what about love? I forget love
not that I am incapable of love
it's just that I see love as odd as wearing shoes—
I never wanted to marry a girl who was like my mother
And Ingrid Bergman was always impossible
And there's maybe a girl now but she's already married
And I don't like men and—
but there's got to be somebody!
Because what if I'm 60 years old and not married,
all alone in a furnished room with pee stains on my underwear
and everybody else is married! All the universe married but me!

Ah, yet well I know that were a woman possible as I am possible
then marriage would be possible—
Like SHE in her lonely alien gaud waiting her Egyptian lover
so I wait—bereft of 2,000 years and the bath of life.

Gregory Corso (1934– )

## *Linda*

Seven, frog-legged among the boys,
even now you realize
what magic holds mechanical toys

have on them. In the green sway
of a sun-burst tree you compromise
the zoom and sputter of their play.

Then you rise, shake off the grass:
you are seventeen, and wise;
their long necks bobble as you pass.

Their gaudy noise halts and garbles.
You know their automatic eyes
are rolling after you like marbles.

John Stone (1936–      )

never falling.
leaning but
thin ladder,
and climb a
filling our heads
their warm song
we must imagine
Nearing the bells,
to each gallery.
turns us darkly
inside this tower
changing angles
The long spiral
curves to the sea.
the bright Arno
rooftops shrink,
drop farther away,
Now the avenues
have climbed in.
thousands like us
worn by leather
on marble steps
finding a balance
of our promises,
how to keep all
here we may see
Love,

*Climbing the Tower at Pisa*

Richard Frost (1935–      )

## *Digging*

Between my finger and my thumb
The squat pen rests; snug as a gun.
Under my window, a clean rasping sound
When the spade sinks into gravelly ground:
My father, digging. I look down

Till his straining rump among the flowerbeds
Bends low, comes up twenty years away
Stooping in rhythm through potato drills
Where he was digging.

The coarse boot nestled on the lug, the shaft
Against the inside knee was levered firmly.
He rooted out tall tops, buried the bright edge deep
To scatter new potatoes that we picked
Loving their cool hardness in our hands.

By God, the old man could handle a spade.
Just like his old man.

My grandfather cut more turf in a day
Than any other man on Toner's bog.
Once I carried him milk in a bottle
Corked sloppily with paper. He straightened up
To drink it, then fell to right away

Nicking and slicing neatly, heaving sods
Over his shoulder, going down and down
For the good turf. Digging.

The cold smell of potato mould, the squelch and slap
Of soggy peat, the curt cuts of an edge
Through living roots awaken in my head.
But I've no spade to follow men like them.

Between my finger and my thumb
The squat pen rests.
I'll dig with it.

Seamus Heaney (1939– )

## *The External Element*

When I was a kid
I had kites & they always
ended entangled in trees
but stronger than the kite memories
is a dream I had at the time
in which my mother climbed a tree
to retrieve one of my smashed kites
& me crying: Ma, don't bother!

& up there she lost balance
fell, landing across the high tension wires
& was electrocuted, the black cinder
of my Ma falling softly to the ground.

For weeks after I couldn't do enough
to help my mother,
                    I was an ideal son
for over a month

                    & even now
I hate poetry with a passion
& write poems.

David McFadden (1940–  )

# Index of Poets and Titles

# Index of First Lines

# Index of Subjects